PROTEST AND SURVIVE

Stop Nuclear War

edited by

E.P. Thompson and Dan Smith

introduction by

Daniel Ellsberg

PROTEST AND SURVIVE
E.P. Thompson and Dan Smith

Published in agreement with Monthly Review Press, New York for publication and sale only in the Indian Subcontinent (India, Pakistan, Bangladesh, Nepal, Maldives, Bhutan & Sri Lanka)

First Published in India, 2009

ISBN 978-93-5002-009-8

Published by
AAKAR BOOKS
28 E Pocket IV, Mayur Vihar Phase I, Delhi-110 091
Phone : 011-2279 5505 Telefax : 011-2279 5641
aakarbooks@gmail.com; www.aakarbooks.com

Printed at
Arpit Printographers
E-mail : arpitprinto@yahoo.com

Contents

A Note from the Publisher

In 1980 the British civil defense department issued a classified pamphlet entitled "Protect and Survive" designed to be distributed if a nuclear attack became imminent. The pamphlet was leaked and became a public scandal. In response, E. P. Thompson, an eminent British historian and already an outspoken critic of British nuclear policy, wrote his pamphlet, "Protest and Survive," a counterblast against official policy that became a rallying cry for the peace movement in England and Europe. Later, this pamphlet in revised form became the leading essay in a book of the same name co-edited by Thompson and Dan Smith, and including essays offering a detailed and factual critique of the official nuclear weapons policy of the United Kingdom, the United States, NATO, the Soviet Union, the Warsaw Pact countries, and the worldwide military industrial complex. Of this book, the *Bulletin of the Atomic Scientists* said, "It seems destined to become the well-thumbed bible of a revitalized international movement."

This volume is a U.S. version of the British edition, with several essays from United States sources replacing certain of the British essays. This broadly ecumenical collection is our attempt to help break the silence on the real and present danger of a nuclear war and its horrible consequences.

Introduction
Call to Mutiny
Daniel Ellsberg

"It has never been true that nuclear war is 'unthinkable.' It has been thought and the thought has been put into effect." E. P. Thompson refers here, in the brilliant and moving essay that opens this volume, to the deliberate destruction of the people of Hiroshima and Nagasaki in August 1945. What he does not mention is that the Americans who conceived and ordered this project, like those who prepared it and carried it out and the great majority of the public who learned of it after the event, regarded the effects of the first nuclear war as marvelously successful. Such thoughts get thought again, and acted on.

The notion common to nearly all Americans that "no nuclear weapons have been used since Nagasaki" is mistaken. It is not the case that U.S. nuclear weapons have simply piled up over the years—we have over 30,000 of them now, after dismantling many thousands of obsolete ones—unused and unusable, save for the single function of deterring their use against us by the Soviets. Again and again, generally in secret from the American public, U.S. nuclear weapons *have* been used, for quite different purposes: in the precise way that a gun is used when you point it at someone's head in a direct confrontation, whether or not the trigger is pulled.

By Harry Truman's own telling, it was just seven months after Nagasaki that he so used the Bomb in the "postwar" world. As he recalled, the effect was immediately as successful as on the first occasion, with no need this time to pull the trigger.

The issue was, as it happens, Russian influence in northern Iran, where the Soviets were prolonging their wartime occupation and supporting separatist regimes in Azerbaijan and Kurdistan, in pursuit of Russian oil leases in that area comparable to those of the British in the south. One version of Truman's account was revealed to *Time* by Senator Henry Jackson in January 1980, the week, by no coincidence, that the Carter

Doctrine was announced. *Time* gave the story the heading, "Good Old Days for the Middle East":

> In a little-known episode of nuclear diplomacy that Jackson said he had heard from Harry Truman, the President summoned Soviet Ambassador Andrei Gromyko to the White House. Truman told Gromyko that Soviet troops should evacuate Iran within 48 hours—or the U.S. would use the new superbomb that it alone possessed. "We're going to drop it on you," Jackson quoted Truman as saying. They moved in 24 hours.

Truman's memory may be faulty in this recounting; Barry Blechman, who believes it was, reports at least seven public or private occasions when Truman discussed what he called his "ultimatum" over Iran, the earliest of these in 1950, but there are inconsistencies and a lack of any supporting evidence. This is not the case with any other of the episodes to be discussed below, for which this anecdote is, in the form Truman presented it, nevertheless archetypal.

The most recent of these, thirty-five years later, brings us back to the very same region and adversary. When outgoing Secretary of Defense Harold Brown told interviewers in January 1981, and President Ronald Reagan reiterated in February—using the same words—that what will keep Russia out of northern Iran and other parts of the Middle East in the 1980s is "the risk of World War III," the threat-strategy each was at the same time describing and implementing was somewhat more complex than that which Truman recollected, but not by much.

And there is no lack, this time, of corroborating elucidations of the nuclear component to the policy. A year earlier, in the weeks before and after Carter's State of the Union message announcing his "doctrine" for the Middle East, the White House almost jammed Washington talk shows and major front pages with authorized leaks, backgrounders, and official spokesmen all carrying the message that the president's commitment to use "any means necessary, including military force" against a further Soviet move into the Persian Gulf region was, at its heart, a threat of possible initiation of tactical nuclear warfare by the United States.

Just after the president's speech, Richard Burt of the *New*

York Times (now a high Reagan official), was shown a secret Pentagon study, "the most extensive military study of the region ever done by the government," which lay behind the president's warning. It concluded, as he summarized it, "that the American forces could not stop a Soviet thrust into northern Iran and that the United States should therefore consider using 'tactical' nuclear weapons in any conflict there" (*New York Times*, February 2, 1980).

Even before the president spoke, this same conclusion was reflected in White House backgrounders given to *Los Angeles Times* reporters Jack Nelson and Robert Toth. Heralding the president's message, "White House and other senior officials dealing with national security" told them that "if the Soviet Union carried its expansionism into Iran or Pakistan, the United States would have little choice but to oppose it militarily." These officials went on to say what the president, speaking to the public a few days later, did not put into words: such a war with the Soviet Union "would almost certainly become a nuclear war" (*Los Angeles Times*, January 18, 1980). This information was the lead front-page story, under the headline "Russia vs. Iran: U.S. Ponders Unthinkable." The same story reprinted next day in the *San Francisco Chronicle* bore the headline, "Doomsday Talk in Washington."

The revelation in *Time* of Senator Jackson's old conversation with Truman, appearing on newstands the day before the president's speech, was part of this same chorus. It was particularly well suited to administration purposes—evident in the unusual publicity given to threats usually kept highly secret—of legitimizing and gaining public acceptance for the president's own policy. The Truman anecdote displayed a precedent of nuclear threats against the Russians, involving Iran (or really, in both cases, the transcendent issue of Middle East oil), invoking just the image of feisty, now-popular Harry Truman (re-elected against all odds, now enshrined in history after the lowest ratings in popular support until Jimmy Carter) that the president sought to associate with his own shift to a new Cold War: above all, a precedent of success.

But there was still another reason to evoke the memory of

Harry Truman in this context. For all the talk and posturing, for all the military analyses, plans, and recommendations, even the deployments, the question remained: Could the Russians, could anyone, come to believe that the president of the United States, if challenged, might really *carry* out such threats, accepting the prospects *at best*—if the war, improbably, stayed regionally limited—of annihilating the local population along with troops? Indeed, was he not bound to the contrary—as most Americans still imagine, quite falsely—by an explicit or at least tacit "no first-use" commitment, never to be the first to use nuclear weapons in a crisis or non-nuclear conflict?

It was the official function of William Dyess, assistant secretary of state for public information, to interpret the president's meaning to the public in the week following the speech, and to address in particular just these questions. In an arresting exchange on television (*Newsmakers*, NBC Television, February 3, 1980) one day after Burt's leak of the Pentagon study, Dyess answered the second question crisply and correctly, and the first as well:

> *Q: In nuclear war are we committed not to make the first strike?*
>
> Dyess: No sir.
>
> *Q: We could conceivably make an offensive . . .*
>
> Dyess: We make no comment on that whatsoever, but the Soviets know that this terrible weapon has been dropped on human beings twice in history and it was an American president who dropped it both times. Therefore, they have to take this into consideration in their calculus.

But the Soviets, better than most, know a good deal more than this about past uses and near-uses of U.S. nuclear weapons. What Dyess might have mentioned (but almost surely does not know) is that in the thirty-six years since Hiroshima, *every* president from Truman to Reagan, with the possible exception of Ford, has felt compelled to consider or direct serious preparations for possible imminent U.S. initiation of tactical or strategic nuclear warfare, in the midst of an ongoing, intense, non-nuclear conflict or crisis.

The Soviets know this because they were *made* to know it—often by explicit threats from the Oval Office, even when White House considerations of use of nuclear weapons was secret from other audiences—since they or their allies or client states were the intended targets of these preparations and warnings. Moreover, the Soviets will recall that the U.S. Strategic Air Command was established in early 1946 with the function of delivering nuclear attacks upon Russia when so directed, at a time when it was publicly proclaimed by the president and high military that the Soviet Union was not expected to possess operational nuclear weapon systems for a decade or longer. SAC's *only* mission in that initial period—which included the formation of NATO—was to threaten or carry out a U.S. first strike: *not at all* to deter or retaliate for a nuclear attack on the United States or anywhere else.

It is not the Russians but the rest of us who need to learn these hidden realities of the nuclear dimension to U.S. foreign policy. As important background for the essays that follow and for much else, here, briefly listed, are most of the actual nuclear crises that can now be documented from memoirs or other public sources (in most cases after long periods of secrecy; footnotes indicate the most accessible references):

- Truman's deployment of B-29s, officially described as "atomic-capable," to bases in Britain and Germany at the outset of the Berlin Blockade, June 1948.[1]
- Truman's press conference warning that nuclear weapons were under consideration, the day after marines were surrounded by Chinese Communist troops at the Chosin Reservoir, Korea, November 30, 1950.[2]
- Eisenhower's secret nuclear threats against China, to force and maintain a settlement in Korea, 1953.[3]
- Secretary of State Dulles' secret offer to Prime Minister Bidault of three tactical nuclear weapons in 1954 to relieve the French troops beseiged by the Indochinese at Dienbienphu.[4]
- Eisenhower's secret directive to the Joint Chiefs during

the "Lebanon Crisis" in 1958 to prepare to use nuclear weapons, if necessary, to prevent an Iraqi move into the oilfields of Kuwait.[5]

- Eisenhower's secret directive to the Joint Chiefs in 1958 to plan to use nuclear weapons, imminently, against China if the Chinese Communists should attempt to invade the island of Quemoy, occupied by Chiang's troops, a few miles offshore mainland China.[6]
- The Berlin crisis, 1961.[7]
- The Cuban Missile Crisis, 1962.[8]
- Numerous "shows of nuclear force" involving demonstrative deployments or alerts—deliberately visible to adversaries and intended as a "nuclear signal"—of forces with a designated role in U.S. plans for strategic nuclear war.[9]
- Much public discussion, in newspapers and in the Senate, of (true) reports that the White House had been advised of the possible necessity of nuclear weapons to defend marines surrounded at Khe Sanh, Vietnam, 1968.[10]
- Nixon's secret threats of massive escalation, including possible use of nuclear weapons, conveyed to the North Vietnamese by Henry Kissinger, 1969–72.[11]
- The Carter Doctrine on the Middle East (January 1980) as explained by Defense Secretary Harold Brown, Assistant Secretary of State William Dyess, and other spokesmen,[12] reaffirmed, in essence, by President Reagan in 1981.[13]

Although the current warnings and preparations for nuclear war in the Middle East are the most *public* threats since the crises over Berlin and Cuba a generation ago, it follows from this listing that there has been no thirty-six-year moratorium upon the active consideration and use of nuclear weapons to support "nuclear diplomacy." Indeed, many of the recurrent circumstances were remarkably similar to the first use at Hiroshima.

In none of these cases, any more than in 1945, was there

apprehension among U.S. officials that nuclear war might be initiated by an adversary or needed urgent deterring. In most of them, just as against Japan, the aim was to coerce in urgent circumstances a much weaker opponent that possessed no nuclear weapons at all. In the remaining cases the object—already important in August 1945—was to intimidate the Soviet Union in an otherwise non-nuclear conflict.

And even against the Soviets most of these threats were seen as effective, just as the first two bombs were. U.S. marines, who had fought their way out of Chinese encirclement at the Chosin Reservoir without carrying out Truman's 1950 warning, were never finally assaulted at Khe Sanh, in 1968. The Chinese accepted and kept our 1953 armistice terms in Korea; in 1958, they ceased abruptly their daily shelling of Quemoy. The Russians backed down over Berlin in 1961 and again, spectacularly, in Cuba the next year.

Whether the nuclear component of U.S. threats to escalate the level of hostilities was actually critical to the behavior of opponents is not the issue here. (That question is still hotly controversial for the 1945 case itself.) What matters, if we are to understand this record, is that presidents *believed* that past and current threats had succeeded: this was why, as they understood it, they or their predecessors had not been forced to carry them out, and why they and their successors kept making such threats, and buying more and more first-use and first-strike nuclear weapon systems to maintain and increase the credibility and effectiveness of threats they expected to make in the future. It is why, after all, each president has refused to make a "no first-use" commitment, even when the Soviet Union has proposed such a commitment bilaterally.

The objection to these tactics is not that such threats cannot possibly "work." However, it is important to observe that most of these known incidents—*and all of the apparently successful ones* (except Khe Sanh)—occurred under earlier conditions of American strategic nuclear superiority so overwhelming as to amount to monopoly.

Thus, in mid-1961, the year of the projected "missile gap" favoring the Russians, the United States had within range of

Russia about 1000 tactical bombers and 2000 intercontinental bombers, 40 ICBMs, 48 Polaris missiles, and another 100 intermediate range missiles based in Europe. The Soviets had at that time some 190 intercontinental bombers and exactly *four* ICBMs: four "soft," nonalert, liquid-fueled ICBMs at one site at Plesetsk that was vulnerable to a small attack with conventional weapons.

When Kennedy urged the American people to prepare fallout shelters during the Berlin crisis that year, it was not for a nuclear war that would be started by the Soviets. Nor was it to avert Soviet superiority, nor to deter a Soviet nuclear first strike, that Kennedy fixed on the figure of 1000 missiles as the projected size of the Minuteman force in November of that year, well *after* the intelligence community had concurred on the conclusive estimate that the Soviets possessed less than ten ICBMs.

Officially, the precise figure cited above for Soviet ICBMs in the period from early 1960 to early 1962—four—is guarded as a classified secret today just as it was twenty years ago; the number presented in nearly all public sources—"about fifty"—is wrong by an order of magnitude. The true figure remains secret for the same reason as before: because public knowledge of the *scale* of the "missile gap" hoax would undercut the recurrently-necessary tactic of whipping up public fears of imminent U.S. "inferiority" to mobilize support for vastly expensive arms spending intended, in fact, to assure continued and increased—or in the present instance, regained—U.S. superiority.

The Soviets did acquire a large and growing ability to devastate Western Europe from the mid-fifties on (with short- and medium-range bombers and rockets). But (a) the ability to disarm the opposing superpower of its strategic forces in a first strike, and (b) the ability to retaliate against the homeland of the opposing superpower in a second strike, were both capabilities strictly monopolized by the United States until the late sixties. Not until 1967 did the Russians begin to put their ICBMs into "hardened" concrete silos and deploy advanced missile submarines, thereby acquiring the second capability and depriving the U.S. of the first.

For most of two decades, it is now clear, the Soviets chose

not to seriously challenge what amounted to U.S. strategic monopoly. But the cost to U.S. security interests of *using* that monopoly repeatedly, most dramatically over Quemoy, Berlin, and Cuba—while increasing spending sharply to maintain it and refusing to put a ceiling on U.S. technological superiority by a comprehensive, bilateral test ban on warheads or missiles—was to discredit Khrushchev's reliance on cheap bluffs and to help him lose his job. Brezhnev, displacing Khrushchev in 1964, seems to have promised the Soviet military to spend whatever it would take to eliminate inferiority. The Soviets proceeded to outspend the U.S. in the seventies, as they finally duplicated the huge investments in strategic capabilities that the U.S. had made in the fifties and sixties. In the course of the decade, they succeeded in buying "rough equivalence" or parity, thus drastically eroding the credibility of the U.S. first-strike threat, and along with it, the credibility of threats to escalate lesser levels of conflict if necessary to avoid tactical defeat or stalemate.

Americans are now being mobilized for a massive attempt to buy back these two lost pillars of U.S. foreign policy. The damaged credibility is to be partially restored by adding to our sizeable (and unique) antisubmarine capability the highly precise counterforce capabilities for a disarming first strike against landbased forces represented by the MX, Trident II, Pershing, and cruise missiles (with antiballistic missile systems and civil defense as logical and likely complements, when the public is ready). So far (July 1981) Congress is not balking at a projected price tag of several hundred billion dollars, even though the significant superiority sought (under the consciously deceptive public slogan of "avoiding inferiority") seems most unlikely to be achieved, in face of the evident Soviet determination to deny it.

Meanwhile, as the Nixon, Carter, and Reagan examples demonstrate, presidents continue to issue threats of U.S. nuclear initiatives, even in the era of superpower parity that has lasted now about a dozen years. The White House backgrounders cited earlier explain why, for the case of the Carter Doctrine. Thus the secret Pentagon study of U.S. capabilities in the

Middle East is quoted by the *New York Times* as concluding: "To prevail in an Iranian scenario, we might have to threaten or make use of tactical nuclear weapons." The reason given is that the Soviets could move twenty-three divisions with 200,000 troops into their neighboring country within thirty days, confronting the 20,000 Americans and equipment that could be brought in by then with "more than a five-to-one advantage in forces." In the *Los Angeles Times* backgrounder, White House officials explained that even a local conflict with Soviet troops "would almost certainly become a nuclear war, because the United States has concentrated on its nuclear weapons rather than on matching the Soviet Union's massive strength in conventional warfare" (January 18, 1980).

Of course, as the leaked Pentagon study makes clear, even if the U.S. did match Soviet conventional strength in overall global terms, it could hardly aspire to do so in a region bordering Russia, any more than the Soviet Union, for all its vast army and growing navy, could ever hope to outweigh U.S. conventional strength on our own borders, in order, say, to block U.S. access to the oil in Mexico or Canada (or, for that matter, to protect states in the Caribbean or Central America from determined U.S. intervention). This regional disadvantage for the exercise of unilateral U.S. military power in at least the northern part of the Persian Gulf region would not be reduced at all by instituting the draft, or by enlarging a Rapid Deployment Force, or, indeed, by combat employment (as distinct from threat) of tactical nuclear weapons, with which the Soviet forces are well equipped.

It is in these unchanging circumstances that the *deterrent* tactic has recommended itself to a succession of U.S. administrations of *threatening* and preparing to initiate tactical nuclear warfare in the region, and to escalate if necessary, risking Soviet preemption or counter-escalation. In plainer language, the tactic is to threaten regional annihilation, with a link to global holocaust. Within their persistent frame of reference, these policy-makers see simply no alternative.

Nor is this true only of the Middle East. Look again at the list of nuclear crises. In fact nearly *all* of them, except for Cuba, focus on countries bordering the Soviet Union or China (with Berlin actually within the Soviet zone of occupation). The current "dilemma" in the Middle East merely highlights the historical legacy of an earlier generation in which strategic nuclear monopoly permitted and encouraged the United States to claim rights to intervention in what amounted to a "sphere of predominant influence" that ran right up to the borders of Soviet or Chinese occupation *everywhere in the world*, including (from early 1946) northern Iran. Now, a decade after that monopoly has vanished, U.S. commanders-in-chief still feel compelled to defend and assure U.S. influence within that same immense, global sphere. They believe, and they are right to believe, they cannot do so everywhere without being ready to ignite thermonuclear war whenever "necessary."

Within that sphere of influence, the incentive to threaten or launch nuclear weapons to protect U.S. interventionary troops is not limited, either, to prospective confrontations with Russian forces. Again, the list of incidents above reveals a clear pattern. In *every one* of the half-dozen cases when U.S. or allied tactical units were surrounded or cut off and in danger of defeat—at the Chosin Reservoir, Dienbienphu, Berlin, Quemoy, Khe Sanh—the administration secretly gave consideration, far more seriously than was ever admitted to the public, to the use of tactical nuclear weapons to defend them. In the light of this secret history, it is worth reflecting on the potential nature of the Rapid Deployment Force, limited in size and equipment and intended for distant intervention, as a portable Dienbienphu. Perhaps its major function would be as an instrument of real and visible commitment to the possible first-use of nuclear weapons by the United States. Indeed, that is pretty much how its purpose is described, to a careful reader of official statements. Analogy is often explicit to the nuclear "tripwire" function of U.S. forces stationed in Western Europe.

In an interview in his first weeks in office (*New York Times*, February 3, 1981), President Reagan was asked if the U.S. was "capable, now, militarily of backing-up" his threat to "use arms to prevent any Soviet move in the Persian Gulf to cut off oil to the United States."

Reagan replied that what he called for, "is a presence in the Middle East. . . . Not the stationing of enough American troops that you say we could stop the Soviet Union if they set out to advance logistically; we know that we couldn't do that.

"What is meant by a presence is that we're there enough to know and for the Soviets to know that if they made a reckless move, they would be risking a confrontation with the United States."

Why wouldn't that be, he was then asked "an empty threat that the Soviets could see through?"

Reagan's reply: "Well, it's not—you don't just plant a flag in the ground and walk away and leave it. There would be Americans there. But I think there should be some kind of American presence. Well, we're doing it right now with the Navy in the Indian Ocean. But I think we need a ground presence also.

"But it's based on the assumption—and I think a correct assumption—the Soviet Union is not ready yet to take on that confrontation which could become World War III."

There are, currently, a few weak links in that threatened sequence, but measures to strengthen them are all included in the current defense budget. Production of "neutron" warheads, is one: with their relatively precise killing zone, they are "optimal" for close-in nuclear defense of protected troops (not only against tanks, not only in Europe). Precisely accurate delivery vehicles for such low-yield warheads as air- or sea-launched cruise missiles, are another.

But how might the Soviets be deterred from retaliating in kind, at least, to such short-range attacks on their forces (or on their allies)? Or, if some retaliation was unavoidable, how might it be kept to an "acceptable" level, the prospect of which would not deter the U.S. from the initial attacks? The Pentagon's answer is to be able to pose a threat of further escalation that is more credible than the Soviets can make.

This is where the Pershing and cruise missiles to be stationed in Europe come in, and precisely with reference to the Middle East. With their extreme accuracy, unmatched by anything the Soviets possess (an order of magnitude better than the Russian SS-20), these promise great effectiveness against military targets even with relatively small-yield warheads, which need not destroy nearby population centers. Thus, the theory goes, the Russians might be deterred from retaliating against a U.S. carrier that had just destroyed their forward units in Iran, by fear that the U.S. would then use the unique capabilities of its Pershings to eliminate "surgically" all the bases, depots, command posts, and reserves in Eastern Europe and western Russia that support Soviet Middle Eastern theater operations. The Pershings could (on paper) do this while leaving most Russian cities (and ICBMs) intact, thus daring the Soviets to *start* an all-out city-busting exchange by replying with their large-yield, "indiscriminate" warheads (all they have, supposedly). This they might not do, even in a retaliation limited regionally to Europe, for fear the U.S. might then take out their ICBMs and a good deal more, with the MX, Trident II, and air-launched cruise missiles newly bought for this purpose.

In the words of E. P. Thompson: "If all this sounds crazy, then I can only agree that crazy is exactly what it is." Yet there is a short-run, narrow-focus rationality, a certain coherent, if reckless, logic to the traps the Pentagon planners are so carefully setting for themselves, and all of us on earth. If they did *not* develop and deploy these new first-strike weapons, they could no longer even pretend that threats to initiate, or escalate nuclear war *against Soviet forces* were anything but hollow. But if they do invest several hundred billion dollars to achieve a first-strike capability, the Soviets could not be *sure* they had not convinced themselves they had succeeded.

If all these threats really were hollow, and if presidents were content to let this be perceived, the strategy would not be so dangerous; but then, it could not possibly succeed. Because they do rely on such means to protect what they see as vital interests, and because they do face up, in a sense realistically, to the credibility problem posed by the real craziness of the threats, decision-makers take positive measures to enhance that credibility. And these measures tend to be committing, that is, they actually do increase the likelihood that the threats will be carried out if they should happen to be defied.

Thus, the Carter Doctrine itself, the president's public pledge of effective action ("any means necessary") has this effect. More concretely, nuclear-armed carriers are deployed to the area, where their vulnerability as tempting and urgent targets for retaliatory or preemptive attack by the Soviets (or others) commits the U.S. to the possibility of nuclear escalation just as much as does their own capability to launch nuclear strikes. Exactly the same is true for the presence in Europe of the far-from-invulnerable Pershing and cruise missiles (or, on the Soviet side, SS-20s), which makes quite realistically credible the prospect of escalation *by one side or the other* from a Middle East conflict to the heart of Europe.

And it is not only from the Middle East that a regional nuclear conflict can "spill over" into Europe; *all* the non-Soviet targets of U.S. nuclear warnings in the list above were allies or clients of the Soviet Union, and the possibility of such spill-over (e.g., by Soviet retaliation against Berlin or U.S. missiles in Turkey, or against Japan) was vividly present in the minds of U.S. planners, even in the bygone era of U.S. superiority.[11]

Carter and Reagan are right; their policy cannot safely be regarded by the Russians, or anyone else, as mainly bluff. To make first-use warnings in a world so loaded with nuclear weapons that both threaten and invite preemption is *really* to play Russian roulette, with a gun pointed at the heads of all our children. It was thirty years ago that their White House predecessors pioneered an essentially terrorist strategy based on threats of regional genocide: the indiscriminate, massive slaughter of innocents foreseeable even in the most "limited" one-sided nuclear war. Their own current pursuit of superiority—in the face of present parity and of Soviet efforts to maintain it—is intended to prolong that strategy into an era when such threats are vastly more dangerous than before: likely now to be suicidal as well as genocidal, yet more likely to be challenged, and then, to be carried out. For their deliberate arms policies *are* effectively committing, making it likely that sooner or later—unless U.S. threats always work perfectly, which they will not—a U.S. president will turn a non-nuclear conflict into a nuclear one, or a local nuclear exchange into a global one.

The whole panoply of new arms and deployments, the "usable" neutron warhead and the Rapid Deployment Force to the Pershings and the MX, serve to implement presidential claims to have wired up the Middle East to a Doomsday Machine, in the same way Iranian captors of American hostages in Teheran claimed to have wired the U.S. Embassy for total demolition in the event of attack.

It is not reassuring to recall that the latter warning did not, in fact, deter President Carter from launching a "rescue" raid, despite official estimates that it would cost the lives of some and perhaps most of the hostages. (They all lived to come home, after all, only by an "act of Allah" in the form of a sandstorm, which did not, however, spare the lives of all the raiders.)

Nevertheless, such threats can work, and in the larger case as well. The Russians may not tread, in some future year of crisis, on the nuclear tripwires that have been laid around their present zone of occupation, protecting "our" oil in the Middle East. But the scale of risk is different. By the Carter/Reagan policy, every human life in the Middle East and every city in the northern hemisphere is held hostage.

Even when such a policy is challenged, the demolitions *may* not be triggered. But the historical political conditions for that deserve to be studied. The one clear example among past nuclear crises is the failure of Nixon's direct, secret threats to the Hanoi regime in 1969. As H. R. Haldeman has revealed (see note 11), Henry Kissinger conveyed the warning to the Vietnamese that Nixon would escalate the war massively, including the possible use of nuclear weapons, if they did not accept his terms, which Nixon describes in his memoirs as his "November ultimatum." Roger Morris, who worked on these escalation plans under Kissinger, reports seeing the actual mission folders, including photographs, for the nuclear targets recommended to the president; one of them was a railhead in North Vietnam a mile and a half from the Chinese border. Hanoi never did accept the terms of Nixon's ultimatum; and Nixon's discussion and his later actions indicate strongly that it was not a bluff. Why then was the escalation not carried out?

Nixon himself gives the reason, one only, in his memoirs.

There were too many Americans on the streets, demonstrating nonviolently against the war, on October 15, and again on November 15, 1969, the days of the Vietnam Moratorium actions and the Washington March Against Death, which happened to straddle his secret November 1 ultimatum. Nixon realized by October 16, he reports, that the protest movement had so "polarized" public opinion that he would not have sufficient support for his planned escalation. As he saw it, the antiwar movement had kept him from ending the war—his way—his first year in office. From another point of view, the protest actions—whose actual power and effect Nixon kept at the time as secret from the public as his ultimatum—has prolonged the moratorium on the combat use of nuclear weapons by a dozen years so far.

But presidents learn, too, from such setbacks. In the era of parity (which had arrived a few years before Nixon took office) public support for nuclear threats is both harder to come by and more necessary—if the threat is to work—than in the golden age of U.S. near-monopoly. A demonstration, in advance, of public support of the threat policy seems now almost essential to its prospects of success (as well as to containing the political risks if it should fail). Following the onset of the emotional hostage crisis, the Russian invasion of Afghanistan provided a near-perfect occasion for Carter to bid for this public support, which had become urgent, in White House eyes, almost a year earlier with the fall of the Shah as protector of U.S. interests in the Gulf. (Almost equally ominous for the prospects of client dictators of the U.S. was the triumph of liberation forces over Somoza a few months later, July 19, 1979, in Nicaragua.)

By deliberately making *public* what the Soviets had undoubtedly always regarded as sufficiently obvious implicit threats of nuclear initiatives to preserve U.S. influence in the Gulf oil regions, Carter was also acting to legitimize such threats in future cases where the public was less likely to perceive either an urgent threat from a rival superpower or a "vital national interest." Such threats would be used primarily, as in the past, against adversaries who did not yet have any nuclear weapons with which to retaliate: in particular, to U.S. troops who were defending other Shahs and Somozas from their own people.

Before long some such threat would be called and carried out. Even if such a war, outside NATO or the Middle East, should be limited in area and intensity, it would be a precedent for other nuclear wars that eventually would escape any such limits. And the next such outbreak would not again await thirty-six years; more likely it would not take thirty-six weeks for the earliest example of nuclear first-use to be repeated, by the U.S. or others.

The onset of this fatal epoch of limited—and then less limited—nuclear wars will be hastened if the open advocacy by the White House and Pentagon of nuclear superiority, first-strike forces, and first-use threats continues to meet either a positive or a passive response. What Carter sought with his draft registration, what Reagan now seeks with his trillion-dollar-plus arms build-up, what some NATO leaders have intended by pressing the "token" deployment of Pershing and cruise missiles to Europe, are active expressions of consent and commitment from their publics, the nuclear hostages in Europe and America. It is what the Reverend Jim Jones wanted with his suicide drills in Guyana.

Jones called the practice sessions "White Nights," rehearsing his followers in the gestures of sacrificing their children and themselves, training them to react passively to his message (in the recurrent tones of every American president and every other leader of a nuclear weapons state since 1945): "Trust me. This time it's only a drill. *I* will decide . . . when the time has come for us to meet together on the other side; the time for the cyanide." That time finally came for Jones and his followers in mid-November 1979, just weeks before the NATO governments announced in December their decision, prepared in secret with no prior public discussion, to accept in the name of their citizens the stationing of U.S.-controlled Pershing and cruise missiles on European territory.

But in Europe, now, public consent to these preparations and rehearsals for "omnicide" is beginning to be denied. In many parts of West Europe, in fact, more broadly than in the United States as yet, an active movement of education and protest is well past the stage of beginnings. Reacting in particular to the December 1979 decision, in Holland, Norway, Britain, West Germany, to a lesser extent Denmark and Belgium, public movements are already approaching what is required—a movement of protest and resistance on the scale of that which blocked Nixon from escalating in 1969—to restrain their national leaderships from following the catastrophic overall course proclaimed by the U.S. administration.

This book, and each of its authors, is part of that movement. Along with the "Appeal for European Nuclear Disarmament" which he initially drafted, E. P. Thompson's opening essay, in particular, has played the role of awakening that movement of Tom Paine's *Common Sense*. As a participant myself in such projects in the United States in recent years as the teach-ins and demonstrations of the Mobilization for Survival, the Continental Walk for Disarmament and Social Justice, civil disobedience at Wall Street, the Pentagon, the Department of Energy, Rocky Flats Nuclear Production Facility, and the University of California (designer of all U.S. nuclear warheads), I can testify to the existence of a variegated and growing movement against the nuclear arms race in the United States, which also includes campaigns of civil disobedience organized by Jonah House and by the Pacific Life Community, broad-based regional protests against the MX basing plans in Utah and Nevada, and massive non-compliance with draft registration. Yet it is my impression from several visits that West Europe is at this moment the focal point for effective resistance to official American-led nuclear policies, and that the current movement there is potentially an important source of energy and inspiration for Americans. Which is to say that the movement in Europe deserves close attention in America, and the essays in this book are a good place to start.

The emphasis in these papers on unilateral measures of disarmament and on nuclear-free zones in England and West Europe has little counterpart in the U.S. movement, except for the regional anti-MX activities, and (like the latter) may at first glance seem parochial or unrealistically limited in scope to American readers: perhaps easily circumvented by national leaderships simply by changing the basing modes—putting the cruise missiles out to sea or among more compliant nationals, putting the MX missiles into Minuteman silos—without any fundamental change in the policy or its risks.

Actually, the differences in tactical focus reflect mainly different backgrounds, different national roles within the NATO alliance, and a European perspective that is simply unfamiliar to most Americans but that is important to come to understand. The immediate aims of END (European Nuclear Disarmament), in fact, logically *complement* objectives that have received more attention in the United States, such as a superpower freeze (a bilateral halt to the testing, production, and deployment of all new nuclear weapons and vehicles), bilateral no-first-use commitments, and sharp reduction in superpower stockpiles, leading toward the general abolition of nuclear weapons. For example, to reject the deployment of neutron warheads and Pershing and cruise missiles and to demand the removal of the U.S. and Soviet nuclear weapons that now exist in West and East Europe, as END does, can be understood not only as part of the freeze demand but as calling for the effective implementation of a no-first-use commitment, since none of these forward-based weapons have much function other than first-use. What is more, the impulse to rid one's own neighborhood of the poisoned bait is a natural and appropriate basis for mobilization, if it comes to be understood within a framework of broader objectives and global concern.

We all live in Guyana now, and there is no place to run to. From Utah to Norway to east of the Urals, we must take our stand where we live, and act to protect our home and our family: the earth and all living beings. The slogan of the Dutch Interchurch Council (IKV)—"Rid the earth of nuclear weapons; let it begin in Holland"—can inspire the commitments of individuals and communities in the superpowers and other countries of the world: "Let it begin here, now, with us."

As this is being written (July 1981) more than a thousand citizens of Europe (including delegations from East Germany and Yugoslavia) are on the road, walking from Copenhagen to Paris on a March for Peace, with the theme: "A Nuclear-free Europe, from Poland to Portugal." The symbolism of the action, launched by three women from Norway and scheduled to arrive in Paris on August 6, seems just right; without relying on jet fuel, it is moving across national boundaries, at the steady pace of humans walking, together, in contact with the earth. As they proceed, holding rallies and teach-ins at each night's stop, others are joining the march: many of them, no doubt, from among the million Dutch citizens who petitioned and demonstrated against the neutron bomb in 1978 and the million West Germans who have petitioned (the Krefelder Appel) and demonstrated against the stationing of cruise and Pershing missiles this spring of 1981.

Like Americans resisting "symbolic" draft registration or sitting on railroad tracks at Rocky Flats, these European marchers are saying with their presence on the road what the mothers and fathers at Jonestown waited too long to say, what they should have said when the cyanide shipments first arrived or at the first rehearsals for murder and suicide: "No! Not our children! This is craziness; we won't be part of it." It is none too soon to be saying this to the President/Prime Minister/Chairman Jim Jones's of the world; nor is it, yet, too late. It is mutiny time in Jonestown: the revolt of the hostages.

Notes

1. Gregg Herken, *The Winning Weapon* (New York: Knopf, 1980), pp. 256–74.

> . . . the important feature of the bombers—to British strategy —was that it worked—or at least many Americans believed it worked. By the end of July [1948] the absence of any Soviet military countermoves to the airlift that had effectively broken the blockade of Berlin was attributed in substantial part to the deterrent effect of the "atomic-capable" bombers within range of Russian cities. (p. 260)

> Even Marshall—who throughout the year had been concerned that the United States not "provoke" the Russians into military action—now expressed optimism for the future. His change in attitude had been partly motivated, he confided to Forrestal, by his belief that "the Soviets are beginning to realize for the first time that the United States would really use the atomic bomb against them in the event of war." (p. 274)

2. Press Conference, November 30, 1950. Also Truman's memoirs, *Years of Trial and Hope*, Vol. II (New York: Signet, 1965), pp. 450–51. Dean Acheson, *Present at the Creation* (New York: W. W. Norton, 1969), pp. 472–85. (See note 14.)
3. Eisenhower's memoirs, *Mandate for Change*, Vol. I (New York: Doubleday, 1963), pp. 178–81.

> In the light of my unwillingness to accept the status quo, several other moves were considered in the event that the Chinese Communists refused to accede to an armistice in a reasonable time. These possibilities differed in detail, but in order to back up any of them, we had to face several facts.
>
> First, it was obvious that if we were to go over to a major offensive, the war would have to be expanded outside of Korea—with strikes against the supporting Chinese airfields in Manchuria, a blockade of the Chinese coast, and similar measures. . . . Finally, to keep the attack from becoming overly costly, it was clear that we would have to use atomic weapons. . . . One possibility was to let the Communist authorities understand that, in the absence of satisfactory progress, we intended to move decisively without inhibition in our use of weapons, and would no longer be responsible for confining hostilities to the Korean Peninsula. We would not be limited by any world-wide gentleman's agreement. In India and in the Formosa Straits area, and at the truce negotiations at Panmunjom, we dropped the word, discreetly, of our intention. We felt quite sure it would reach Soviet and Chinese Communist ears.

See also, Alexander L. George and Richard Smoke, *Deterrence in American Foreign Policy* (New York: Columbia University Press, 1974), pp. 237–41.

According to Sherman Adams, Eisenhower's White House chief of staff (Firsthand Report, pp. 48–49),

> Long afterward, talking one day with Eisenhower about the events that led up finally to the truce with Korea, I asked him what it was that brought the Communists into line.

> "Danger of an atomic war," he said without hesitation. "We told them we could not hold to a limited war any longer if the Communists welched on a treaty of truce. They didn't want a full-scale war or an atomic attack. That kept them under some control."

In the above passage of his memoirs, Eisenhower also mentions: "Meanwhile, General Mark Clark (who had succeeded Ridgway as United Nations commander) began to suspect that the Communists were building up forces in the Kaesong 'sanctuary' area. He requested permission to launch an attack in the event he became convinced that a Communist attack there was pending. This authority I thought unwise to delegate at that time" (p. 181). But recently declassified minutes of the National Security Council meeting on February 11, 1953, to which this refers, record a noteworthy exchange at this point, omitted from the memoirs:

> [The President] then expressed the view that we should consider the use of tactical atomic weapons on the Kaesong area [an area of approximately twenty-eight square miles, which was according to Clark, "now chock full of troops and material"], which provided a good target for this type of weapon. In any case, the President added, we could not go on the way we were indefinitely.
>
> General Bradley thought it desirable to begin talking with our allies regarding an end of the sanctuary, but thought it unwise to broach the subject yet of possible use of atomic weapons.
>
> Secretary Dulles discussed the moral problem and the inhibitions on the use of the A-bomb, and Soviet success to date in setting atomic weapons apart from all other weapons as being in a special category. It was his opinion that we should try to break down this false distinction.
>
> The President added that we should certainly start on diplomatic negotiations with our allies. To him, it seemed that our self-respect and theirs was involved, and if they objected to the use of atomic weapons we might well ask them to supply three or more divisions needed to drive the Communists back, in lieu of use of atomic weapons. In conclusion, however, the President ruled against any discussion with our allies of military plans or weapons of attack.

The corresponding discussion in Eisenhower's memoirs does raise the subject of allied attitudes (and perhaps, implicitly, those of the American public as well) in remarks that seem highly pertinent to a number of the essays that follow:

If we decided upon a major, new type of offensive, the present policies would have to be changed and the new ones agreed to by our allies. Foremost would be the proposed use of atomic weapons. In this respect American views have always differed somewhat from those of some of our allies. For the British, for example, the use of atomic weapons in war at that time would have been a decision of the gravest kind. My feeling was then, and still remains, that it would be impossible for the United States to maintain the miliary commitments which it now sustains around the world (without turning into a garrison state) did we not possess atomic weapons and the will to use them when necessary. But an American decision to use them at that time would have created strong disruptive feelings between ourselves and our allies. However, if an all-out offensive should be highly successful, I felt that the rifts so caused could, in time, be repaired.

Of course, there were other problems, not the least of which would be the possibility of the Soviet Union entering the war. In nuclear warfare the Chinese Communists would have been able to do little. But we knew that the Soviets had atomic weapons in quantity, and estimated that they would soon explode a hydrogen device. Of all the Asian targets which might be subjected to Soviet bombing, I was most concerned about the unprotected cities of Japan. (p. 180)

4. Prime Minister Bidault in the film *Hearts and Minds*, and in Roscoe Drummond and Gaston Coblentz, *Duel at the Brink* (New York: Doubleday, 1960), pp. 121–22. Also see, Richard Nixon's memoirs, *RN* (New York: Grosset & Dunlap, 1978), pp. 150–55.

As he told Drummond and Coblentz,

Bidault understood Dulles, on two separate occasions, to have offered him the use of American atomic bombs by French forces in the Indochina war.

By Bidault's account, both offers were made before the fall of Dienbienphu; prior, that is, to the Geneva Conference. According to Bidault, both offers were made to him personally by Dulles in Paris.

The first is recalled by Bidault as an offer of one or more atomic bombs to be dropped on Communist Chinese territory near the Indochina border in a countermove against the Chinese supply lines to the Vietminh Communists.

The second is recalled as an offer of two atomic bombs against the Vietminh forces at Dienbienphu.

Bidault, by his account, declined both offers. He told

> Dulles that it would be impossible to predict where the use of nuclear weapons against Red China would end, that it could lead to Russian intervention and a world-wide holocaust. In the case of the second offer, he considered the French and Vietminh forces to be by then too closely engaged at Dienbienphu to permit the use of atomic weapons.

5. Barry M. Blechman and Stephen S. Kaplan, *Force Without War* (Washington: Brookings Institution, 1978), pp. 238, 256.
6. Morton H. Halperin, *The 1958 Taiwan Straits Crisis: A Documented History* (formerly Top Secret), RAND Corporation Research Memorandum RM-4900-ISA, December 1966.
7. Blechman and Kaplan, *Force Without War*, pp. 343–439.
8. R. F. Kennedy, *Thirteen Days* (New York: W. W. Norton, 1971). (See note 14.)
9. Blechman and Kaplan, pp. 47–49, with a table listing nineteen such incidents between November 1946, and the worldwide SAC alert of October 1973.
10. Herbert Schandler, *The Unmaking of a President* (Princeton: Princeton University Press, 1977), pp. 86–91. Also see, General Westmoreland's memoirs, *A Soldier Reports* (New York: Doubleday, 1976), p. 338.

> Because the region around Khe Sanh was virtually uninhabited, civilian casualties would be minimal. If Washington officials were so intent on "sending a message" to Hanoi, surely small tactical nuclear weapons would be a way to tell Hanoi something, just as two atomic bombs had spoken convincingly to Japanese officials during World War II and the threat of atomic bombs induced the North Koreans to accept meaningful negotiations during the Korean War. It could be that use of a few small tactical nuclear weapons in Vietnam—or even the threat of them—might have quickly brough the war there to an end.

Or as General Nathan Twining, U.S. air force chief of staff at the time of Dienbienphu and later elevated by Eisenhower to be chairman of the Joint Chiefs of Staff, recollected in tranquility:

> I still think it would have been a good idea [to have taken] three small tactical A-bombs—it's a fairly isolated area, Dienbienphu—no great town around there, only Communists and their supplies. You could take all day to drop a bomb, make sure you put it in the right place. No opposition. And clean those Commies out of there and the band could play the Marseillaise and the French could march out

of Dienbienphu in fine shape. And those Commies would say, "Well, those guys might do this again to us. We'd better be careful." And we might not have had this problem we're facing in Vietnam now if we'd dropped those small A-weapons. (Dulles Oral History Project, Princeton; cited in Carl Solberg, *Riding High*, [New York: Mason & Lipscomb, 1973], p. 230)

11. H. R. Haldeman's memoirs, *The Ends of Power* (New York: Times Books, 1978), pp. 81–85, 97–98; and Richard M. Nixon's memoirs, *RN*, pp. 393–414; and personal interviews with Roger Morris and Eqbal Ahmad.

Haldeman's account:

> When Nixon spoke of his desire to be a peacemaker, he was not just delivering words his listeners wanted to hear. Nixon not only *wanted* to end the Vietnam War, he was absolutely convinced he *would* end it in his first year. I remember during the campaign, walking along a beach, he once said, "I'm the one man in this country who can do it, Bob." . . .
>
> He saw a parallel in the action President Eisenhower had taken to end another war. When Eisenhower arrived in the White House, the Korean War was stalemated. Eisenhower ended the impasse in a hurry. He secretly got word to the Chinese that he would drop nuclear bombs on North Korea unless a truce was signed immediately. In a few weeks, the Chinese called for a truce and the Korean War ended.
>
> In the 1950s Eisenhower's military background had convinced the Communists that he was sincere in his threat. Nixon didn't have that background, but he believed his hardline anti-Communist rhetoric of twenty years would serve to convince the North Vietnamese equally as well that he really meant to do what he said. He expected to utilize the same principle of a threat of excessive force. He would combine that threat with more generous offers of financial aid to the North Vietnamese than they had ever received before. And with this combination of a strong warning plus unprecedented generosity, he was certain he could force the North Vietnamese—at long last—into legitimate peace negotiations.
>
> The threat was the key, and Nixon coined a phrase for his theory which I'm sure will bring smiles of delight to Nixon-haters everywhere. We were walking along a foggy beach after a long day of speechwriting. He said, "I call it the Madman Theory, Bob. I want the North Vietnamese to believe I've reached the point where I might do *anything* to stop the war. We'll just slip the word to them that, for God's

> sake, you know Nixon is obsessed about Communism. We can't restrain him when he's angry—and he has his hand on the nuclear button—and Ho Chi Minh himself will be in Paris in two days begging for peace."
>
> As it turned out, it wasn't Bill Rogers, the future secretary of state, who slipped the word to the North Vietnamese, but a brilliant, impulsive, witty gentleman with an engaging German accent—Henry Kissinger. (pp. 82–83)

12. References in text.
13. References in text.
14. Eisenhower's self-appointed concern (see note 3) about retaliation against "the unprotected cities of Japan" (which were, and are, of course, neither more nor less unprotected against nuclear attack than every other city in the world) if he should carry out his nuclear threats against China in 1953 would have been equally appropriate in connection with his offer of nuclear weapons for use in Indochina in 1954 and his plans for use over Quemoy in 1958. But his concern not only failed to preclude the threats and serious preparations; it did not lead him to alert the Japanese, or others including close allies, to the danger he perceived himself as imposing on them.

    Immediately after Truman's announcement of U.S. consideration of nuclear weapons in Korea, December 1950, British Prime Minister Atlee flew to Washington, wishing, in Acheson's words, "Britain to be admitted to some participation with us in any future decision to use nuclear weapons," specifically an agreement "that neither of us would use these weapons without prior consultation with the other" (*Present at the Creation*, pp. 478, 484). Like other U.S. allies, Britain failed to get any such assurance, then or later.

    The main effect of Atlee's "scurrying across the ocean" in response to Truman's "unfortunate" candor at his press conference (Acheson's words, in an account contemptuously patronizing of the British leader) was to make later presidents more circumspect with their nuclear threats, usually cutting out U.S. allies and the American public from knowledge of them.

    Even the Cuban Missile Crisis is only a partial exception to this. In an account unique for its vividness and its authority, Robert Kennedy reports an episode in that crisis when the navy was preparing to force a Russian submarine to the surface, a few minutes which

    > were the time of gravest concern for the President. Was the world on the brink of a holocaust? Was it an error? A mis-

> take? Was there something further that should have been done? Or not done? His hand went up to his face and covered his mouth. He opened and closed his fist. His face seemed drawn, his eyes pained, almost gray. We stared at each other across the table. For a few fleeting seconds, it was almost as though no one else was there and he was no longer the President.
>
> Inexplicably, I thought of when he was ill and almost died; when he lost his child; when we learned that our oldest brother had been killed; of personal times of strain and hurt. The voices droned on, but I didn't seem to hear anything until I heard the President say: "Isn't there some way we can avoid having our first exchange with a Russian submarine—almost anything but that?" "No, there's too much danger to our ships. There is no alternative," said McNamara. "Our commanders have been instructed to avoid hostilities if at all possible, but this is what we must be prepared for, and this is what we must expect."
>
> We had come to the time of final decision. "We must expect that they will close down Berlin—make the final preparations for that," the President said. I felt that we were on the edge of a precipice with no way off. . . . One thousand miles away in the vast expanse of the Atlantic Ocean the final decisions were going to be made in the next few minutes. President Kennedy had initiated the course of events, but he no longer had control over them. (*Thirteen Days*, p. 48)

Minutes later a messenger brought in a report that Russian ships approaching the blockade line had stopped dead in the water, and Kennedy *then* cancelled the intercept orders. But three days later, the Executive Committee of the NSC with the president presiding was considering an imminent U.S. air strike and invasion.

> The NATO countries were supporting our position and recommending that the U.S. be firm, but, President Kennedy said, they did not realize the full implications for them. If we carried out an air strike against Cuba and the Soviet Union answered by attacking [U.S. Jupiter intermediate-range missiles—comparable to Pershing IIs—stationed in] Turkey, all NATO was going to be involved. Then, immediately, the President would have to decide whether he would use nuclear weapons against the Soviet Union, and all mankind would be threatened. . . . We had to be aware that we were deciding, the President was deciding, for the U.S., the Soviet Union, Turkey, NATO and really for all mankind . . . (*Ibid.*, pp. 74, 77; final dots in original)

Later that evening, alone with Robert Kennedy, the president

> talked about the miscalculations that lead to war. War is rarely intentional. The Russians don't wish to fight any more than we do. They do not want to war with us nor we with them. And yet if events continue as they have in the last several days, that struggle—which no one wishes, which will accomplish nothing—will engulf and destroy all mankind. . . . It was not only for Americans that he was concerned, or primarily the older generation of any land. The thought that disturbed him the most, and that made the prospect of war much more fearful than it would otherwise have been, was the specter of the death of the children of this country and all the world—the young people who had no role, who had no say, who knew nothing even of the confrontation, but whose lives would be snuffed out like everyone else's. They would never have a chance to make a decision, to vote in an election, to run for office, to lead a revolution, to determine their own destinies. (*Ibid*., pp. 84–85.)

These reflections had (only) the effect of leading President Kennedy to send his brother to convey an explicit, secret, forty-eight-hour ultimatum to Khrushchev through Ambassador Dobrynin, rather than simply to attack two days later without warning. According to Theodore Sorensen, "[T]he odds that the Soviets [sic] would go all the way to war," President Kennedy later said, "seemed to him then 'somewhere between one out of three and even'" (*Kennedy*, [New York: Harper & Row, 1965], p. 705).

PART I

1
A Letter to America
E. P. Thompson

America's Europe: A Hobbit Among Gandalfs

I do not think that I can be accused of being anti-American. It would be strange if I were, for I am ethnically half-American myself. My mother came of stock reaching back to seventeenth-century New England immigrants, and surely three centuries is long enough to establish some ethnic credentials?

I first crossed the Atlantic from England when I was a child of five, in 1929. The Atlantic seemed to me then, as I clambered about the decks of an ocean liner, to be an immense stretch of water. But the faces and gestures which I met with in America appeared as reassuring and familiar.

What bothers me now, as a frequent visitor to the States, is that the Atlantic seems to be growing wider, even though it now takes only some six hours to cross. The gestures, the voices, indeed the whole mind-set of the dominant politics and media are becoming more and more unfamiliar. There are times when Europe and America appear to have drifted beyond range of communication.

This drift is bringing both continents into immense danger. And a European feels the need to raise his voice and shout out some warning to his American friends.

But how is this to be done? There are already sufficient authoritative voices on this side of the Atlantic, ready, at the drop of a fee, to expound to the American public what Europeans think and need. What they need (it seems) is to be defended by the United States, by the most advanced and hideous nuclear weapons imaginable; and they want the United States to be strong, decisive, and to pay the bill. The more querulous commentators grumble that Europeans don't want to pay much for their own protection, and—the Blessed Mrs. Thatcher apart—they want, in their decadent materialist way, to benefit from trading and money-lending to the Warsaw Pact nations while Uncle Sam holds a nuclear umbrella over their chiming tills. It will therefore be necessary for the vigorous new administration of President Ronald Reagan to bring Europeans to a proper sense of their duties to the Free World.

This is what the American public has been told, in various places, throughout 1980, and what it will be told, more loudly, in 1981. For example, Flora Lewis, who has the reputation of being an able columnist, informed readers of the *New York Times* (October 17, 1980) of "the dominant European view" of United States diplomacy and military postures, and she reassured them as to "basic Western solidarity" and an increased European "sense of dependence" on the U.S.A.

One answer to this kind of statement is that "Europeans" are not, any more than Americans, of some kind of standard issue. I am sure that Ms. Lewis will have been told this kind of thing by public relations operators around the Foreign or Defense Ministries of certain Western European nations—that is, by persons who are employed to tell American columnists whatever they have come to hear. But there is rather a lot of evidence, about which readers of the American press have been left singularly ill-informed, as to what other Europeans have been thinking and doing in 1980.

If we leave the Warsaw Pact populations aside (although these are also Europeans), a brief summary would show this. Sweden, Austria, and Yugoslavia have continued to pursue policies of active nonalignment, pressing disarmament upon both superpowers. Norway and Denmark refused even to consider harboring cruise missiles on their territories. (The Norwegian Prime Minister, in his New Year's message for 1981, has now called for a nuclear-weapons-free zone embracing five northern European nations.) The Dutch and Belgian Governments, which initially went along with the NATO decision (of December 12, 1979) to "modernize" theater nuclear weapons, have been forced to backtrack on their agreement in the face of nationwide agitation extending from the churches to the far left. In West Germany only Chancellor Helmut Schmidt's dexterous political ambiguities are postponing the moment when a smoldering political revolt will flare up in his own party and far beyond. In Greece it is now considered probable that Andreas Papandreou's Pasok, with nonaligned, anti-NATO policies, will head the polls in the 1981 elections.

In Britain the main opposition party, the Labour Party—which is now way ahead in all opinion polls—is committed to policies of unilateral nuclear disarmament and outright opposition to the introduction of cruise missiles, and the Labour Party's leader, Michael Foot, has promised that if Mrs. Margaret Thatcher's Government introduces these missiles, the next Labour government will send them back across the Atlantic. And on October 26, 1980, some 70,000 people assembled in Trafalgar Square, London, to signal their outright opposition to every measure of nuclear menace and weaponry.

This great meeting signaled the re-entry into British political life—but at an even broader and higher level—of the old C.N.D. (Campaign for Nuclear Disarmament) founded in the 1950s by Bertrand Russell, J. B. Priestley, Canon Collins, and others—a campaign long quiescent. It is now supported, right across the spectrum, by academics and trade unionists, Liberals and Labourists, ecologists and Welsh nationalists, church men and women, feminists, and by the youth culture in the popular music world. New C.N.D. branches, local antimissile groups, women's groups, specialist groups (of scientists, doctors, university teachers) have proliferated.

I have not discussed the similar movements in Spain, Portugal, France, and Italy but, altogether, this amounts to quite a few Europeans who, unaccountably, do not take what is supposed to be "the European view." I did attempt to draw the attention of readers of the *New York Times* to this evidence, but without success. My letter went unpublished, although Ms. Lewis herself was kind enough to send me a courteous note of acknowledgment.

Since her letter to me was private I am not entitled to quote it here. But, in brief, she argued that, since the elected governments of certain NATO powers were endorsing NATO plans for nuclear rearmament, she was correct in reporting this as "the dominant European view."

Now such a reply is formally acceptable—and it was nice of her to write back—but it is not good enough. I can recall a time when liberal opinion in the United States was finely attuned to the causes and issues of other nations, a time when New York was a great internationalist city which listened to the world—and when we, in Europe, listened back to the causes and arguments of New York.

What Ms. Lewis seemed to be signaling to me was the end of that sort of tradition, when not only ruling parties and great blocs (Europe, NATO) were attended to but when minorities also were allowed voices—and I have been speaking of very substantial minorities, strong enough to defeat governments—and when we tried, across national barriers, to exchange arguments and to work for common causes. There is a substantial, growing, well-informed tide of opinion in Europe which considers that both superpowers—under the pressure of their rival military establishments—are on a collision course which will prove, within some two decades, to be terminal: that is, terminal for *all* of us. The survival of civilization in the Northern Hemisphere might appear to be a common cause whose movements and arguments merit reporting.

It is not because I am "anti-American" but because I am pro-American—that is, because I think that, on balance, it would be a good thing if American civilization survived—that I am asking for attention to these arguments. And I must add one more personal note.

In the past two decades I have benefited greatly from intellectual exchanges with American scholars in my own discipline of social history, and I have enjoyed the hospitality of several American universities. There can be no doubt as to the internationalism of the American academic community—it is to the United States that one comes to find out what is happening in many other parts of the world. There is no honor which has delighted me more than election as a foreign honorary Fellow of the American Academy of Arts and Sciences.

I am therefore baffled to know what to make of the Winter 1981 issue of *Daedalus*. *Daedalus* is the journal of the American Academy and it has a distinguished reputation. This current issue is the second of two numbers devoted to "U.S. Defense Policy in the 1980s," and it is largely concerned with NATO and with European arrangements. The concern is phrased, throughout, in such terms as this: "Are new doubts about the American commitment to its defense taking hold in Western Europe?"

I have read this special issue with attention and with growing astonishment. I find it to be a barbaric utterance, made up of chapters of bad advice from Satan's Kingdom, and in its sum a signal that civilization is already defeated beyond remedy. (And I would add that the views expressed in this particular issue of *Daedalus* are representative of the larger community of "defense intellectuals" in the United States.)

Indeed, this defeat is *assumed*, as a first proposition, from the first page to the last. It is assumed that two great blocs in the world are in a state of permanent war (restrained only by something called "deterrence") and will, forever, remain so. The expertise of the authors—for they are, all of them, undoubtedly very great experts—is contained within an infantile political view of the world, derived, I suppose, from too much early reading of Tolkien's *Lord of the Rings*. The evil kingdom of Mordor lies there, and there it ever will lie, while on our side lies the nice republic of Eriador, inhabited by confused liberal hobbits who are rescued from time to time by the genial white wizardry of Gandalf-figures such as Henry Kissinger, Zbigniew Brzezinski or, maybe, Richard Allen.

That is an overstatement, for in fact the contributors to this issue say little about politics at all. A Manichaean, black-white, world-view is assumed, and the rest is politically null. That is, perhaps, what a top-flight "defense expert" is: a person with a hole in the head where politics and morality ought to be, who can then get along all the better with moving around the acronyms, in a vocabulary of throw-weight, delivery-systems, megatons, and the extrapolation of ever-more-tenuous worst-case scenarios.

"Controlling the escalation process by providing NATO with a wider menu of realistic nuclear options has become an important priority." That is a sample of the use of English of one of these experts, Mr. Richard Burt, whose extremist views were represented extensively in the *New York Times* in the period of the late election. And another notable expert, Professor Michael Nacht, comes forward proudly as the inventor of a new "defensive" concept, that of "pre-emptive deterrence." Pre-emptive deterrence consists in preemptive *aggressive* actions around the world in pursuit of strategic advantage or scarce minerals, raw materials, oil and so forth, and he recommends this brave new concept (although I had thought the concept to be as old as Roman or British imperialism) to the attention of the new U.S. administration—but in a moderate kind of way, of course, and only when "U.S. security interests" or "the intrinsic value of the assets" are important and, even then, only in "favourable circumstances."

I have been puzzling, as a European, to work out how this "wider menu" of "nuclear options" might affect us, and what "pre-emptive deterrence" might lead on to. The view of Europe of several of these distinguished contributors is somewhat hazy. Scholars so high in the world, whose advice is solicited by statesmen and editors, must take a large and distant view of things. One expert notes that "Western Europe (like South Korea) amounts geographically to a peninsula projecting out from the Eurasian land mass, a land mass dominated by the Soviet Union, a land mass from which large contingents of military force can emerge on relatively short notice to invade the peninsula."

Undoubtedly a sage comment. But it puzzles me as a historian. South Korea has not, I think, ever been invaded by Russians, although those new-found friends of the United States, the Chinese, did once enter *North* Korea in force. Nor is Western Europe *exactly* like South Korea. Nor, come to think of it, has the traffic, since the time of the Visigoths, always been that way, with invading hordes bearing down on the "peninsula" from the "land mass." I seem, dimly, to recall movements the other way—and on two occasions to the gates of Moscow. I believe that there are Russians still living (for many millions did not survive it) who recall the second occasion.

But these are expert matters which we must leave to the

experts. What we cannot leave to the experts are the *politics* of human survival: and on this small matter, one might have supposed, the American Academy of Arts and Sciences might (in two generous issues) have solicited a contribution. This matter confuses me very deeply: I feel myself severed in half, as a citizen of Europe and as a visiting scholar enjoying American hospitality.

For the editor of *Daedalus*, Professor Stephen Graubard, is a member of the history department at Brown University (where I have been teaching), and he has an office at the top of the same pleasant old house in which I work. We have not been introduced to each other, but no doubt we have met and nodded genially on the stairs. No doubt, if he has heard of me at all, he thinks of me as a *very* confused hobbit, needing all the protection that American Gandalfs can bring.

Professor Graubard's own introduction to this special issue is bland, and it might even be thought that he has done no more than exercise his necessary editorial duties in putting this Satanic handbook together. Yet, at a second view, it is clear that he is very much in accord with the first assumptions of his contributors. He shares the prime assumption, upon which all else is erected, that there is "a potential Soviet threat to the very heart of Europe," and that this must be so, forever and ever, amen. The "gravity of our predicament" stems from the loss of United States "dominance" in Europe, and this loss "can only be thought of as tragic." The growing desire, even lust, of Europeans, East and West, for nuclear disarmament and for detente, is seen by Graubard (as by several of his contributors) as regrettable and as something presenting "problems" to defense experts and to Western politicians, who must somehow—by fictive gestures at arms control—negotiate around the susceptibilities of their electorates. And Graubard shares with other contributors a sense of alarm at the possible "Finlandization" of Europe, while, at the same time, writing that "Europeans are openly shocked by evidences of American indecision and incompetence."

Now I wonder who these "Europeans" are? I think that they may be fictions of defense experts and editors, counters in the rhetorical games of the Cold War. If Professor Graubard and I were to stop on the stairs one day and exchange courtesies, I would feel bound to go on, beyond courtesy, to ask him some questions. I would ask him why he assembled for this number this set of contributors and not others: for example, those many distinguished American scientists, arms-control experts, and others (some of them longstanding Fellows of the Academy) who have, over the years, in such places as the *Bulletin of the Atomic Scientists*, performed a service to the entire world by presenting seriously researched information and by proposing alternatives to the never-ending arms race? And if Professor Graubard replied that "defense experts," in Western Europe as well as the United States, are into this kind of Satanic vocabulary and are prisoners of their own discipline, then I would readily agree; and would agree, also, that a similar compilation of worst-case scenarios and tabulations of megatonnage could be put together in the Soviet bloc as well. But I would go on to ask whether the discipline itself may not be suspect, corrupt and at enmity with the universal principles of humane scholarship; whether it was the business of scholarship; whether it was the business of scholars, at a time when civilization itself is threatened, to serve as the (well-funded, and -rewarded) apologists of military establishments and states?

I would then tell him that I do not know what "Finlandization" means, but that if it means a process by which, in the Warsaw bloc, the bankrupt ideology and methods of Soviet Communism give way before increasing pressures for democratization, while in Western Europe the pressures grow for disarmament, trade and cultural exchange, this is an end devoutly to be hoped for. And what shocks my kind of European is not American "indecision and incompetence" but its menacing measures of military deployment and nuclear armament, its refusal to engage in any disarmament negotiations in plain earnest, its ridiculous and threatening claim of the Persian Gulf as an American sea, the manifest desire of its strategists to reduce Western European nations to an inert state of cliency, its instrumental and opportunist use of the issues of civil rights in the Soviet Union and Eastern Europe, not as causes which can actually be *won* but as amazing propaganda-fodder in the media cold war, and, in sum, exactly that infantile and self-confirming view of hostilities in perpetuity which is the premise of this issue of *Daedalus*.

I would have to go on to explain why I do not wish to be "defended" by American nuclear weaponry, and more than this, why increasing numbers of Western Europeans regard the proposed introduction of cruise missiles and Pershing IIs onto their territory as, so far from being any defense, a move that, by making them priority targets in any nuclear war, threatens their existence. And I would then have to explain how I came to be one of the speakers at Trafalgar Square on October 26, in a demonstration under the slogan "Protest and Survive"—a slogan which was taken from a pamphlet of that title issued last April.

The editor of *The Nation*, who holds to the old and estimable tradition of international exchanges, has done me the honor of proposing that some large part of this pamphlet, *Protest and Survive*, may be of concern to American readers. And I must ask these readers, in what follows, to have the courtesy to place themselves for a while in an alternative, European, perception. I have struck out some merely local British passages, but I have not attempted to adjust the argument as a whole. This would not be possible, and it is, in any case, precisely the alternative perception which I wish to convey. If readers will do me the kindness, for a while, to consider themselves as Europeans or even—painful as this may be—as British protesters, then I will attempt, in the conclusion, to return them to themselves.

"Modernizing" NATO: The Mendacity Game

We have academic defense "experts" in Europe also, who are on very much the same circuit as the contributors to *Daedalus*. One such is Professor Michael Howard, until lately Chichele Professor of the History of War, and now promoted to be Regius Professor of History at Oxford, perhaps the most eminent position in the British historical profession.

Professor Howard wrote to *The Times* of London (January 30, 1980) urging extensive provisions for civil defense, as a component in British "defense posture." And he continued:

> The presence of cruise missiles on British soil makes it highly possible that this country would be target for a series of preemptive strikes by Soviet missiles. These would not necessarily be on the massive scale foreseen by Lord Noel-Baker in your columns of January 24. It is more likely that the Russians would hold such massive strikes in reserve, to deter us from using our sea-based missiles as a "second strike force" after the first Soviet warheads had hit targets in this country.
>
> This initially limited Soviet strike would have the further objective, beyond eliminating weapons in this country targeted on their own homeland, of creating conditions here of such political turbulence that the use of our own nuclear weapons, followed as this could be by yet heavier attacks upon us, would become quite literally "incredible."

On these grounds Professor Howard argued that "civil defense on a scale sufficient to give protection to a substantial number of the population" is "an indispensable element of deterrence."

What such measures of civil defense might be, or what scale would be necessary to protect a "substantial number" of the population Professor Howard did not explain. I therefore consulted the letter which he cited by Philip Noel-Baker in *The Times*. Lord Noel-Baker is the recipient of the Nobel Peace Prize for his work for international conciliation over very many years. We may take it that he keeps himself well informed. In his letter he notes that "many voices are being raised in the United States, Britain and elsewhere to argue that nuclear wars could be fought without total disaster; some even suggest that nuclear war can be won." He then goes on to detail the findings of Mr. Val Peterson, who was appointed United States Civil Defense Administrator some twenty-five years ago, and who organized many exercises, national, regional, and local, at the height of a previous Cold War.

Mr. Peterson drew the following conclusions from his successive exercises. In 1954 the national exercise was estimated to have had a yield of twenty-two million casualities, of whom seven million would have been dead. In 1956 fifty-six million, or one-third of the population of the United States, were presumed as casualties. In 1957:

> If the whole 170 million Americans had Air Raid Shelters, at least 50 percent of them would die in a surprise enemy attack. In the last analysis, there is no such thing as a nation being prepared for a thermonuclear war.

From evidence of this order Lord Noel-Baker concludes:

> Any use of nuclear weapons will escalate into a general war. . . . There is *no* defense against such weapons; and . . . nuclear warfare will destroy civilization, and perhaps exterminate mankind. To hope for salvation from Civil Defense is a dangerous self-deluding pipe dream.

There is a good deal of talk around today, from defense "experts," military strategists, and the like, which leads us to suppose that the military, on both sides of the world, are capable of delivering very small nuclear packs, with the greatest accuracy and with no lethal consequences outside the target area. In the bright vocabulary of "deterrence" they chatter on about "surgically clean strikes" with "minimum collateral damage." Professor Howard's speculations were evidently supported by some such assumptions: thus the Russians are supposed to "eliminate" the 160 cruise missiles which the United States is bent on placing in England, but only local damage will be done.

Now there are two matters here which require examination. The first concerns the known power and probable effect of these weapons. The second concerns the strategic assumptions of those "experts" who suppose that any nuclear war could be limited in this way. We will now turn to the first.

In the autumn of 1979, Lord Zuckerman delivered a major address in Philadelphia to the American Philosophical Society, which was published in its *Proceedings* of August 1980. It is an address which Europeans (and Americans also) should study. The author was the British Government's chief scientific adviser from 1964 to 1971 and, in addition to drawing upon his own extensive experience, he also draws upon that of a number of eminent U.S. scientists and advisers.

Lord Zuckerman's testimony (which should be read in full) is wholly dismissive of the notion of a "limited" nuclear strike, confined to military targets only:

> It is still inevitable that were military installations rather than cities to become the objectives of nuclear attack, millions, even tens of millions, of civilians would be killed, whatever the proportion of missile sites, airfields, armament plants, ports, and so on that would be destroyed.

And he explains that strategists, in calculating the estimated effects of missile strikes, employ the acronym C.E.P. (Circular Error Probable) for the radius of a circle within which 50 percent of the strikes would fall.

Thus we have to deal with two factors: the 50 percent of the missiles which fall *within* the C.E.P., and the 50 percent which fall *without* and which "would not necessarily be distributed according to standard laws of probability." Lord Zuckerman does not tell us the presumed C.E.P. for a "limited" strike aimed at a single missile base, and this is perhaps an official secret. But in the debate that was eventually held in the Commons *after* NATO's decision to base cruise missiles in Britain, statements were made which enable an impression to be offered.

I must first explain that the strategy of nuclear warfare has now become a highly specialized field of study, which has developed its own arcane vocabulary, together with a long list of acronyms: C.E.P., MIRV (multiple independently targeted re-entry vehicle), ICBM (intercontinental ballistic missile), ECCM (electronic counter-countermeasures), MEASL (Marconi-Elliot Avionics Systems, Ltd.), and as the plum of them all, MAD (mutual assured destruction).

In this vocabulary, nuclear weapons are subdivided into several categories: *strategic*––the intercontinental missiles of immense range and inconceivable destructive power, which may be submarine-launched or sited in silos and on tracks behind the Urals or in the Nevada desert; *theater* (long-, middle-, or short-range), which may be bombs or missiles, carried on aircraft or permanently sited, or moved around at sea or on land on mobile launch platforms; and *tactical*. Sometimes NATO strategists refer to "theater" weapons as "tactical" ones, and sometimes they are referring to smaller battlefield nuclear devices—land mines, artillery shells, etc., which could be mixed in with "conventional weapons."

These several degrees of weaponry form "a chain of deterrence." Mr. Pym, the British Defense Secretary, spoke in the House of Commons of "an interlocking system of comprehensive deterrence . . . a clear chain of terrible risk," with the pistol and the grenade at one end and the MX missile at the other.

It is generally agreed that "the West" has some advantage in *strategic* weapons, although this fact has been concealed from the Western public in recent months in order to direct attention to long- and medium-range *theater* weapons, where it is said that the Soviet Union has recently attained an advantage by replacing the SS-4 and SS-5 missiles with the very deadly SS-20, and by introducing the Backfire bomber. It is to meet this "threat" to parity in the middle link of the chain that cruise missiles are to be introduced by NATO in Western Europe.

On December 3, 1979, Mr. David Fairhall, the *Guardian*'s defense correspondent and a very zealous apologist for NATO, published a map which illustrated how NATO apologists perceived the European "balance." It could be seen from this map that the Soviet threat was very serious, since it was marked in heavy dotted lines and thick arrowheads, whereas NATO's response was delicately etched. It could also be seen that NATO's existing, premodern weaponry (the Pershing I, the F-111, and the Vulcan) was pitiful, and would not even be able to destroy Rome or Naples, nor any part of Greece. So that if it were not for the submarine-launched ballistic missiles (Polaris, Poseidon, and Trident), NATO would be reduced in a nuclear war to stinging itself, like a scorpion, to death.

Either NATO or the map is pretty silly, or both. The point, however, is that present strategic thinking supposes a limited nuclear war, with theater weapons. Europe is such a theater, and this limited war will be localized to a small area from the Urals to the western coast of Ireland. In this scenario, strategic weapons (ICBMs and the like) will be held back for a second strike, so that neither Siberia nor the North American continent will be under any immediate threat.

Before we go further, we should note the fact that, when we come to hard information—and in particular to the trading of estimated numbers of missiles and other weapons—the air is very much fouled up today.

The reasons for this are easy to identify, but they illuminate a part of the problem, so we will digress to explain them. First, it is axiomatic that each military bloc has an interest in misleading the other, and this is done both by concealing information and by deliberately spreading disinformation.

In general, each bloc is at pains to deny and conceal its own areas of greatest military strength, and to advertise a pretense to strength in areas where it is weak. The intelligence agencies that report on each other's resources are themselves an interest group, with high ideological motivation, and on occasion they deliberately manufacture alarmist reports.

Lord Zuckerman gives evidence as to the steady flow of "phony intelligence" and "farfetched" predictions as to Soviet military power which have influenced United States planning over the past twenty years. There is no reason to suppose that this fouling-up of information takes place only in Western capitals.

The name of the game, on both sides, is mendacity. Indeed, "deterrence" might itself be defined as the biggest and most expensive lie in history; and it has, in effect, been defined in this way by British Defense Secretary Pym: "Deterrence is primarily about what the other side thinks, not what we may think."

The second reason why the air is fouled up is that the military and security elites in both blocs, and their political servitors, cannot pursue their expensive and dangerous policies without continually terrifying the populations of their own countries with sensational accounts of the war preparations of the other bloc.

To be sure, the plain facts are terrifying enough without any embroidery. But it is necessary to persuade the native populations that the other side is stealing a lead in order to justify even greater preparations and expenditure at home.

This is as necessary in the Soviet Union as it is in the West, despite the absence of any open public debate there on the issues. For the Soviet military budget is very heavy, and this entails the continual postponement and disappointment of people's expectations as to improving services and goods. In particular, a quite disproportionate concentration of the nation's most advanced scientific and technological skills takes place in the military sector—as it does, increasingly, in the West. The threat from the West, whether it exists or not (and in Soviet perception it certainly does), has become a necessary legitimation for the power of the ruling elites, an excuse for their many economic and social failures and an argument to isolate and silence critics within their own borders.

In the West we have "open debate," although it is contained by bipartisan "consensus" and is not permitted to intrude in any sharp way into our major media. An interesting example of this manipulation came out in the House of Commons debate when the British Under Secretary for Defense (replying to suggestions that the NATO program of missile "modernization" might not be *large* enough to keep up with Soviet missile programs) replied:

> The United States is planning to introduce cruise missiles, carried on B-52 bombers, for the strategic role. It is planning an armory of 2,000 or 3,000 missiles . . . forming only one part of a huge strategic triad alongside ICBMs and submarine-launched ballistic missiles, and all due to enter service in two or three years' time.

This program is to be *in addition* to the existing U.S. strategic resources (which are generally agreed to be already in excess of Russia's, and which have always been so).

Now I am not an expert in these matters, and I do not usually follow the specialist press. But in the previous three months, and especially in the weeks preceding the NATO decision of December 12, 1979, I had followed the general press with care. I have still a thick file of clippings from the defense correspondents of the more serious British daily, weekly, and Sunday papers. Yet this was the first mention I met with of these rather substantial U.S. plans, which are to be added to NATO's little provision.

The entire "debate" in Britain prior to the NATO decision was not a debate at all but an exercise in official information. It was conducted in the press and television on the basis of letting the people believe that there was a massive build-up of Soviet SS-20s and Backfire bombers, all aimed at NATO, but with the United States, the dominant power in NATO, removed from the equation. NATO's program of nuclear weapons "modernization" could then be presented as a tardy and inadequate response to the Soviet threat. Nothing at all was mentioned, in the general press, as to this little addition to the Western sum ("2,000 or 3,000 missiles") as part of "a huge strategic triad."

Since that decision—and as some members of the British public have begun to ask awkward questions—official information has given way, in some quarters, to downright official lying. I am not complaining at the fact that Mr. Pym, when, on June 17, 1980, he announced on television the sites chosen by the U.S. Air Force for their missiles, pleaded, with a catch in his throat, that these were intended only for the "defense" of our peace and our liberty. This is exactly what Mr. Brown, Mr. Ustinov, or any other Minister of Defense (as Ministers of War are now laughably called the world over) tells his own people. That is only to be expected.

I am objecting more to the kind of statement given, with increasing frequency, in Parliament and in the press, of the following order:

> One new Russian SS missile, with all Europe in its sight, is installed every five days; there are already 160 of these monsters in place. . . . The Russian nuclear force threatening Europe's cities will build up to something like 2,000-3,000 warheads by the mid-1980s. Against it is a NATO plan, still on paper, to deploy Pershing II and cruise missiles—but only some 500 of them.

That is from the leading editorial of the *Sunday Times* of

London for July 6, 1980. I am sorry to single out this newspaper, since it is only repeating what is said on all sides. But a paper that pretends to objectivity and authority ought to be judged by stricter standards than those which pretend only to propaganda.

What is directly false in this passage is that 160 of "these monsters" (the SS-20s) are faced only by "a NATO plan, still on paper" to introduce Pershing IIs and cruise missiles. What they and other Russian forces face are substantial long-range nuclear weapons assigned to the NATO theater: these include F-111 and Vulcan bombers, with a range of some 3,000 nautical miles; the British "independent" Polaris, which is assigned to NATO command, as well as (in Soviet perception) the French "independent" weapons; and the United States Poseidon, forty of which are also assigned to NATO command. These U.S. Poseidons each carry some ten independently targeted warheads. This is before we take into any account the U.S. carrier-based aircraft in the Mediterranean and further American strategic resources, which can be attached to any particular theater at will.

The SS-20 is based on land and the Poseidon is based at sea, and, until lately, it had been supposed, in the wargames rooms, that they traded off against each other. What has happened is not the introduction of some wholly new dimension of threat (the SS-20 came into production in 1976, the Backfire bomber in 1974) but a redefinition of the rules of the game. Our Western experts have suddenly decided to hold their hands over Poseidon, Polaris, etc., and to pretend that they do not exist. This is done as a public information exercise, aimed not at the Russians but at us, to frighten us into believing that we are naked and defended by only a plan "still on paper" against Russian "monsters."

This is a contemptible exercise, since the truth could easily be ascertained by any editorial writer. And, indeed, any competent Russian editorialist can make a very much better case against cruise missiles than our "experts" can make against the SS-20. For the plain fact is that the critical accounting must be done, not between the Warsaw Pact and NATO (with the U.S.A.

removed from the equation) but between the two giant superpowers. And in this accounting, the cruise missile can hit targets in western Russia, whereas the SS-20 can get nowhere near the U.S.A. Hence in Russian perception these lethal and accurate weapons, all under American control, are being given forward bases on the European continent where they can strike at Russian installations or cities, thus creeping beneath the "strategic" thresholds negotiated for the SALT II agreement.

Moreover, they can strike at Russia both fast and far. The Pershing II, from its West German bases, could descend on Russian targets in only four minutes. Mr. Pym, on that same telly fireside chat (June 17), assured the British people, with tears in his eyes, that cruise missiles did not "escalate" nuclear armaments—no, not at all. For each cruise missile, one F-111 or older warhead would be withdrawn. What he neglected to mention was that the cruise can stretch into Russian territory some 500 miles deeper than the existing theater bombers. Where Vulcan bombers can hit Leningrad, the cruise and Pershing IIs can (like Polaris or Poseidon) hit Kiev, Moscow, and beyond.

If I were a Russian this would seem to me like escalation. It might make me feel uneasy, just as, if the Russians had a category of very swift and accurate weapons that could just hit Buffalo and Rochester, and then replaced these with missiles with a stretch to reach Boston, New York, and Philadelphia, Americans would feel uneasy also.

In Russian perception the placing of Pershing IIs, under U.S. operation, on the advanced soil of West Germany bears an exact analogy with Nikita Khrushchev's attempt to place missiles in Cuba. As Dr. Robert Havemann, a well-known East German champion of civil liberties and no kind of Russian apologist, has recently noted, these missiles present to Russian military strategists a worst-case scenario in which the United States might launch a sudden preemptive strike simultaneously from Germany and from Alaska, and take out the greater number of Soviet ICBMs in something less than ten minutes. Hence Europe, in 1981–83, will be living through a slow-motion "Cuban missile crisis" in reverse, when at any moment Leonid

Brezhnev might remember the example of President Kennedy and reach for the button.

I am not suggesting that Russian missiles are not multiplying, nor that they are not menacing. They are both. The mobile SS-20, with its triple warhead, is a foul, unnecessary, and threatening weapon, supported by arguments of "deterrence" quite as ugly as those of British or American "experts." The European Nuclear Disarmament movement (END), which is opposing cruise missiles, has made its opposition to the SS-20 equally clear. But I have been illustrating two different points. First, that the logic of "deterrence," that compels both sides to play a never-ending game of leapfrog, justifying their actions at each stage by blaming the other, whereas in fact a good deal of the thrust to modernize weapons is planned quite independently (ten or twenty years ahead of the event) by the armorers of each side. Second, I have sought to emphasize that the whole basis of our information is corrupt, and that every official statement, on both sides, is either an official lie or a statement with direct propagandist intent that conceals as much as it reveals.

As to the actual facts of the nuclear balance, objective research by such bodies as the Stockholm International Peace Research Institute and the Center for Defense Information in Washington, D.C., gives rise to conclusions more complex than anything that we have been offered in our press or on our screens. Thus, in one count of strategic missiles, the Soviet Union appears to be a little ahead of the United States, whereas by a different count of actual warheads (that is, MIRVs) the United States appears as having many more weapons (9,000 to 5,000) than Russia. This is, of course, before "modernization."

This counting is, in any case, nothing but nuclear war carried on by rhetorical means. Much of it consists in redefining unilaterally the counting rules, as in the NATO definition of a European theater in which only ground-launched missiles may be counted and submarine- or carrier-launched missiles are forgotten. It is also obscene and so irrational that only an academic "expert" could believe in it for one moment, since, as everybody knows, both sides already have enough missiles to exterminate each other many times over, and whatever chatter goes on about "surgical strikes" and "taking out" each other's case-hardened ICBM silos, the first rule of every war is always general balls-up (as the Iranian helicopter fiasco reminded us) and enough missiles will survive any attack on each side to finish off the other. As two more serious authors note in the current *Daedalus*, "a mere 1 percent of the Soviet strategic forces reaching the United States could destroy more than fifty of our largest cities (each to a far greater extent than Hiroshima)."

That the numbers game is obscene and irrational does not make it any less dangerous. For these are the terms in which the steady escalation of weaponry and the growing collision course of the superpowers are justified and rationalized. The apologists for this process are perhaps even more dangerous than are the manufacturers of the weapons or the generals who will order them to be fired. For they force us into a cul-de-sac at the end of which is only reciprocal extermination.

Whether the balance of evidence or perception is tilted toward the West or the East (how many delivery systems, what worst-case expectations), the historical outcome is compressed within the same parameters: that is, the leapfrog logic of "deterrence," within which the hawks of each side feed to each other arms and provocations, strive for "parity," envisage fictitious "gaps" and "windows of opportunity," adumbrate through never-ending negotiations at the highest level elaborate devices of "control" (which their clever games-players then seek to evade or to turn to new advantage), and generate more thrust in the ongoing course toward collision.

The SS-20, as we have seen, is the theater missile which we are warned may strike Britain. Its destructive capacity is many times that of the bomb which was dropped on Hiroshima. This bomb caused the deaths of 100,000 persons within hours, and of about a further 100,000 who have died subsequently, in the main from radiologically related diseases.

The SS-20 is reputed to be an accurate missile, although not as accurate as the cruise, and the C.E.P. might be down to a few hundred yards. But the meditated strategy of both sides is to send, not one accurate missile at each target but missiles in clutches of thirty or forty. The late arrivals will be buffeted about a good deal by the immense detonations of the first-comers (the genial expert jargon for this is missile "fratricide") so that the C.E.P. for a clutch is likely to be enlarged to several miles. Within the C.E.P. we must suppose some fifteen or twenty detonations at least on the scale of Hiroshima, which will then discharge immense quantities of radioactive effluvia over the surrounding countryside.

This is to suppose that the Soviet strike is homing on to clearly defined and immobile targets. But this is not the case. We are not told that the missiles will be carried in packs of four on mobile launching vehicles, and in times of "emergency" will be dispersed from their bases into the surrounding districts.

There has been a great deal of double talk about all these questions. On the one hand, we have been told that these are defensive weapons, which could never be used for a first strike. But if we are to suppose the Russians to be a hideous enemy, plotting an aggressive preemptive strike with "monsters," then packing away all these missiles at advertised bases (Greenham Common near Newbury and Molesworth near Huntingdon) is to present them with perfect targets for two immense Pearl Harbors. And, equally, the sudden deployment of missile-launchers from these bases (which would be monitored by satellite observation) would be the signal to an enemy that the moment of emergency had come.

In any case, it may not matter all that much where the missiles are sited. In response to questions in the House of Commons, British Defense Minister Pym responded, "It is a mistake for anyone to think that the siting of a weapon in a particular place . . . makes it more or less vulnerable. We are all vulnerable in the horrifying event of a holocaust." The American officers who alone will "own and operate" these missiles have indicated that they intend to spread and scatter them from 50 to 100 miles from the bases in emergency, so that the enemy will have to spread and scatter his strike over the same huge area in order to have any hopes of "eliminating" them.

Thus, if the Russians really wanted to find the cruise missile-launchers out, then there would have to be C.E.P.s dotted all across southern, central, and eastern England. There is nothing very special being prepared by NATO for Newbury or Huntingdon: Luton, Sheerness, and Southhampton will be just as vulnerable, and there is no way of describing a series of nuclear strikes against cruise missiles except as a holocaust.

This is before we take account of Lord Zuckerman's other variable—the 50 percent of strikes which would fall outside the Circular Error Probable. These will be missiles whose navigational or homing devices are inaccurate or which, perhaps, are brought down on their path. I have taken a ruler to a map of Europe, and I cannot see any way in which an SS-20 dispatched from Russia could home in on Newbury without passing directly over central London.

If by misadventure a strike outside the C.E.P. fell on a major city, the damage would be considerable. Lord Mountbatten told an audience in Strasbourg in May 1979 that "one or two nuclear strikes on this great city . . with what today would be regarded as relatively low-yield weapons would utterly destroy all that we see around us and immediately kill half of its population." And Lord Zuckerman adds that a single one-megaton bomb—and the warhead of the SS-20 is said to be one and a half megatons—"could erase the heart of any great city—say, Birmingham—and kill instantly a third of its citizens."

There is no room in Britain to "scatter" missiles without bringing multitudes into mortal danger, and there is no room to "search" without inflicting a holocaust. As Lord Zuckerman has said:

> There are no vast deserts in Europe, no endless open plains, on which to turn war-games in which nuclear weapons are used into reality. The distances between villages are no greater than the radius of effect of low-yield weapons of a few kilotons; between towns and cities, say a megaton.

We are now at last prepared to cast a more realistic eye upon Professor Howard's scenario.

According to this, the "initially limited Soviet strike" might, in the absence of civil defense precautions, create conditions of "political turbulance" which would prevent "us" from using our own nuclear weapons in retaliation. This would be regrettable, since it would inhibit the escalation from tactical or theater to second-strike, sea-based nuclear war. But he envisages civil defense measures "on a scale sufficient to give protection to a substantial number of the population," enabling this number to endure the "disagreeable consequences" which would ensue.

The object of civil defense, then, is not so much to save lives as to reduce the potential for "political turbulence" of those surviving the first strike, in order to enable "us" to pass over to a second and more fearsome stage of nuclear warfare. It is Professor Howard's merit that he states this sequence honestly, as a realist, and even allows that the consequences will be disagreeable.

We are still entitled, however, to inquire more strictly as to what measures would be *on a scale sufficient*, what proportion of the population might constitute *a substantial number*, and what may be indicated by the word *disagreeable*.

It is not as if nuclear weapons are a completely unknown quantity, which have only been tested in deserts and on uninhabited islands. They have been tested upon persons also, in 1945, at Hiroshima and Nagasaki, and to some effect. These effects have been studied with care, and the beneficiaries of this sudden donation of advanced technology were so much struck by the disagreeable consequences that they have continued to monitor the effects to the present day.

One remarkable consequence of those two detonations is that the survivors in those two cities, and the descendants of the sufferers, were transformed into advocates, not of revenge but of international understanding and peace. To this day, work for peace is regarded as a civic duty, and the mayors of Nagasaki and Hiroshima regard this work as the principal obligation of their office.

For example, in 1977 an International Symposium on the damage and aftereffects of the bombing of these two cities was inaugurated, and a number of reports of this work are now in translation. I have read condensations of these, as well as other materials from Nagasaki.

It had been my intention to condense this material still further, and to remind readers of the effects of the first atomic bombings. I have now decided to pass this matter by, for two reasons. The first is that I have found the task beyond my powers as a writer. After reading these materials, whenever I approached my typewriter I was overcome by such a sense of nausea that I was forced to turn to some other task.

The second reason is that, at some point very deep in their consciousness, readers *already know* what the consequences of these weapons are. This knowledge is transmitted to children even in their infancy, so that as they run around with their space-weapons and death-rays they are re-enacting what happened thirty years before they were born.

There is, however, one area of convenient forgetfulness in this inherited memory. The moment of nuclear detonations is remembered vaguely, as a sudden instant of light, blast, and fire, in which instantly tens of thousands of lives were quenched. It is thought of as a stupendous but instantaneous moment of annihilation, without pain or emotional suffering.

But this is not accurate. It is now estimated that 140,000 were killed directly by the bomb on Hiroshima, and 70,000 by that on Nagasaki, with an allowance for error of 10,000 either way in each case. But the bombs were dropped on August 6 and 9, and the accounts for *immediate* casualties were closed on December 31, 1945. This reflects the fact that a very great number of these deaths—especially those from burns and radioactivity—took place slowly, in the days and weeks after the event.

Michiko Ogino, 10 years old, was left in charge of his younger sisters when his mother went out to the fields to pick eggplants. The bomb brought the house down on them all, leaving his 2-year-old sister with her legs pinned under a crossbeam:

> Mamma was bombed at noon
> When getting eggplants in the field
> Short, red and crisp her hair stood
> Tender and red her skin was all over

So Mrs. Ogino, although her clothes were burned from her

body and she had received a fatal dose of radiation, could still run back from the fields to succor her children. One after another, passing sailors and neighbors heaved at the beam to release the trapped 2-year-old, failed, and, bowing with Japanese courtesy, went on their way to help others.

> Mother was looking down at my little sister. Tiny eyes looked up from below. Mother looked around, studying the way the beams were piled up. Then she got into an opening under the beam, and putting her right shoulder under a portion of it, she strained with all her might. We heard a cracking sound and the beams were lifted a little. My little sister's legs were freed.

> Peeled off was the skin
>   over her shoulder
> That once lifted the beam
>   off my sister
> Constant blood was spurting
> From the sore flesh opening

Mrs. Ogino died that night. Fujio Tsujimoto, who was 5 years old, was in the playground of Yamazato Primary School, Nagasaki, just before the bomb dropped. Hearing the sound of a plane he grabbed his grandmother's hand and they were the first into the deepest part of the air-raid shelter. The entrance to the shelter, as well as the playground, was covered with the dying. "My brothers and sisters didn't get to the shelter in time, so they were burnt and crying. Half an hour later, my mother appeared. She was covered with blood. She had been making lunch at home when the bomb was dropped."

> My younger sisters died the next day. My mother—she also died the next day. And then my older brother died. . . .
>
> The survivors made a pile of wood on the playground and began to cremate the corpses. My brother was burned. Mother was also burned and quickly turned to white bones which dropped down among the live coals. I cried as I looked on the scene. Grandmother was also watching, praying with a rosary. . . .
>
> I am now in fourth grade at Yamazato Primary School. That playground of terrible memories is now completely cleared and many friends play there happily. I play with my friends there

> too, but sometimes I suddenly remember that awful day. When I do, I squat down on the spot where we cremated our mother and touch the earth with my fingers. When I dig deep in the ground with pieces of bamboo, several pieces of charcoal appear. Looking at the spot for a while, I can dimly see my mother's image in the earth. So when I see someone else walking on that place, it makes me very angry.

I will not quote any more of the testimony of the children of Nagasaki *(Living Beneath the Atomic Cloud)*. What it makes clear is that the "instant" of detonation was protracted over days and weeks, and was full, not only of physical misery but of unutterable yearning and suffering. A great river runs through Hiroshima, and each year the descendants set afloat on it lighted lanterns inscribed with the names of family dead, and for several miles the full breadth of this river is one mass of flame.

After this we still have to consider the future tens of thousands who have died subsequently from the aftereffects of that day—chiefly leukemia, various cancers, and diseases of the blood and digestive organs. The sufferers are known as *hibakashu*, a word which ought to be international. Some *hibakashu* suffer from the direct consequences of wounds and burns, others from premature senility, others from blindness, deafness, and dumbness, others are incapable of working because of nervous disorders, and many are seriously mentally deranged. Only two comforts can be derived from the expert *Nagasaki Report: hibakashu* have been distinguished by their mutual aid, sometimes in communities of fellow-sufferers, and the genetic effects of the bomb (which are still being studied) do not as yet appear to have been as bad as was at first apprehended.

We may now push this distressing matter back into our subconscious and reconsider the possible effect of "a series of pre-emptive strikes" with scores of weapons very much more powerful than those bombs, upon my own country.

It is true that the inhabitants of Hiroshima and Nagasaki were very little prepared for this advanced technology and, indeed, in Nagasaki the "All Clear" had sounded shortly before the detonation, so that the populace had trooped out of their conventional shelters and the women were working in the fields and the children playing in the playgrounds when the bomb went off.

Our own authorities might be able to manage the affair better. With greater warning, stronger houses and with some more effective measures of civil defense, some lives might be saved, and perhaps even "a substantial number." Indeed, two Conservative M.P.s have calculated that effective measures might reduce deaths in a nuclear war in Britain from about thirty-five million to just twenty million, and I will allow that fifteen million in savings is substantial number indeed.

Nevertheless, two comments must be made on this. The first is that the death or mortal injury of even the small figure of twenty million (or one-third of the British population) might still give rise to conditions of "turbulence." The incidence of disaster would not be evenly spread across the country, with hale and hearty survivors in all parts standing ready, with high morale, to endure the hazards of the second strike.

Air Marshal Sir Leslie Mavor, Principal of the British Home Defense College, addressing a civil defense seminar in 1977, said that "the main target areas would be so badly knocked about as to be beyond effective self-help. They would have to be more or less discounted until adjoining areas recovered sufficiently to come to their aid." Those parts of the country "holding no nuclear targets" might come through "more or less undamaged by blast or fire. Their difficulties would be caused by fallout radiation, a large influx of refugees, survival without external supplies of food, energy, raw materials."

This seems a realistic assessment. There would be some total disaster areas, from the margins of which the wounded and dying would flee as refugees; other intermediate areas would have energy supplies destroyed, all transport dislocated, and persons, food, and water contaminated by fallout; yet others would be relatively immune. But even in these immune areas there would be some persons in a state of hysterical terror, who would be ready (if they knew how) to intervene to prevent the second stage of Professor Howard's scenario.

The second comment is that we do not yet have any realistic notion of what might be *a scale sufficient* to effect *substantial* savings, nor what measures might be taken. We may certainly agree with the professor that no such measures are either planned or contemplated. Measures have been taken to ensure the survival of the high personnel of the state. This has long been evident. There will be bunkers for senior politicians, civil servants, and military, and deep hidey-holes for regional centers of military government. That is very comforting.

The population of Britain, however, will not be invited to these bunkers, and it is an official secret to say where they are. The population will be sent off, with a do-it-yourself booklet (*Protect and Survive**), to wait in their own homes. They will be advised to go down to the ground floor or the cellar and make a cubbyhole there with old doors and planks, cover it with sandbags, books, and heavy furniture, and then creep into these holes with food and water for fourteen days, a portable radio, a portable latrine and, of course, a can opener.

I have for long wondered why sociologists and demographers keep writing about "the nuclear family," but now it is all at length set down and explained.

Now this might save some lives, but it will also make for an unhappy end to others. For the principal effects of nuclear weapons are very intense heat, blast, and radioactive emissions. Within a certain distance of the center of the detonation all houses, cars, clothes, the hair on dogs, cats, and persons, and so on, will spontaneously ignite, while at the same time the blast will bring the houses tumbling down about the cubbyholes. We must envisage many thousands of nuclear families listening to consensual homilies on their portable radios as they are baked, crushed, or suffocated to death.

Those outside this radius might be afforded a little temporary protection. But when they eventually emerge (after some fourteen days) they will find the food and water contaminated, the roads blocked, the hospitals destroyed, the livestock dead or dying. The vice chairman of Civil Aid, who is a realist, advises thus: "If you saw a frog running about, you would have to wash it down to get rid of active dust, cook it and eat it."

---

*An official British civil defense brochure.

If we are to learn from the experience of the people of Nagasaki and Hiroshima, then I think it is, after all, unlikely that many survivors will be devoting their energies to "political turbulence," since, unless they know the entrances to the government deep bunkers, they will have nothing to turbul against. Most will be wandering here and there in a desperate attempt to find lost children, parents, neighbors, friends. A few of the most collected will succor the dying and dig among the ruins for the injured.

The measures outlined in *Protect and Survive* do not seem to me to be on *a scale sufficient* to reduce the consequences of a nuclear strike to the compass of a small word like "disagreeable."

It is possible to imagine measures on a greater scale. One might imagine the excavation of vast subterranean systems beneath our towns, complete with stored food and water, generating systems, air-purifying systems, etc.

This might save *a substantial number* of lives, although one is uncertain what it would save them for, since above-ground no workplaces, uncontaminated crops, or stock would be left. The logic of this development, then, will be to remove these activities underground also, with subterranean cattle-stalls, granaries, bakeries, and munitions works.

It is certainly possible that, if civilization survives and continues on its present trajectory until the mid-twenty-first century, then the "advanced" societies will have become troglodyte in some such fashion. But it would not be advisable to suppose that our descendants will have then at length attained to "security," in the simultaneous realization of the ultimate in "deterrence" with the ultimate in "defense." For the military will by then have taken further steps in technology. Earth penetrators already exist which can drive death underground. All this will be perfected, modernized, and refined. There will be immense thermonuclear charges capable of concussing a whole underground city. And, in any case, by the time that humanity becomes troglodyte, it will then have been already defeated. "Civilization" will then be an archaic term, which children can no longer construe.

Little Theater Wars: Expendable Europe

We must now turn our attention to the second assumption which underpins the arguments of our defense "experts." This concerns "tactical" or "limited" theater nuclear war.

This theory supposes a nuclear war confined to a specific theater—and Europe is the theater most often mentioned—with a range of nuclear "options" and with a progressive series of "firebreaks." It supposes the aforementioned "chain of deterrence," according to which war may not only start at any level but may be confined to that level, since at any point there is a further fearsome threshold of "deterrence" ahead. Hence it envisages a theater nuclear war which does not escalate to outright confrontation between the superpowers.

This is not the same as the proposal that *local* or *regional* wars with nuclear weapons may take place. That is a reasonable proposal. If the proliferation of these weapons continues, it is possible that we will see such wars: as between Israel and Arab states, or South Africa and an alliance of African states. Whether such wars lead on to confrontation between the superpowers will depend not upon the logic of weaponry but on further diplomatic and political considerations.

This proposition is different. It is that nuclear wars between the two great opposed powers and their allies could be confined to this or that level. This is a silly notion at first sight; and, after tedious and complex arguments have been gone through, it emerges as equally silly at the end. For while it might very well be in the *interests* of either the United States or of the USSR to confine a war to Europe, or to the Persian Gulf, and to prevent it from passing into an ultimate confrontation, we are not dealing here with rational behavior.

Once theater nuclear war commences, immense passions, indeed hysterias, will be aroused. After even the first strikes of such a war, communications and command posts will be so much snarled up that any notion of rational planning will give way to panic. Ideology will at once take over from self-interest. Above all, it will be manifest that the only one of the two great powers likely to come out of the contest as victor must be the one which hurls its ballistic weapons first, farthest, and fastest—and preferably before the weapons of the other have had time to lift off.

This was the common-sense message which Lord Mountbatten, shortly before he was murdered, conveyed to the meeting in Strasbourg. He referred to the introduction of tactical or theater weapons:

> The belief was that were hostilities ever to break out in Western Europe, such weapons could be used to field warfare without triggering an all-out nuclear exchange leading to the final holocaust.
>
> I have never found this idea credible. I have never been able to accept the reasons for the belief that any class of nuclear weapons can be categorized in terms of their tactical or strategic purpose. . . .
>
> In the event of a nuclear war there will be no chances, there will be no survivors—all will be obliterated. I am not asserting this without having deeply thought about the matter. When I was Chief of the British Defense Staff I made my views known. . . . I repeat in all sincerity as a military man I can see no use for any nuclear weapons which would not end in escalation, with consequences that no one can conceive.

The same firm judgment was expressed by Lord Zuckerman: "Nor was I ever able to see any military reality in what is now referred to as theater or tactical warfare":

> The men in the nuclear laboratories of both sides have succeeded in creating a world with an irrational foundation, on which a new set of political realities has in turn had to be built. They have become the alchemists of our times, working in secret ways which cannot be divulged, casting spells which embrace us all.

The notion of a limited nuclear war has been around for a long time in American strategic thinking, under such names as "flexible response" or "counterforce." It is, perhaps, the most dangerous, as it is the most irrational, of all the spells that the "alchemists" have cast. For it is in the name of "surgical strikes" and "menus" of "options" that nuclear warfare is being made thinkable—and therefore possible or even probable—once more.

There are two distinct propositions which have been hidden within the single term: "deterrence." The first proposition is that of Mutual Assured Destruction (MAD), and it is that nuclear weapons are capable of inflicting such "unacceptable damage" upon both parties to an exchange that mutual fear ensures peace. The second proposition is that each party is actually preparing for nuclear war and is ceaselessly searching for some ultimate weapon or tactical/strategic point of advantage which would assure its victory.

For a long time the second proposition has been hidden within the mendacious vocabulary of "deterrence," and behind its veils of "posture," "credibility," and "bluff" it has waxed fat. For years we have lived uneasily with the first proposition. Now the second proposition has come to age, and we are looking directly into its eyes.

"Deterrence" has plausibility. It has "worked" for thirty years, if not in Vietnam, Czechoslovakia, the Middle East, Africa, Cambodia, the Dominican Republic, Afghanistan, then in the central fracture between the superpowers which runs across Europe. It may have inhibited, in Europe, major conventional war.

But it has not worked as a stationary state. The weapons for adequate deterrence already existed thirty years ago, and, as the Pope reminded us in his New Year's message for 1980, only 200 of the 50,000 nuclear weapons now estimated to be in existence would be enough to destroy the world's major cities. Yet we have moved upward to 50,000, and each year new sophistications and "modernizations" are introduced.

The current chatter about theater or tactical nuclear war is not a sophisticated variant of the old vocabulary of deterrence; it is directly at variance with that vocabulary. For it is founded on the notion that either of the superpowers might engage, to its own advantage, in a limited nuclear war which could be kept below the threshold at which retribution would be visited on its own soil.

Thus it is thought by persons in the Pentagon that a theater nuclear war might be confined to Europe, in which, to be sure, America's NATO allies would be obliterated, but in which immense damage would also be inflicted upon Russia west of the Urals, while the soil of the United States remained immune. (In such a scenario it is even supposed that President Reagan and Mr. Brezhnev would be on the hot line to each other while Europe scorched, threatening ultimate intercontinental ballistic retribution, but at last making peace.) This has been seen as the way to a great victory for the West, and if worldwide nuclear war seems to be ultimately inevitable, then the sooner that can be aborted by having a little theater war the better.

The trouble with all this, from the Pentagon's point of view, is that it requires rewriting the war games-plan, and in this rewriting Soviet strategists have been unaccountably uncooperative. Mr. Lawrence Freedman, who is Head of Policy Studies at the Royal Institute of International Affairs, and who is evidently a very great expert, noted in *The Times* of London (March 26, 1980):

> Recent moves in NATO have encouraged plans for selective, discrete strikes rather than all-out exchanges. . . . Unfortunately, the Soviet Union has shown little interest in Western ideas on limited nuclear war.

"Missiles in Western Europe would give the American President an intermediate option," stopping short of "putting American cities at risk," writes another expert, Mr. Treverton of the International Institute for Strategic Studies. And President Carter's national security adviser, Zbigniew Brzezinski, discussed the reviews of "our nuclear targeting plans" in the course of an interview in the Sunday *New York Times* (March 30, 1980):

> All of these reviews are designed . . . to avoid a situation in which the President would be put under irresistible pressure to preempt, to avoid leaving the United States only the options of yielding or engaging in a spasmodic and apocalyptic nuclear exchange.
> Question: Are you saying that you want the United States to be able to fight a "limited" nuclear war?

> *Brzezinski:* I am saying that the United States, in order to maintain effective deterrence, has to have choices which give us a wider range of options than either a spasmodic nuclear exchange or a limited conventional war.

That is a politician's way of saying "yes." European war is to be one "choice" or "option" for U.S. strategists, although what might appear to be limited on one side of the Atlantic might appear to be spasmodic and apocalyptic on the other.

In this perspective the famous Presidential Directive 59 (as to which, it seems, Secretary of State Edmund Muskie was not even consulted) is only a confirmation of a longstanding Pentagon policy. The Secretary of Defense, Harold Brown, was at pains to make this clear in a speech at the Naval War College in Newport, Rhode Island, on August 20, 1980. The Directive (he said) was only "a refinement, a codification of previous statements of our strategic policy," although accompanied by "a fundamental review of our targeting policy." As a settled statement of "the same essential strategic doctrine" of the Pentagon, we may expect it to survive the change of administrations, and to be zealously furthered by President Reagan's Administration also.

What is less comforting, for a European, is Brown's statement that "in our analysis and planning, we are necessarily giving greater attention to how a nuclear war would actually be fought," with "more stress on being able to employ strategic nuclear forces selectively." For the cruise and Pershing missiles which are being set up in Western Europe, under sole American ownership and control, are the hardware designed for exactly such a limited war, and the nations which harbor them are viewed, in this strategy, as launching platforms which are expendable in the interests of Western defense. While Russia might not *wish* to rewrite the games-plan, since some of its most populous and highly industrialized regions are *within* the theater whereas all of the United States is not, nevertheless (it is supposed) its hand might be forced if faced with the alternatives of such a war or of outright ICBM obliteration.

If all this sounds crazy, then I can only agree that crazy is exactly what it is. But, then, as a frequent visitor to the United

States I must report that there is a dangerous tendency to craziness in the American view of the world. Protected geographically by two huge oceans, on a continent that has never been invaded or even subjected to aerial attack, the people suffer from a diminished reality-sense in which wars are always something that happen "over there." These illusions are fed with massive media propaganda and are excited by electoral humbug, until crowds can shout (of the Iranians) "Nuke them!" without any notion of what the words mean. It is against all this that the generous and responsible American peace movement has to work.

Cruise and Pershing missiles are *committing:* strategically and also politically. They place Europeans, with finality, within the games-plan of the Pentagon. In each and every crisis, a Pentagon finger will be on the West European trigger: one barrel may be aimed at Russia, but the other will be aimed at Europe's own head. It is for this reason that Senator Nino Pasti, formerly an Italian member of the NATO Military Committee and Deputy Supreme Commander for NATO Nuclear Affairs, has declared: "I have no doubt that the tactical nuclear weapons deployed in Europe represent the worst danger for the peoples of the continent. In plain words, the tactical nuclear weapon would be employed in the view of NATO to limit the war to Europe. Europe is to be transformed into a 'nuclear Maginot line' for the defense of the United States."

Meanwhile, the United States is urgently seeking similar platforms in the Middle East for another small theater war which might penetrate deep into the Caucasus. And an even uglier scenario is beginning to show itself in China, where greed for a vast arms market is tempting Western salesmen while U.S. strategists hope to nudge Russia and China into war with each other—a war which would dispel another Western phobia, the demographic explosion of the East. The idea here is to extract the West, at the last moment, from this war—much the same scenario as that which went disastrously wrong in 1939.

These little theater wars (not one of which would obediently stay put in its theater) are now all on the drawing boards, and in the Pentagon more than in the Kremlin, for the simple reason that every theater is adjacent to the Soviet Union, and any tactical nuclear strike would penetrate deep into Russian territory.

The plans for the European theater war are not only ready—the modernized missiles designed for exactly such a war have been ordered and will be delivered to Europe in 1983. And at this moment, the advocates of civil defense make a corresponding *political* intervention. Let us see why this is so.

These advocates wish to hurry people across a threshold of mental expectation, so that they may be prepared, not for deterrence but for actual nuclear war.

The expectations supporting the theory of deterrence will *work*. Deterrence is effective, because the alternative is not only "unacceptable" or "disagreeable": it is "unthinkable."

Deterrence is a posture, but it is the posture of MAD, not of menace. It does not say, "If we go to nuclear war we intend to win." It says, "Do not go to war, or provoke war, because neither of us can win." In consequence it does not bother to meddle with anything so futile as civil defense. If war commences, everything is already lost.

Those who have supported the policy of deterrence have done so in confidence that this policy would prevent nuclear war from taking place. They have not contemplated the alternative, and have been able to avoid facing certain questions raised by that alternative. Of these, let us notice three.

First, is nuclear war preferable to being overcome by the enemy? Are the deaths of fifteen or twenty million and the utter destruction of the country preferable to an occupation which might offer the possibility, after some years, of resurgence and recuperation?

Second, are we ourselves prepared to endorse the use of such weapons against the innocent, the children and the aged, of an "enemy"?

Third, how does it happen that Britain should find itself committed to policies which endanger the very survival of the nation, as a result of decisions taken by a secret committee of NATO, and then endorsed at Brussels without public discussion or parliamentary sanction, leaving the "owning and operation" of these weapons in the hands of the military personnel of a foreign power, a power whose strategists have contingency plans for unleashing these missiles in a theater war which would not extend as far as their own homeland?

The first two questions raise moral, and not strategic, issues. My own answer to them is "no." They are, in any case, not new questions. The third question is, in some sense, new, and it is also extraordinary, in the sense that even proposing the question illuminates the degree to which the loss of British national sovereignty has been absolute, and democratic process has been deformed in ways scarcely conceivable twenty years ago.

But arguments such as those of Professor Howard are designed to hurry us past these questions without noticing them. They are designed to carry us across a threshold from the *unthinkable* (the theory of deterrence, founded upon the assumption that this must *work*) to the *thinkable* (the theory that nuclear war may happen and may be imminent and, with cunning tactics and proper preparations, might end in "victory").

More than this, the arguments are of an order which permit the mind to progress from the unthinkable to the thinkable *without thinking*—without confronting the arguments, their consequences or probable conclusions and, indeed, without knowing that any threshold has been crossed.

At each side of this threshold we are offered a policy with an identical label: "deterrence." And both parties stink with the same mendacious rhetoric—"posture," "credibility," "bluff." But mutual fear and self-interest predominate on one side, and active menace and the ceaseless pursuit of tactical or theater advantage predominate on the other. Which other side we have crossed over, and now daily inhabit.

Overthrowing the Satanic Kingdom

I have sought in these pages to open up the arguments of the defense "experts," to show what is inside them, which premises and what conclusions. I have not been trying to frighten readers but to show the consequences to which these arguments lead.

Although I am myself by conviction a socialist of William Morris's sort, I have not been grounding any arguments upon premises of that kind. And I certainly do not suppose that all blame for the desperate situation of the world lies with the ideological malice and predatory drives of the capitalist "West," although some part of it does.

I have based my arguments on the *logic* of the cold war, or of the deterrent situation itself. We may favor this or that explanation for the origin of this situation. But once this situation has arisen, there is a common logic at work in both blocs. Military technology and military strategy come to impose their own agenda upon political developments.

This is an interoperative and reciprocal logic, which threatens all, impartially. If you press me for my own view, then I would hazard that the Russian state is now the most dangerous in relation to its own people and to the people of its client states. The rulers of Russia are police-minded and security-minded people, imprisoned within their own ideology, accustomed to meet argument with repression and tanks. But the basic postures of the Soviet Union seem to me, still, to be those of siege and aggressive defense; and even the brutal and botched intervention in Afghanistan appears to have followed upon apprehension as to U.S. and Chinese strategies.

The United States seems to me to be more dangerous and provocative in its general military and diplomatic strategies, which press around the Soviet Union with menacing bases. It is in Washington, rather than Moscow, that scenarios are dreamed up for theater wars; and it is in America that the alchemists of superkill, the clever technologists of "advantage" and ultimate weapons, press forward "the politics of tomorrow."

But we need not ground our own actions on a preference for one or the other bloc. This is unrealistic and could be divisive. What is relevant is the logic of process common to both, reinforcing the ugliest features of each other's societies, and locking both together in each other's nuclear arms in the same degenerative drift.

It is in this sense that NATO's modernization program and the Soviet intervention in Afghanistan, taken together, may perhaps be seen as a textbook case of the reciprocal logic of cold war. NATO's plans were certainly perceived by Soviet leaders as menacing, and vigorous efforts were made by Brezhnev and others to prevent them. This perception of menace hardened, on December 12, 1979, when NATO endorsed the full program at Brussels—and when, in the meantime, the U.S. Senate, under pressure from the arms lobby, failed to ratify SALT II. In response, the hard arguments and the hard men had their way among the Soviet leadership and, two weeks later, the Soviet intervention in Afghanistan took place. NATO modernization was not a decisive factor, in the view of the Russian historian Roy Medvedev (to whom I addressed some questions last June), since the intervention of Afghanistan had been mediated and prepared over a much longer period. But it signaled to those Soviet leaders who favored the military option that, in relation to Europe, they now had nothing to lose.

Throughout this essay I have been attempting to disclose this reciprocal logic of process, which is driven forward by the armorers of both superpowers. And what I have been contending is this: First, I have shown that the premises of nuclear deterrence are *irrational*.

Second, I have been concerned throughout with the use of *language*.

What makes the extinction of civilized life in Europe probable is not a greater propensity for evil than in previous history but a more formidable destructive technology, a deformed political process (East and West) and also a deformed culture.

The deformation of culture commences within language itself. It makes possible a disjunction between the rationality and moral sensibility of individual persons and the effective political and military process. A certain kind of "realist" and "technical" vocabulary effects a closure which seals out the imagination, and prevents the reason from following the most manifest sequence of cause and consequence. It habituates the mind to nuclear holocaust by reducing everything to a flat level of normality. By habituating us to certain expectations, it not only encourages resignation—it also beckons on the event.

"Humankind cannot bear very much reality," T. S. Eliot wrote. As much of reality as most of us bear is what is most proximate to us—our self-interests and our immediate affections. What threatens our interests—what causes us even mental unease—is seen as outside ourselves, as the Other. We can kill thousands because we have first learned to call them "the enemy." Wars commence in our culture first of all, and we kill each other in euphemisms and abstractions long before the first missiles have been launched.

It has never been true that nuclear war is "unthinkable." It has been thought and the thought has been put into effect. This was done in 1945, in the name of allies fighting for the Four Freedoms (although what those Freedoms were I cannot now recall), and it was done upon two populous cities. It was done by professing Christians, when the Allies had already defeated the Germans, and when victory against the Japanese was certain, in the longer or shorter run. The longer run would have cost some thousands more Western lives, whereas the short run (the bomb) would cost the lives only of enemy Asians. This was perfectly thinkable. It was thought. And action followed on.

What is unthinkable is that nuclear war could happen to *us*. So long as we can suppose that this war will be inflicted on *them*, the thought comes easily. And if we can also suppose that this war will save "our" lives, or serve our self-interest, or even save us (if we live in California) from the tedium of queuing every other day for gasoline, then the act can easily follow on. We *think* others to death as we define them as the Other: the enemy: Asians: Marxists: non-people. The deformed human mind is the ultimate doomsday weapon—it is out of the human mind that the missiles and the neutron warheads come.

For this reason it is necessary to enter a remonstrance against those who use this kind of language and adopt these mental postures. They are preparing our minds as launching platforms for exterminating thoughts. The fact that Soviet ideologists are doing much the same (thinking us to death as "imperialists" and "capitalists") is no defense.

It is therefore proper to ask such experts to resist the contamination of our culture with those terms which precede the ultimate act. The deaths of fifteen million fellow citizens ought not to be described as "disagreeable consequences." A war confined to Europe ought not to be given euphemisms of "limited" or "theater." The development of more deadly weapons, combined with menacing diplomatic postures and major new political and strategic decisions, ought not to be concealed with the anodyne technological term of "modernization." The threat to erase the major cities of Russia and Eastern Europe ought not to trip easily off the tongue as "unacceptable damage."

I am thinking of that great number of persons who very much dislike what is going on in the actual world, but who dislike the vulgarity of exposing themselves to the business of "politics" even more. They erect both sets of dislikes around their desks or laboratories like a screen, and get on with their work and their careers. I am not asking these, or all of them, to march around the place or to spend hours in weary little meetings. I am asking them to examine the deformities of our culture and then, in public places, to demur.

I will recommend some forms of action, although every person must be governed in this by his or her own conscience and aptitudes. But, first, I should offer a scenario of my own.

I have come to the view that a general nuclear war is not only possible but probable, and that its probability is increasing. We may indeed be approaching a point of no return when the existing tendency or disposition toward this outcome becomes irreversible.

I ground this view upon two considerations, which we may define (to borrow the terms of our opponents) as "tactical" and "strategic."

By tactical I mean that the political and military conditions for such war exist now in several parts of the world; the proliferation of nuclear weapons will continue, and will be hastened by the export of nuclear energy technology to new markets, and the rivalry of the superpowers is directly inflaming these conditions.

Such conditions now exist in the Middle East and around the

Persian Gulf, will shortly exist in Africa, while in Southeast Asia, Russia and China have already engaged in wars by proxy with each other, in Cambodia and Vietnam.

Such wars might stop short of general nuclear war between the superpowers. And in their aftermath the great powers might be frightened into better behavior for a few years. But so long as this behavior rested on nothing more than mutual fear, then military technology would continue to be refined, more hideous weapons would be invented, and the opposing giants would enlarge their control over client states. The strategic pressures toward confrontation will continue to grow.

These *strategic* considerations are the gravest of the two. They rest upon a historical view of power and of the social process, rather than upon the instant analysis of the commentator on events.

In this view it is a superficial judgment, and a dangerous error, to suppose that deterrence has worked. Very possibly it may have worked, at this or that moment, in preventing recourse to war. But in its very mode of working, and in its "postures," it has brought on a series of consequences within its host societies.

Deterrence is not a stationary state, it is a degenerative state. Deterrence has repressed the export of violence toward the opposing bloc, but in doing so the repressed power of the state has turned back upon its own author. The repressed violence has backed up and worked its way into the economy, the polity, the ideology, and the culture of the opposing powers. This is the deep structure of the Cold War.

The logic of this deep structure of mutual fear was clearly identified by William Blake in his Song of Experience, "The Human Abstract":

> And mutual fear brings peace;
> Till the selfish loves increase.
> Then Cruelty knits a snare,
> And spreads his baits with care. . .
>
> Soon spreads the dismal shade
> Of Mystery over his head;

And the Catterpillar and Fly
Feed on the Mystery

And it bears the fruit of Deceit,
Ruddy and sweet to eat;
And the Raven his nest has made
In its thickest shade.

In this logic, the peace of "mutual fear" enforces opposing self-interests, affords room for "Cruelty" to work, engenders "Mystery" and its parasites, brings to fruit the "postures" of Deceit, and the death-foreboding Raven hides within the Mystery.

Within the logic of deterrence, millions are now employed in the armed services, security organs, and military economy of the opposing blocs, and corresponding interests exert immense influence within the councils of the great powers. Mystery envelops the operation of the technological alchemists. Deterrence has become normal, and minds have been habituated to the vocabulary of mutual extermination. And within this normality, hideous cultural abnormalities have been nurtured and are growing to full girth.

The menace of nuclear war reaches far back into the economies of both parties, dictating priorities and awarding power. Here, in failing economies, will be found the most secure and vigorous sectors, tapping the most advanced technological skills of both opposed societies and diverting these away from peaceful and productive employment or from efforts to close the great gap between the world's north and south. Here also will be found the driving rationale for expansionist programs in unsafe nuclear energy, programs which cohabit comfortably with military nuclear technology whereas the urgent research into safe energy supplies from sun, wind, or wave are neglected because they have no military payoff. Here, in this burgeoning sector, will be found the new expansionist drive for markets for arms, as capitalist and socialist powers compete to feed into the Middle East, Africa, and Asia more sophisticated means of killing.

The menace of this stagnant state of violence backs up also

into the polity of both halves of the world. Permanent threat and periodic crisis press the men of the military-industrial interests, by differing routes in each society, toward the top. Crisis legitimates the enlargement of the security functions of the state, the intimidation of internal dissent and the imposition of secrecy and the control of information. As the natural lines of social and political development are repressed, and affirmative perspectives are closed, so internal politics collapses into squabbling interest groups, all of which are subordinated to the overarching interests of the state of perpetual threat.

All this may be readily observed. It may be observed even in failing Britain, across whose territory are now scattered the bases, airfields, camps, research stations, submarine depots, communications-interception stations, radar screens, security and intelligence HQs, munitions works—secure and expanding employment in an economic climate of radical insecurity.

What we cannot observe so well—for we ourselves are the object which must be observed—is the manner in which three decades of deterrence, of mutual fear, mystery, and state-endorsed stagnant hostility, have backed up into our culture and our ideology. Imagination has been numbed, language and values have been fouled by the postures and expectations of the deterrent state. But this is matter for a close and scrupulous inquiry.

These, then, are among the strategic considerations which lead me to the view that the probability of great-power nuclear warfare is strong and increasing. I do not argue from this local episode or that: what happened yesterday in Afghanistan and what is happening now in Pakistan or North Yemen. I argue from a general and sustained historical process, an accumulative logic, of a kind made familiar to me in the study of history. The episodes lead in this direction or that, but the general logic of process is always toward nuclear war.

The local crises are survived, and it seems as if the decisive moment—either of war or of peacemaking and reconciliation—has been postponed and pushed forward into the future. But what has been pushed forward is always worse. Both parties change for the worse. The weapons are more terrible, the means for their delivery more clever. The notion that a war might be fought to "advantage," that it might be "won," gains ground. There is even a tremor of excitement in our culture as though, subconsciously, humankind has lived with the notion for so long that expectations without actions have become boring. The human mind, even when it resists, assents more easily to its own defeat. All moves on its degenerative course, as if the outcome of civilization was as determined as is the outcome of this sentence: in a full stop.

I am reluctant to accept that this determinism is absolute. But if my arguments are correct, then we cannot put off the matter any longer. We must throw whatever resources still exist in human culture across the path of this degenerative logic. We must protest if we are to survive. Protest is the only realistic form of civil defense.

We must generate an alternative logic, an opposition at every level of society. This opposition must be international and it must win the support of multitudes. It must bring its influence to bear upon the rulers of the world. It must act, in very different conditions, within each national state, and, on occasion, it must directly confront its own national state apparatus.

The campaign for European Nuclear Disarmament, which is already gaining active support in many parts of Western Europe, as well as a more cautious attention in some parts of Eastern Europe, has as an objective the creation of an expanding zone freed from nuclear weapons and bases. It aims to expel these weapons from the soil and waters of both East and West Europe and to press the missiles, in the first place, back to the Urals and to the Atlantic Ocean.

The tactics of this campaign will be both national and international.

In the national context, each peace movement will proceed directly to contest the nuclear weapons deployed by its owns state, or by NATO or Warsaw Pact obligations upon its own soil. Its actions will not be qualified by any notion of diplomatic bargaining. Its opposition to the use of nuclear weapons by its own state will be absolute. Its demands upon its own state for disarmament will be unilateral.

In the international, and especially in the European, context, each national movement will exchange information and delegations, will support and challenge each other. The movement will encourage a European consciousness, in common combat for survival, fostering informal communication at every level, and disregarding national considerations of interest or security.

It is evident that this logic will develop unevenly. The national movements will not grow at the same pace, nor be able to express themselves in identical ways. Each success of a unilateral kind—by Holland in refusing NATO cruise missiles or by Rumania or Poland in distancing themselves from Soviet strategies—will be met with an outcry that it serves the advantage of one or the other bloc.

This outcry must be disregarded. It cannot be expected that initiatives on one side will be met with instant reciprocation from the other. Very certainly, the strategists of both blocs will seek to turn the movement to their own advantage. The logic of peacemaking will be as uneven, and as fraught with emergencies and contingencies, as the logic which leads on to war.

In particular, the movement in West and East Europe will find very different expression. In the West we envisage popular movements engaged in a direct contest with the policies of their own national states. At first, Soviet ideologues may look benignly upon this, anticipating a weakening of NATO preparations which are matched by no actions larger than "peace-loving" rhetoric from the East.

But we are confident that our strategy can turn this rhetoric into acts. In Eastern Europe there are profound pressures for peace, for greater democracy and international exchange, and for relief from the heavy burden of siege economies. For a time these pressures may be contained by the repressive measures of national and Soviet security services. Only a few courageous dissidents will, in the first place, be able to take an open part in our common work.

Yet to the degree that the peace movement in the West can be seen to be effective, it will afford support and protection to our allies in Eastern Europe and the Soviet Union. It will provide those conditions of relaxation of tension which will weaken the rationale and legitimacy of repressive state measures, and will allow the pressures for democracy and detente to assert themselves in more active and open ways. Moreover, as an intrinsic part of the European campaign, the demand for an opening of the societies of the East to information, free communication and expression, and exchange of delegations to take part in the common work will be pressed on every occasion. And it will not only be pressed as rhetoric. We are going to find devices to symbolize that pressure and dramatize that debate.

Against the strategy which envisages Europe as a theater of limited nuclear warfare, we propose to make in Europe a theater of peace. This will not, even if we succeed, remove the danger of confrontation in non-European theaters. It offers, at the least, a small hope of European survival. It could offer more. For if the logic of nuclear strategy reaches back into the organization and ideologies of the superpowers themselves, so the logic of peacemaking might reach back also, enforcing alternative strategies, alternative ideologies. European nuclear disarmament would favor the conditions for international detente.

When I first sat down to write this essay, in February 1980, it seemed to the handful of us in Britain, France, West Germany, and Eastern Europe who were then discussing such a campaign that we were only whistling in the dark. On every side of us the armorers were having their way. Only in Norway, Holland, and Belgium did it seem that a popular movement of conscience could still bring any influence to bear upon political decisions.

Now we know differently. The movement has taken off, and it is moving rapidly across Europe, west, north, and south. It is, already, too large and too various for any group or interest to manipulate it for sectional ends. No one is going to nobble it: this is a movement of people for themselves.

And we have seen, in the last six months of 1980, another movement of quite extraordinary resilience among the Polish people. There have been all the usual attempts—among the Soviet and NATO military—to translate this movement into the habitual terms of the Cold War. These attempts continue, and I have no doubt as to their dangers. Yet the movement of

Polish Solidarity is, in a critical sense, *of the same kind* as the movement in West Europe to resist nuclear rearmament. Both are movements of Europeans for autonomy—away from cold-war cliency—and movements, by Europeans, to resume a political space for themselves.

The Western European initiative for nuclear disarmament is no more "pro-Communist" than Polish Solidarity is "pro-capitalist." These movements, taken together, offer more hope of some way out of the world's appalling impasse than delivery systems, megatonnage, or throw-weight can ever do. They offer a very difficult—barely possible—path forward, whose ultimate end would be, not only the dismantling of some nuclear weapons but the dismantling of the blocs which would throw them. A more limited success might offer, at the least, a nuclear-weapons-free space, in the heart of Europe, holding the superpowers apart—a space of quiet within which alternatives could grow.

I cannot see how such an outcome could be against the true interests of either the American or the Russian people. The rising mood in Europe is neither "anti-American" or "anti-Soviet": it is antimilitarist, and it is opposed to the militarism of both blocs. For militarism, in its rivalry and even more in its reciprocity, is bringing out the worst features in both superpowers. It is containing the forces making democratic transition in the East, so that the aging old guard of Stalinism is now propped up by the weaponry of the West and given fresh transfusions of legitimation by the Western threat. I will not say what I consider that militarism is doing to the political and cultural life of the United States. That is a problem which readers of *The Nation* know only too well.

I promised to conclude by returning you from European perceptions to yourselves. But there is nothing that I can say that readers do not already know. I have described a militarist logic whose outcome must be terminal for civilization in the Northern Hemisphere. The absurd scenarios of counterforce menus and options and theater wars are quite as menacing to Americans as they are to Europeans: only a day or a week will divide us in our common fate. What happens then will make the worst possible outcome of Three Mile Island appear as no more than a pistol shot.

This is what is being prepared, steadily, year by year, and I think it probable that it will come to its conclusion—through accident or miscalculation, through the paranoia of the Russian old guard or the brash theatricals of American preemptive deterrence and, above all, through the steady growth in influence, in both superpowers, of the military-industrial forces and their Satanic "experts"—and that the conclusion will be in the next two or three decades.

On July 25, 1945, President Truman scrawled in his personal notebook: "We have discovered the most terrible bomb in the history of the world. It may be the fire destruction prophesied in the Euphrates Valley era, after Noah and his fabulous ark." The President's literal biblical reference is touching, and touching also was his confidence that his instructions to the Secretary of War that the weapon be used on a "purely military target" only, and not "women and children," would be obeyed by the military executors. For from that very moment it is the logic of weaponry which has been in the saddle, and which has been riding the horse of the Apocalypse remorselessly into the Valley of the Shadow of Death.

What deterrence has done has been to strike into immobility every normal political process of human negotiation or reconciliation. For decades the rival military blocs, like inadequate personalities, have postponed dealing with the problems of today, and, in the name of deterrence, have tied these problems to the backs of missiles and sent them on into the future. Which future we are now fouling up today, just as the experts of the late 1950s fouled up our own present day.

The R and D for the weapons which will kill our children and grandchildren in the twenty-first century is now in hand and is being paid from our current taxes. The leaders of your country and of mine have no political remedy of any kind. None. Nor have those immensely expert contributors to *Daedalus*. From all of them—nothing. They show a process without end, except the terminus of nuclear war.

We offer, cautiously, a possible politics of protest and survival: the different END of European Nuclear Disarmament. It is a politics which commences, not at the top with diplomats and abortive SALT negotiations but with popular movements and with scores of less formal lateral exchanges. As we proceed we may build around the small nonaligned core of Europe (Sweden, Austria, Yugoslavia) a more influential alliance of political parties and of governments.

I doubt whether we can succeed: nothing less than a world-wide spiritual revulsion against the Satanic Kingdom would give us any chance of bringing the military riders down. What might make it just possible that we could succeed would be if the "we" become not just European but truly international—if there should be, first of all, a profound shift in American public opinion, and then, and alongside this, by all our combined efforts and skills, an extension deep into Russian opinion also.

Impossible? It may seem so. That is not the way things are going in the West just now. Dominant American policy appears to be intent upon freezing Europe in the postures of war forever, while enhancing daily the means of that war's final execution. Europeans watch your new administration enter into Washington and await the outcome with fear.

PART II Armaments and Armorers

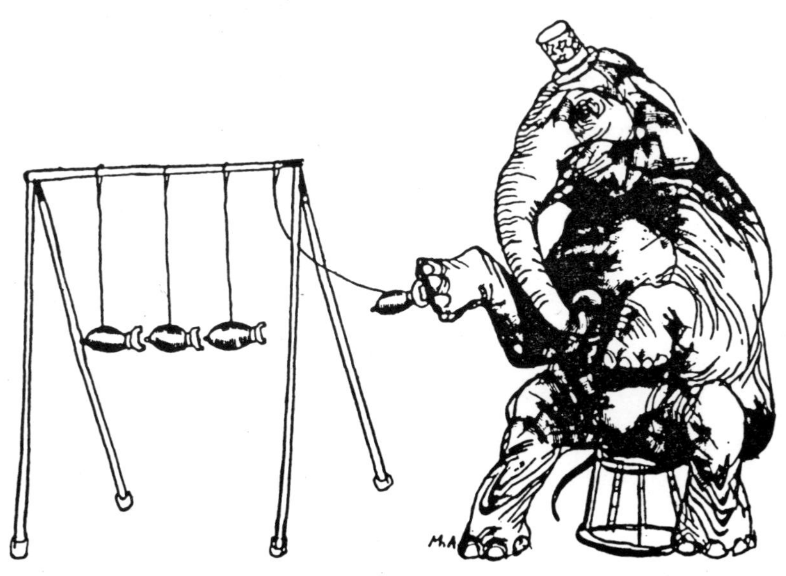

2
The European Nuclear Theater
Dan Smith

In December 1979 NATO decided it would deploy 572 new American nuclear missiles in West Europe. One hundred and eight of them will be Pershing II ballistic missiles, which have a range of about 1,000 miles, and the other 464 will be Tomahawk ground-launched cruise missiles. The NATO plan is for all 108 Pershing IIs plus 112 of the cruise missiles to be based in the Federal Republic of Germany, while Britain takes 160 cruise missiles and Italy 96. Belgium and the Netherlands are marked down to take 48 cruise missiles each, but, because of popular pressure, it looks as if neither of these two countries will take them.

Unlike ballistic missiles, cruise missiles fly all the way to their targets under power—essentially, they are pilotless aircraft. The missile's guidance system works by matching radar readings of the ground over which it is flying with a preprogramed contour map. Flying at low altitude at just below the speed of sound, it can take as direct or circuitous a route to its target as its programmer wishes. Its low-level flight and small size—around fourteen feet long, depending on the particular version, with a diameter of twenty inches—mean it will be hard to detect on its way to the target, while the guidance system will be able, it is claimed, to provide such accuracy that on average half the missiles launched would fall within a few yards of their targets, having flown distances of 2,000 miles or so from their launching points.

At this stage, however, it is not clear that their technology will actually work reliably. There has been a series of mishaps during U.S. testing of cruise missiles over the past few years. But the U.S. military is so enamored of them that in March 1980 the U.S. Air Force announced it planned to purchase 3,400 air-launched cruise missiles over the next seven years, at a cost of $4,000 million.[1] These are different cruise missiles from the ones coming to Europe; the air-launched types are to be produced by Boeing, whereas the Tomahawks are a General Dynamics product. Boeing's product will be carried, twenty at a time, on B-52 bombers, while the Tomahawks will be mounted in fours on trucks.

The 160 Tomahawks expected in Britain will be based at Greenham Common near Newbury and at Molesworth near Huntingdon. In times of emergency they will be dispersed around the countryside on their trucks, up to 100 miles away from their bases. Each truck with its four Tomahawks will be a small target, but the area in which they deploy will be one big target. These missiles, in Britain as elsewhere in Europe, will be completely under U.S. control.

At the time the decision was announced, and in all government statements and most press discussion since, the impression has been given that the new missiles represent no more than a response to a new threat from the USSR, and that without them NATO is virtually defenseless. In military policy and in the arguments used to legitimate major decisions, distortions, half-truths, and downright lies are common currency. But in the period just before and since NATO's December 1979 decision, new standards have been set.

Europe remains the main site of the military confrontation between the U.S. and the USSR and their respective allies in NATO and the Warsaw Pact. Detente in Europe removed some of the main bones of regional contention, but military confrontation continued and escalated through the 1970s. European members of NATO now mount armed forces employing 2,779,000 personnel in uniform, in addition to which the U.S. has 279,700 military personnel in Europe (222,400 in ground forces, the bulk of them in Germany) plus the sailors in its Mediterranean Sixth Fleet, while Canada chips in with 3,000 soldiers. Non-Soviet members of the Warsaw Pact have 1,105,000 people in uniform, in addition to which the USSR has some 618,000 soldiers in the countries of East Europe, plus airmen and ground crew at airfields, together with the sailors of its various fleets in the surrounding seas. This all adds up to well over 5,000,000 people in the regular armed forces of the two alliances in Europe and the seas around it. Further thousands are in the reserves: 3,473,000 in European NATO countries and 2,148,000 in the Warsaw Pact apart from the USSR.[2]

But the numbers of people serving in the military forces in Europe do not tell the whole story. These forces mount weaponry on an unimaginably destructive scale. Part of the confrontation of these forces consists of around 11,000 nuclear warheads for use in Europe. Of these, about 7,500 are deployed by NATO, while around 3,500 are deployed by the Warsaw Pact. The exact figures on either side are not publicly available, and in recent years estimates for Warsaw Pact nuclear warheads for use in Europe have ranged from 1,750 to 5,000.[3]

These figures may surprise readers who have been led to believe that NATO's tactical or theater nuclear warheads (TNW) were vastly outnumbered by the Warsaw Pact's. But the figures are taken from impeccably militaristic Western sources, and, like most such figures, derive by one means or another from U.S. intelligence.

Many of NATO's TNW, however, are mounted on relatively short-range weapon systems, and the complaints about the Warsaw Pact's numerical superiority in TNW have focused on the long-range systems. Even here we shall find that the picture is rather different from the overwhelming superiority the Warsaw Pact is usually claimed to have. But before looking a little closer at the weapons and the numbers, some further points should be made about these misleading presentations.

Nuclear weapons were first introduced into Europe by the U.S. when it stationed strategic nuclear bombers in Britain in 1948. In the mid-1950s NATO took the decision which built the TNW arsenal up to its present size. Not only did NATO deploy TNW in Europe first, but it has always had a large numerical superiority over the Warsaw Pact in this respect. NATO's emphasis on relatively short-range weapons systems is due to its own preferences and decisions; at any time since the mid-1950s it had the technology and capability to deploy long-range missiles for TNW had it so chosen. It did not. It has now. It has done so, not because there is a qualitatively new threat from the USSR in the form of the SS-20—the USSR has had long-range nuclear missiles targeted on Western Europe since the early 1960s. Rather, its December 1979 decision was taken because NATO has come to different views about how it wants to prepare for nuclear war in Europe.

In other words, and this brings us to the second point, NATO was not forced into the decision by the Warsaw Pact; it moved into it of its own volition. If NATO spokesmen and government ministers are right that the new missiles represent an important new capability for NATO, then they cannot deny that it is NATO rather than the Warsaw Pact which has given this particular aspect of the arms race its latest new twist. At one time NATO was happy not to have this new capability. Now it wants it. The comparable TNW on the Warsaw Pact side are today much the same as they have been for many years, but rather more modern. But with NATO we are dealing not with more modern versions of the same weapon, but with a totally new capability, and that means NATO's decision bears a particular burden of responsibility for the dangers we now face.

This also means that the term "modernization" used to describe the decision is thoroughly inappropriate. It is a gentle word which implies nothing more than routine procedure in the arms race, not something which is qualitatively new. In fact, NATO's TNW modernization program dates back to 1969, the first year of the first Nixon administration. It is almost totally a U.S. program which the other NATO states have accepted. It has included the efforts to introduce "mini-nukes" and the neutron bomb. In both cases, the basic theme was that the greater precision of the weapons permitted realistic options to be developed for fighting a nuclear war in Europe. Other aspects of the program include the "hardening" of airfields and other military facilities so that they remain serviceable in nuclear war and the development of communication systems which would not be blacked out by the effects of nuclear explosions. The accuracy of the cruise missiles is the counterpart of the supposed precision of mini-nukes and the neutron bomb. The theme throughout is the attempt to make nuclear war in Europe more "thinkable."

But, unless the Warsaw Pact decides to join in the rules

of this macabre game, none of it will do anything to reduce the destructiveness of nuclear war, which was supposed to be the main problem for NATO in planning to fight one. As it has done for at least twenty-five years, NATO war planning amounts to preparing to defend Europe by blowing it up. The main difference today is that the planning appears to be more enthusiastic.[4]

The Warsaw Pact's TNW

Nuclear weapons grouped under the heading of TNW vary widely in the means of delivery to targets, the ranges over which they can be delivered, and their explosive power. The picture is further confused because both blocs possess "dual capable" systems—systems capable of delivering either nuclear or non-nuclear munitions. What follows is a brief description of some of the main TNW of each side, separated into three categories according to their range (over 1,000 miles; between 100 and 1,000 miles; and less than 100 miles), together with some estimates of the numbers. For numbers of TNW carried by "dual capable" systems I am using estimates from the International Institute for Strategic Studies (IISS) of how many of the total number of systems available would actually be used to carry nuclear weapons.[5]

For longer-range TNW the USSR has land-based missiles and bombers. The SS-4 and SS-5 missiles were first seen publicly in 1961 and 1964 respectively; the SS-4 has a range of about 1,200 miles, while the SS-5's is about 2,300, and both carry single one-megaton warheads. In December 1979 NATO stated that the USSR had 400 of these two missiles.[6] Now replacing these missiles is the SS-20, which has figured so prominently in recent Western news coverage of Soviet armaments. Unlike the older missiles it is mobile on the ground (like Tomahawk cruise missiles) and carries three warheads, each independently targeted, over a range of between 3,000 and 4,000 miles. In December 1979 the U.S. Department of

Defense stated that 100 SS-20s had been deployed, sixty of them targeted against Western Europe and the rest against China.[7] We might therefore estimate that another forty SS-20s may have been produced by October 1980, of which perhaps twenty-five would be targeted against Western Europe, raising this figure to eighty-five. SS-20 warheads would thus number about 255.

It is now thought in NATO that, since the lead-up to NATO's decision to deploy new American missiles to Europe, the USSR has stopped phasing out the older missiles, in which case the SS-20 would be augmenting rather than replacing the SS-4 and SS-5s.[8]

The USSR also has about 450 copies of two bombers with ranges around 1,700 miles, the Badger and the Blinder (these are NATO code-names), which were first seen in 1954 and 1961 respectively. Since early 1975 the USSR has also deployed a supersonic bomber, Backfire, with a range above 3,000 miles. At one time the U.S. was asserting that Backfire was intended for use against it, with the pilots making a one-way trip, but it always seemed more likely that Backfire was meant for use against Western Europe and maritime targets and that if the USSR wanted bombers to attack the U.S. it would make them specifically for that. Assurances that Backfire is not aimed at the U.S. were included in a Soviet statement attached to the Strategic Arms Limitation agreement signed with the U.S. in June 1979, where it is also stated that the production rate will not exceed thirty per year.[9] On the basis of IISS' 1979 estimate of the total number of Backfires, and the proportion of them deployed against Western Europe, it seems likely that by October 1980 the USSR had about 70 Backfires able to carry TNW.

For shorter-range delivery systems, the Warsaw Pact has about 3,600 aircraft, with ranges varying from 275 to 600 miles, capable of delivering nuclear weapons. By no means all of them would be used for that task. The IISS estimates that aircraft from within this total carry about 700 nuclear warheads. These aircraft are based not only in the USSR but also, in varying numbers, in every other Warsaw Pact country. Non-Soviet Warsaw Pact countries also provide sites for Scud nuclear missiles, with a range of 185 miles. Another missile, the SS-12, with a range of about 500 miles, is based in the USSR, as are some Scuds. There are a little over 400 of these two missiles, all carrying single warheads. Finally, the USSR is thought to have about fifty-four missiles deployed on submarines in the Baltic and North Sea; the range is about 700 miles, and, again, each missile carries a single warhead.

For sending nuclear weapons over ranges less than 100 miles the Warsaw Pact has nuclear artillery and mortars deployed in the USSR (though one assumes they would be moved forward for war) and large numbers of a group of artillery rockets known as FROG. These have a range less than forty miles, are capable of having nuclear warheads, and are deployed in all the Warsaw countries.

NATO's TNW

NATO currently has no land-based missiles with ranges over 1,000 miles. This is the "gap" the Tomahawks and Pershing IIs are supposed to fill. But NATO does have long-range submarine-launched missiles, which are usually conveniently forgotten when the time comes round to moan about Warsaw Pact superiority and convince us we need the new missiles. There are sixty-four British Polaris missiles, with a range of 2,880 miles, and forty or forty-five U.S. Poseidon missiles, carrying a total of 400 warheads over a similar range. In addition, France, which is a member of NATO but whose forces are not under NATO's military command, has eighty-two submarine-based missiles.

For long range TNW, NATO has preferred aircraft to missiles. It has a little less than 1,000 bombers with ranges between 1,000 and 3,000 miles. Among several types included here are British Vulcans, now rather aged, and the American F-111s stationed in Britain. If French long-range bombers are counted, the total of aircraft increases to just on 1,000, and the IISS estimates that about 870 TNW (950 including the French) would be carried by aircraft within this total. Britain is now introducing Tornado multi-role aircraft into its forces, and some will be used to replace Vulcans.

For shorter-range TNW, NATO has 180 Pershing I missiles, with a range of 450 miles, and 490 aircraft (660 including the French) with ranges between 350 and 800 miles. According to the IISS these aircraft would probably carry about 175 warheads (230 including the French).

NATO also has over 780 pieces of nuclear artillery and large numbers of short-range missiles, especially Lance and the French Pluton, with ranges of well under 100 miles. Finally, NATO has TNW in the form of nuclear depth bombs (as does the Warsaw Pact) for antisubmarine warfare; it has some old nuclear-tipped anti-aircraft missiles; and it has atomic demolition munitions, which would be placed in the ground and detonated to put obstructions in the way of Warsaw Pact forces.

Comparing Numbers

The way in which the military strength of NATO and the Warsaw Pact are compared by most orthodox Western commentators is extremely misleading, very often incompetent, and occasionally downright dishonest. At one level the problem starts because these comparisons are usually designed to show that NATO needs more forces. At another level the problem starts because of the habit of comparing numbers, which, even if the quality of weapon systems is taken into account, is not the whole story: tactics and roles, morale and the quality of command, timing, terrain, and several other factors ought by rights to enter into the equation. Having said that, I am now going to join in the numbers game, not in order to arrive at a genuine comparison of the two blocs' military might, but to show how misleading the stock propaganda is (and thus to show that calling it "propaganda" is an accurate analytical term and not a simple slur).

I have already pointed to NATO's overall numerical superiority in TNW—approximately 7,500 to 3,500. This is not enough for NATO strategists, who have broken the total down (and there is nothing wrong with that in principle) into different categories in order to reveal the Warsaw Pact superiority in land-based missiles with ranges over 1,000 miles, against which Tomahawk and Pershing II are presented as a defensive response. Everything depends on the choice of categories.

If one took all missiles and aircraft able to deliver TNW over ranges above 1,000 miles, and worked from IISS estimates of how many would carry TNW and how many would be serviceable at the right time, the picture is a little different. In that category, NATO has 1,300 warheads, 1,420 if the French are included, against the Warsaw Pact's 1,040. That is, NATO has a numerical superiority, not a large one (the ratio is 1.3 or 1.4 to 1), in precisely that category into which Tomahawk cruise missiles and Pershing IIs will fit. This is a far cry from the crippling NATO inferiority we hear bemoaned so frequently and furiously. However, for aircraft and missiles with ranges between 100 and 1,000 miles, the Warsaw Pact has a larger numerical superiority in warheads: 1,030 to 340 (or 390 if the French are counted). Overall, for TNW which can be delivered over ranges above 100 miles, the Warsaw Pact has the lead: 2,070 to 1,640 (1,810 counting the French). But the ratio of about 1.3 or 1.1 to 1 is not large, and the lower ratio that includes the French on the NATO side, which is how the Soviets must see it, is within the margin of error for estimates of this kind.

I should repeat that this is really an interesting exercise rather than a genuine comparison of military strength. But it may alert readers to a future possibility—the discovery of a new gap in TNW deliverable over ranges between 100 and 1,000 miles. I think I shall not reveal yet the way in which I will play that particular numbers game if and when the time comes.

European Nuclear Disarmament

All this fooling around is interesting and necessary given the way in which government justifications for the new NATO missiles are presented. But it should not distract attention from two critical points. First, these weapons represent an enormous amount of destructive power and the potential for many millions of deaths within the first few hours of a nuclear war in Europe, with many millions more of horrible casualties, a devastated continent in which the basic structures of society apart from the authority of the central state will totally collapse. Second, with the exception of the British and French weapons, they are all under the direct control of the superpowers (and some of the British weapons are only semi-independent).

The appeal for European nuclear disarmament launched in April 1980 is directed against these weapons, against that war, and against that superpower dominance. The idea and the campaign for it are discussed in more detail in other contributions to this book. My business is to consider two likely objections to European nuclear disarmament: First, the objection that if NATO has no TNW, even if the Warsaw Pact has none, NATO will be the worse off because of its inferiority in non-nuclear forces; second, the objection that the implementation of the idea would weaken the unity of NATO at exactly the time when it should be standing more closely together than ever.

Non-Nuclear Forces

The point about the first objection is that, when the problem is closely studied, NATO's inferiority in non-nuclear forces is extraordinarily elusive. It has always been the basis for arguments for having large numbers of TNW in Europe, and it has long been an obsession in NATO. In fact, in the 1960s and again in the 1970s, the U.S. Department of Defense conducted analyses of both sides' non-nuclear forces which showed that Warsaw Pact superiorities in some categories were more than offset by NATO advantages in other categories it thought were more important. Naturally, these studies never received the kind of coverage from either official spokespeople or the press which is given to the more common reports of Warsaw Pact superiority. It can be added that a comparison of IISS estimates over the years, and these estimates need to be treated with a great deal of care, shows that the Warsaw Pact's military build-up through the 1970s was at least matched by NATO's own military build-up.[10]

I am not going to enter deep into the non-nuclear numbers game here, but just one example may be worthwhile. It is the example of tanks. For years NATO has expressed its anxieties about the much larger number of tanks held by the Warsaw Pact. The Conservatives in the 1980 defense White Paper, like their Labour predecessors in the five previous years, churned out the usual diagram showing NATO tanks outnumbered by 2.8 to 1.[11] This is about the same figure as the IISS gives. But that same diagram somehow forgot to mention NATO's extremely accurate antitank weapons. By late 1978, excluding short-range types carried and fired by individual soldiers, NATO had around 193,000 antitank guided missiles. This represented an increase of one-third over its inventory two years previously. By early 1979 there were over 17,000 ground-based launchers for these missiles, with yet more on helicopters and fixed-wing aircraft. If this rate of deployment has continued, then by October 1980 NATO probably had getting on for 240,000 antitank guided missiles; the 1980 White Paper stated that the Warsaw Pact had 18,300 tanks. The age and quality of Warsaw Pact tanks are not usually mentioned either. Non-Soviet countries use Soviet tanks from the 1950s and before. The Soviet tanks produced in the 1960s are almost universally agreed to be of lower quality than the tanks NATO deploys, and these constitute the bulk of Soviet tank forces in Europe. The newer Soviet tanks probably are superior in some respects to NATO's current tanks, but Britain, the U.S., and West Germany are now in the process of developing and producing new types. It is also not usually mentioned that NATO took a deliberate decision at the start of the 1970s not to match the Warsaw Pact tank for tank—which reveals the dishonesty of comparing tank against tank—and has a policy of going for weapon systems of higher quality—which reveals further dishonesty, since high quality generally means lower numbers.

Of course, the Warsaw Pact may be right from a military perspective to go for quantity rather than quality, and NATO may be wrong to have decided not to match its adversary tank for tank. The point is that the current situation, usually presented as the result of the USSR's unilateral military build-up, is actually the result also of a series of specific and deliberate decisions by NATO, and that the current situation is always incompletely described by the British government and several others.

If NATO and Warsaw Pact forces are examined in this kind of detail across the board, two main conclusions emerge. First, as far as it can be quantified there is a rough balance of forces in Europe; neither side has an important advantage overall. Second, these forces, even without nuclear weapons, would be immensely destructive of each other and everything around them if war came. Neither conclusion forms the basis for objecting to European nuclear disarmament on the basis of a NATO inferiority in non-nuclear forces.

NATO's Unity

The second objection is that if nuclear weapons are removed from Europe, NATO's unity would suffer. In fact, there is much to be said for this objection; I think it is essentially correct to say that European nuclear disarmament would weaken NATO's unity. In the Warsaw Pact it would have a similar effect, though perhaps weaker in the short term. This objection actually provides an important insight into the role of nuclear weapons in the current constitution of NATO and into the type of unity we are talking about.

The point is, of course, that these are American weapons. They provide the U.S. with important strategic and thereby political leadership over the West European NATO states. In general terms, American leadership is under challenge from West Europe and Japan and is suffering; but within NATO the currency of American TNW in Europe and of the "nuclear umbrella" of U.S. strategic forces still buys U.S. hegemony.

Indeed, it is precisely when American leadership is sharply challenged in other arenas that one might expect it to try and strengthen its strategic leadership in NATO, and the most obvious way of doing this would probably be to plan to deploy more U.S. nuclear weapons in Europe. Since meetings of the NATO Nuclear Planning Group, which are supposed to involve the rest of NATO in this aspect of strategic planning, are largely taken up by American lectures, it is not too hard to develop momentum behind any American proposal in this field.

Thus unity in this context means acceptance of U.S. leadership. And that brings with it acceptance of U.S. plans for nuclear war in Europe, for fighting a limited nuclear war, limited in the sense that the U.S.'s own territory is not directly involved. Their limited war—our holocaust. Whether the USSR would permit war to remain limited in this sense is very dubious, but beside the point. For the issue which is of overriding importance for West Europeans is that NATO unity means agreeing to be an expendable American asset, a forward line of defense, a battlefield for the two superpowers. For East Europeans, the issue is essentially the same.

The movement for European nuclear disarmament thus gets to the heart of the matter. Precisely because it does challenge NATO's unity it could create the space for developing new and safer ways of ensuring some degree of security in a dangerous world. It is the confrontation between the U.S. and the USSR which is leading us toward war. European nuclear disarmament offers a possibility for Europe to disengage from that confrontation, to challenge the right of the superpowers to have the power over our fate that they now do, and eventually to eliminate that power. It opens a perspective of new political movement in both East and West Europe, breaking out of the suffocating effects on domestic politics of the superpowers' military confrontation, leading to a greater variety of social and political systems among wholly or partially nonaligned nations. European nuclear disarmament threatens both American and Soviet hegemony. It therefore demands the rethinking of some of the basic and most cherished precepts in both NATO and the

Warsaw Pact; for example, it demands seeing a challenge to NATO unity as positive. It thus involves a head-on collision with what NATO would have us believe are the basic "facts of life" of international politics. Unless we undertake that task, we are all too likely to have those "facts of life" draw us over the brink into nuclear war.

Notes

1. The *New York Times*, March 26, 1980.
2. These figures are taken from *The Military Balance 1979–1980* (London: International Institute for Strategic Studies, 1979), with the exception of the figure for Soviet troops in Europe, which was not given. I therefore took the figure given in the previous year's edition and subtracted from it the 20,000 troops unilaterally withdrawn from the German Democratic Republic by the USSR since. The figures for NATO include French forces.
3. See, for example, M. Leitenberg, "Background Information on Tactical Nuclear Weapons," in *Tactical Nuclear Weapons: European Perspectives* (London: Taylor & Francis, 1978); *World Armaments and Disarmament: SIPRI Yearbook 1978* (London: Taylor & Francis, 1978), pp. 426–29. The usual figure given for NATO tactical nuclear warheads is about 7,000, but the U.S. Department of Defense has now made it clear that its Poseidon missiles designated for use in Europe are not included in that total, and the higher figure of about 7,500 therefore becomes appropriate: *Department of Defense Annual Report Fiscal Year 1981* (U.S. DOD, 1980), p. 92.
4. This issue is discussed in more detail in my *The Defence of the Realm in the 1980s* (London: Croom Helm, 1980), chapter 4.
5. *The Military Balance 1979–1980*, pp. 114–19. In addition I have taken information from *Jane's Weapon Systems* and from *SALT and the NATO Allies* (U.S. Senate, Committee on Foreign Relations, Staff Report, October 1979) as well as sources cited below.
6. NATO press statement, December 5, 1979, cited by M. Leitenberg, *NATO and WTO Long Range Theater Nuclear Forces*, mimeo, April 1980 (available from the Armament and Disarmament Information Unit, University of Sussex); the figure is some 190 missiles lower than the one given by the IISS in *The Military Balance 1979–1980*.

7. U.S. International Communication Agency, December 6, 1979, cited by Leitenberg, *NATO and WTO Long Range Theater Nuclear Forces*; again the figure is a good deal lower than the one given by the IISS.
8. *Guardian*, October 15, 1979; *International Herald Tribune*, October 15, 1979.
9. Reprinted in *Survival*, September/October 1979.
10. These issues and those in the following paragraph are discussed in detail in Chapter 4 of *The Defense of the Realm in the 1980s*.
11. *Defence in the 1980s*, Cmnd 7826-I (London: HMSO, 1980), p. 18.

3
War, Militarism, and the Soviet State

David Holloway

In the military structure of the world the Soviet Union and the United States stand in a class by themselves. They mount the two largest military efforts and between them account for one half of the massive resources which the world devotes to arms and armed forces. There are, it is true, considerable differences between the military forces of the Soviet Union and the United States, but these are insignificant when compared with the differences between them and the forces of other states.

From the armed forces it maintains and the weapons it produces, it is clear that the Soviet military effort is large. It is difficult, however, to say precisely what resources it consumes. The Soviet Government publishes a figure for the defense budget each year, but this is of little help in estimating the military burden because it is not clear what the budget covers. In any event, observers outside the Soviet Union agree that the Soviet armed forces could not be paid for by the official defense budget without the help of very large hidden subsidies. Western attempts to assess Soviet defense spending must be treated with caution too because of the intrinsic difficulties of making such estimates.[1] It is evident, nevertheless, that only a major commitment of resources has enabled the Soviet Union in the last twenty years to attain strategic parity with the United States, maintain large well-equipped forces in Europe and along the frontier with China, extend the deployment of the Soviet Navy throughout the world, and engage in continuous modernization of arms and equipment.

A military effort of this scale necessarily has a far-reaching impact on the Soviet economy. An extensive network of military

---

*This article was originally prepared for the Demilitarization Working Group of the World Order Models Project and was in a more extended form in *Alternatives: A Journal of World Policy* 6, no. 1 (March 1980). It is reprinted here with permission of *Alternatives* and the author.

research and development establishments is required to develop armaments, while a major sector of industry is needed to produce them in quantity. The Soviet Union has amassed military power roughly comparable to that of the United States, even though its Gross National Product is only about half as large. Consequently, a higher rate of extraction of resources has been necessary, with consequences which will be examined below.

The maintenance of standing forces of some 4 million people (mainly men) has not only economic, but also social and political consequences.[2] Institutional arrangements exist to draft a substantial proportion of each generation of young men into the armed forces. A considerable effort is made to ensure that reserves are available for mobilization if necessary. Voluntary military societies provide moral support for the armed forces and military training for the population at large. Secondary school children are given pre-induction military training from the age of fifteen. In recent years there has been a growing campaign of military-patriotic education which tries to instil in the population the values of patriotism and respect for military virtues. Party leaders seemingly believe that obligatory military service can help to foster social discipline and to bring the different nationalities closer together. They also appear to believe that association of the Party with the armed forces will strengthen Soviet patriotism and the commitment of the people to the existing political order.[3] At the highest political level the close relationship between Party and army has been underlined by the awarding to General Secretary Brezhnev of various military honors, including the rank of Marshal of the Soviet Union.

All this is a far cry from the vision of a socialist society which the founders of Marxism and the makers of the Bolshevik revolution held. Marxist thought has traditionally been marked by a strong antipathy to militarism, seeing war and armies as the product of the world capitalist system. Before 1917 socialists agreed that standing armies were instruments of aggression abroad and repression at home; the proper form of military organization for a socialist state would be the citizen army which would not degenerate into a military caste or create a military realm separate from other areas of social life. Although he had to lead the young Soviet republic against the White armies and foreign intervention, Lenin never succumbed to the worship of things military or tried to enhance his own authority by the paraphernalia of military command.

Why is it then that the country in which the first socialist revolution took place is so highly militarized? Why is Soviet military organization so different from original socialist concepts, with rank and hierarchy distinguished in a very marked way? Why is the defense sector accorded a special place in the economy? Why are the values of military patriotism given so much emphasis? The object of this essay is to examine the obstacles to disarmament and demilitarization in the Soviet Union and to see whether there exists in Soviet society the possibility for initiatives in that direction.

Methodological Issues

Soviet writers claim that there is nothing intrinsic to Soviet society that would generate arms production or armed forces, and that the military effort has been forced on the Soviet Union by the enmity of the capitalist world. This claim is not usually argued at length, and is based on a general statement about the nature of socialism rather than on a specific analysis of the Soviet system. A contrast is drawn with the fundamentally aggressive nature of imperialism and the incentives which the capitalist system offers for arms production. In this view Soviet military policy is purely a response to external stimuli. (Interestingly, the same writers often claim that Soviet society is, for various reasons, peculiarly suited to building up military power; among the reasons given are the disciplined, hierarchical, military-like organizations of the Party, and the planned economy which enables the Party to mobilize resources for military purposes.[4])

A rather different view is given by those peace researchers who argue that the East-West arms race is now firmly rooted in the domestic structures of the two military superpowers. The military competition between East and West, it is claimed, did have its origins in international conflict, but has now become institutionalized in powerful military-industrial-scientific complexes. This is why the settlement of major political disputes in Europe in the early 1970s was not accompanied by any significant moves toward demilitarization. This argument points not to specific features of socialism or Russian history, but to characteristics which the Soviet Union shares with the United States.[5]

The Soviet Union has been subjected to this kind of critical analysis primarily since its emergence as a full-fledged military superpower. The attainment of strategic parity with the United States has made the Soviet Union seem to share full responsibility for the continuing arms race. Soviet arms policies in the 1970s have proved profoundly disappointing to those who hoped that the SALT I agreements would lead to a slackening of the arms race. They, and others, have come more insistently to ask: What drives Soviet arms policies? What are the domestic roots of those policies?

The problem of militarization is, however, wider than that of disarmament. Andreski has pointed out that the term militarism is used in a number of different senses: First, an aggressive foreign policy, based on a readiness to resort to war; second, the preponderance of the military in the state, the extreme case being that of military rule; third, subservience of the whole society to the needs of the army, which may involve a recasting of social life in accordance with the pattern of military organization; fourth, an ideology which propagates military ideals.[6] In this essay I shall use the term militarization to refer to the third of these phenomena, specifying the others when necessary.

In an essay on the militarization of Soviet education William Odom argues that Soviet militarism is to be explained by two major factors.[7] The first of these is the similarity that exists between socialism and the war system. By this he means that both socialism and a state of war "sacrifice individuals and their private interests for the state's political objectives." (This is akin to the argument made by Soviet writers who point to the capacity of the Soviet system for creating powerful armed forces.) The second factor is the inheritance by the Soviet state of the military-political tradition of tsarism. The very process of consolidating Soviet power against external and internal enemies meant that the Bolshevik state "had to accept as its birthright most of the tensions that had made militarization of the old state seem imperative to the imperial leadership."[8] The argument here is not that socialism is inevitably militarist, but that the imperial military tradition combined with the Soviet experience to create a form of socialist militarism. In other words, Odom sees the militarization of Soviet society as primarily a product of Russian history and the Soviet system.

There are, of course, many who see the militarization of Soviet society as a consequence of both external and internal factors and explain it in terms of the Cold War rather than of the Russian past. Many socialists and liberals in the West, for example, held the view—particularly in the early years of de-Stalinization—that if the tensions of the Cold War could be relaxed, this would facilitate not only a shift of resources away from military purposes, but also political change in the direction of freedom and democracy. In other words, many of the distortions of Soviet socialism could be explained in terms of the international pressure under which socialist construction had to be carried out in the Soviet Union.

In the mid-1970s E. P. Thompson wrote of the policy of nuclear disarmament and positive neutrality which the New Left advocated in Britain in the late 1950s and the 1960s:

> It was a critical part of our advocacy that with each effective movement of detente there would follow a relaxation in military and bureaucratic pressures within the United States and the Soviet Union. Thus the relaxation of Cold War tensions was a precondition for further destalinization, and a precondition for resuming socialist and democratic advances, East or West.

Thompson went on to ask whether Soviet policy in the early 1970s—detente with the West allied with sharper repression of dissidents at home—invalidated this argument. He concluded that it did not, on two grounds: that the detente of the early

1970s amounted only to great power agreement to regulate their interests from above; further, that the repression of dissidents was a sign that even a little detente sharpens internal contradictions in the Soviet Union by threatening to deprive the bureaucracy of its functions and the official ideology of its credibility. Over the long run, he argued, international tension helps to justify repression, while detente will help to weaken that justification and increase the possibilities of movement toward democracy.[9]

It is precisely this kind of argument that has been challenged by those peace researchers who claim that the arms race is so deeply rooted in domestic structures that the lessening of international tension will have no effect on it. Some see the arms race and detente coexisting for a long time; others see detente falling victim to tensions generated by the military-industrial complexes. In either case, the peace research argument is that the resolution of international political disputes may be a necessary condition for disarmament and demilitarization, but that it is by no means a sufficient condition.

This is not a comprehensive, much less an exhaustive, survey of the approaches that have been taken in examining the obstacles to disarmament and demilitarization in the Soviet Union. But it does provide some helpful pointers to the relationships that have to be analyzed. The first of these is the interaction of internal and external factors. The particular form which socialist construction has taken in the Soviet Union cannot be understood without reference to the international context in which the Bolsheviks undertook the transformation of Russian society. Consequently, the militarization of Soviet society has to be examined in the light of international, as well as of domestic, relationships. Moreover, some attempt must be made to discuss what is specific to militarism in the Soviet Union, and what it shares with militarism elsewhere.

Secondly, it has been seen that different historical perspectives—some rooted in the Russian Empire, some in the Cold War—have been adopted, and this raises interesting questions about the way in which patterns of political relationships are reproduced in a given society. Although it is important to provide a historical perspective, there is the danger that the Russian tradition will be presented as monolithic, and that militarism will be seen as a genetic inheritance, transmitted from one generation (or even one social formation) to the next. This would be disheartening in its suggestion that no change is possible, and also wrong. The Russian political tradition is diverse, embracing not only militarism, but also the antimilitarism of Tolstoy and Kropotkin. The Soviet tradition too contains various strands, and the diversity is very wide if the views of contemporary dissidents are taken into account. Consequently it would be a mistake to begin this analysis by portraying this militarization as either inevitable or all-embracing.

War and the Soviet State

Analyzing the militarization of Soviet society involves much more than an effort to identify a military-industrial or military-bureaucratic complex, elimination of which would remove the internal dynamic of Soviet military policy and leave the rest of the social system untouched. The history of the Soviet state is intimately bound up with war and the preparation for war. This is true both in the classical sense that armed force has established the territorial limits of the state and secured internal rule, and in the sense that war and the preparation for it have profoundly affected the internal structure of the state.

It is one of the striking features of the history of tsarist Russia and the Soviet Union that rivalry with other, economically more advanced, states has provided a major stimulus to economic and political change. This was true of Peter the Great's reforms and of the reforms which followed the Crimean and Russo-Japanese wars; it was a major factor in Soviet industrialization, too. One consequence of this pattern has been the role of the state as the dominant agency of change; it was through the state that social and economic relationships were altered with the aim of mobilizing resources to increase the power of the state.

When the Bolsheviks seized power they faced the problem of consolidating their rule in the face of enemies at home and abroad. The early experience of the young Soviet state—civil war, foreign intervention, and internal unrest—had a profound impact on Bolshevik ideas about military organization. The early vision of militia-type forces did not survive the realization that the Bolsheviks faced considerable opposition from inside Soviet society and from foreign powers. The military reform of 1924–25 created a mixed system, with the main emphasis on standing forces; the territorial-militia element was retained for economic reasons rather than on grounds of principle. Trotsky's project of combining labor with military training was not implemented. Of more immediate practical importance was the view advanced by Frunze, Trotsky's successor as Commissar of War, that, in conditions of economic constraints on defense, every civilian activity ought to be examined for the contribution it could make to military preparedness. By the late 1920s the Red Army did have features which distinguished it from the armies of bourgeois states—its social composition and the commissar system, for example—but it was far from embodying the earlier socialist ideas of military organization.[10]

With the failure of revolution in Europe, the Soviet Union was left largely isolated in a hostile world. This helped to stimulate a great debate about the direction of socialist construction, and in the mid-1920s the idea of building "socialism in one country" began to gain ground in the Bolshevik Party. This idea, as E. H. Carr has noted, marked the marriage of Marxist revolutionary goals and Russian national destiny.[11] The policy of industrialization which was embarked on toward the end of the decade was the practical offspring of this marriage. In 1931 Stalin, now the dominant leader, who had set his own brutal stamp on the industrialization drive, justified the intensity of the policy by referring to the need to overcome Russia's backwardness and thus prevent other powers from beating her.

> Do you want our Socialist fatherland to be beaten and to lose its independence? If you do not want this you must put an end to its backwardness in the shortest possible time and develop

> genuine Bolshevik tempo in building up its Socialist system of economy. There is no other way. That is why Lenin said during the October Revolution: "Either perish, or overtake and outstrip the advanced capitalist countries."
>
> We are fifty or a hundred years behind the advanced countries. We must make good this distance in ten years. Either we do it, or they crush us.[12]

Although this justification was not explicitly military, it did prove a clear rationale for the development of the defense industry.

Industrialization was made possible by a massive extraction of resources from the population and their investment in heavy industry. A vast and powerful party-state bureaucracy ensured that resources were forthcoming, enforced the priorities set by the Party leaders, and managed the new industrial economy. The defense sector was given high priority in the allocation of investment funds, scarce materials, able managers, and skilled workers. During the 1930s a powerful defense industry was created which produced large quantities of weapons, some of which were of high quality. The Soviet Union had rejected the idea, which was popular in the West at the time, of building a small, highly mechanized army and sought instead to marry mass and technology—to create a mass army equipped with the best possible armaments. The territorial-militia element of the armed forces was gradually abandoned. Yet for all that had been done, the Winter War of 1939–40 with Finland exposed serious weaknesses in the Red Army, some of which resulted from the great purge which Stalin had inflicted on Soviet society in the late 1930s.

The German invasion of June 22, 1941 took Stalin by surprise, and found the Red Army in a state of unreadiness. The opening months of the war proved disastrous, with the German forces advancing to the outskirts of Moscow. Only by an enormous effort over the next four years was the Soviet Union able to halt the German advance, turn the tide of war, and push the German armies back to Berlin. The degree of industrial mobilization was much greater in the Soviet Union than in the other belligerent states, and Soviet losses of people and material goods were immense. The Soviet name for the war with Germany—the Great Patriotic War—symbolizes the appeal which Stalin made to the Soviet people's patriotism. In contrast to the bitter social and political tensions of the 1920s and 1930s, state and people were largely united in the common effort to defeat the Nazi enemy.[13]

Victory brought the Soviet Union gains of territory and influence which had seemed inconceivable in the early months of the war. But victory also brought political conflicts with the war-time allies, and these soon found their expression in intense military rivalry, which centered on the development of nuclear weapons and their means of delivery. By 1947 the Soviet Union had four major military research and development programs under way: nuclear weapons, rockets, radar, and jet-engine technology. After Stalin's death the implications of this "military-technical revolution" became more pressing. The existence of nuclear weapons in growing stockpiles raised fundamental questions about the relationship of war to policy, and about the appropriate structure for armed forces in the nuclear age—questions which have dominated Soviet military policy ever since.

Khrushchev now put greater stress on peaceful coexistence between East and West, and set in motion major changes in military doctrine and military institutions. In the late 1950s and early 1960s he tried to devise a new military policy, based on nuclear-armed missiles, that would be militarily and diplomatically effective, while freeing resources for civilian purposes. He even floated the idea of restoring the territorial-militia element in the armed forces. But internal opposition, which was strengthened by a succession of international crises (the U-2 incident in 1960, the 1961 Berlin crisis, and the Cuban missile crisis of 1962) and by the Kennedy administration's build-up of strategic forces, finally defeated Khrushchev's efforts.[14]

If we can speak of a "Soviet military build-up," then its origins lie in the defeat of Khrushchev's policy. His successors have devoted considerable attention to the all-round strengthening of Soviet military power. A major increase in strategic forces has brought parity with the United States. The Ground Forces have been expanded, in particular along the frontier with China, and have received more modern equipment. The Air Forces too have been modernized. Soviet naval presence has been extended throughout the world. Arms transfers to third world countries have grown substantially in this period. Certainly Soviet policy has been subject to many rash and alarmist interpretations in the West, but the evidence does point to a steady and significant increase in Soviet military power since the early 1960s.[15]

In the first ten years after the end of the Second World War a clear bipolar structure emerged in world politics, with the United States and the Soviet Union as the dominant powers. Since that time new forces have emerged to transform the international system. The creation of the third world as a political force was helped by the existence of the Soviet bloc, which could provide a counterweight to Western power. Fissiparous tendencies, both East and West, have further complicated international politics. By the late 1960s Japan and the EEC had become major centers of economic power, while the rivalry between the Soviet Union and China had assumed military form. From the Soviet point of view the international environment had become more complex, with the ever-present danger that the various centers of power would combine in opposition to it. Indeed, elements of such a combination have been evident in the 1970s, motivated in large part by the desire to offset growing Soviet military power; in its turn, this countervailing power has provided the Soviet leaders with further reasons for military forces.

The Soviet Union now possesses large armed forces, an advanced defense industry, and an extensive military R and D network. In no other area has the Soviet Union come so close to achieving the goal of "catching up and overtaking the advanced capitalist powers." As a consequence, the law of comparative advantage seems to operate in Soviet external policies, giving a major role to the military instrument. The Soviet Union conducts its central relationship with the NATO powers from a position of military strength but economic weakness. In Eastern Europe the Soviet Union has suffered political setbacks but has used military force, and the threat of military force, to underpin its dominant position. Soviet relations with China have now acquired an important military dimension with the build-up of forces along the Chinese frontier. In the third world the Soviet Union has used arms transfers and military advisers as a major instrument of diplomacy. Thus in spite of the fact that the Soviet concept of the "correlation of forces," in terms of which international politics is analyzed, does not place primary emphasis on military force, military power has become a basic instrument of Soviet external policy.

It is not surprising that the present generation of Soviet leaders should see military power as the main guarantee of Soviet security and of the Soviet position in the world. The men now at the top levels of leadership came to positions of some power in the late 1930s, and Brezhnev and Ustinov are only the most prominent members of this generation to have had a direct part in managing the development and production of arms. Victory in the war with Germany, the attainment of strategic parity with the United States, and the long period at peace since 1945—these are regarded by this generation as among its greatest achievements. When one considers the course of Soviet history from 1917 to 1945, it is no surprise that this should be so.

It should be clear from this brief outline how important war and the preparation for war have been in the formation of the Soviet state. This is not to say that the course of Soviet development has been determined by forces outside the Soviet Union or that every event in Soviet history is to be explained in terms of external conditions. The rise of Stalin and his system of rule cannot be explained without reference to social, economic, and political conditions in the Soviet Union. Moreover, not everything in the Stalinist period can be seen as a response to external threats. The great purge of 1936–38 was justified in this way, but the justification was patently false and the purge greatly weakened the Red Army. But the Stalinist industrialization drive had as its major goal the development of heavy industry as the basis for economic growth and military power, and it was in these terms that it was justified.

This policy involved the extensive mobilization of the resources and energies of Soviet society and the extraction from society of those resources by the state, which then channelled them toward the ends laid down by the Party leadership. The process was dominated by the Party-state apparatus which forced changes in social and economic relationships, extracted the resources from an often unwilling population, and managed the new economic system. In order to secure the loyalty of the Party-state apparatus special social and economic privileges and distinctions were introduced. (It was at this time that prerevolutionary ranks began to be reintroduced into the Red Army.) The rate of extraction was very high, leaving the mass of the population with minimal living standards and sometimes (as when famine occurred) not even those. Coercion was an intrinsic part of this policy.

Victory in the war seemed to show that, whatever the "mistakes" of Stalin's policies in the immediate prewar years, the general emphasis on industrialization had been correct. After the war the high rate of extraction continued as industry was reconstructed and military rivalry with the West pursued. But since Stalin's death important changes have taken place which have a bearing on the questions of disarmament and demilitarization. The first is that the rate of economic growth has slowed considerably, provoking intensive debate about economic reform. It has been widely argued inside and outside the Soviet Union that the system of economic planning and administration was suited to the industrialization drive, but has now become a brake on industrial development and in particular on technological innovation. Second, terror has been abandoned as a system of rule and the Party leadership has been searching for new sources of legitimacy for the state. Repression of opposition and dissent still takes place, but greater effort has been made to secure popular support. Among the ways in which this has been done is through the provision of more and better goods and services to the mass of the population, and through appeals to nationalist sentiments. Third, as a result of the greater attention that has been paid to the living standards and welfare of the population, the priorities of resource allocation have become more complex than they were under Stalin.

The Defense Sector and the Soviet Economy

The organization of the defense sector is similar to that of the rest of Soviet industry.[16] The enterprises that produce arms and equipment are controlled by a series of ministries which have responsibility for the different branches of the sector. The work of these ministries is in turn planned by the central planning agencies (in line with the general policy laid down by the Politburo), since the activities of the defense sector must be coordinated with those of the rest of the economy. There are, however, special institutional arrangements in the defense sector which are designed to ensure that military production has priority claim on scarce resources. In this sense the defense sector is distinct from the rest of the economy.

Since the war some important changes have taken place in the defense sector. It has expanded to include new branches of production, in particular nuclear weapons, rockets, and electronics. Along with this expansion has come the creation of an extensive network of research and development (R and D) establishments to provide the basis for innovations in weapons technologies. These establishments are controlled by the production ministries in the defense sector. The size of the network is impossible to establish with any precision, but the number of establishments must be in the hundreds, while those engaged in military research and development must number in the hundreds of thousands. Research institutes from outside the defense sector—for example, from the Academy of Sciences—are also drawn into military work.

Military R and D is more effective than civilian R and D in the Soviet Union. The defense sector is well suited to the development and production of follow-on systems (for example, of tanks) where no great shift of mission or technology is required. The Soviet Union has also been able to organize large-scale innovation when the political leaders have deemed it necessary; the R and D system is well suited to the concentration of resources on specific goals such as the development of the atomic bomb or the development of the intercontinental ballistic missile. It is not so well adapted to the lateral or horizontal transfer of technology across departmental boundaries, unless this is organized as a matter of priority from above.[17]

Soviet military-economic policy is supposed to be guided by three main principles: (1) to maintain a high level of armaments production; (2) to ensure the flexibility of the economy (for example, in shifting from civilian to military production, in raising the rate of arms production or in introducing new weapons); and (3) to secure the viability of the economy in war-time.[18] These principles were elaborated in the 1930s and are still taken as the most important indicators of the state's economic potential—that is, of its ability to provide for the material needs of society while producing everything necessary for war.

In spite of the flexibility recommended by these principles the available evidence suggests that there is considerable stability in the defense sector and that this has a major influence on its mode of operation. The research institutes and design bureaus, where new weapons are created, are funded from the budget and their finances do not seem to depend directly on orders for specific systems. Coupled with the institutional continuity of the military R and D network, this provides the basis for a steady effort in the design and development of weapons. Consequently a strong tendency to create "follow-on" systems can be discerned. Stable production appears also to be a feature of the defense sector, with no major variation in output from year to year.

Besides the stability of its structure and its operations, the defense sector is marked by the continuity of its leading managers. For example, D. F. Ustinov, the present Minister of Defense, became People's Commissar (i.e. Minister) of Armament in 1941 and until his appointment to his present position in 1976 played a major role in weapons development and production.

Another example: Ye. P. Slavskii, the Minister of Medium Machine-Building (in charge of nuclear weapons development and production) has held that position since 1957 and has been involved in the nuclear weapons program since 1946.

The managers of the defense industry form a coherent group, with interlocking careers. There is, however, little evidence that they have acted together as a lobby. The one occasion on which they seem to have done so was in the period 1957 to 1965 when they took part, with some success, in resistance to Khrushchev's decentralization of the system of economic planning and management. In 1963, after some recentralization had taken place, Khrushchev indicated his dissatisfaction with Ustinov and the "metal-eaters" and complained that secrecy made it difficult to criticize the shortcomings of the defense industry.[19]

This is the only occasion on which the performance of the defense sector emerged into the open as an issue in the arguments about economic reform. In the post-Stalin period there have been intensive debates about the need to reform the system of economic planning and administration in order to stimulate technological innovation. In the 1960s it was widely held by Soviet and foreign economists alike that sooner or later the Soviet leaders would have to choose between plan and market, and that any significant reform would involve a move toward some form of "market socialism." Such a reform would not be incompatible with a high level of defense expenditure. Even if the Soviet Union now devotes 12 to 15 percent of its GNP to defense (and this is the upper range of Western estimates) this level could be maintained in an economy where the market played a significant role; after all, some capitalist countries devote a higher proportion of the GNP to defense without instituting a "war economy." Thus the present Soviet system of economic planning and management cannot be said to be entailed by the level of defense expenditure. This is not to deny, of course, that the managers who have been used to working the present system might be fearful of changes on the grounds that their high priority position would be jeopardized.

In any event the choice of market socialism has not been

made in the Soviet Union. The Czechoslovak crisis of 1968 was a major setback for the Soviet advocates of far-reaching reform, because political developments in Czechoslovakia were widely seen as the consequence of economic reform. The problems of economic growth and technological progress have not vanished in the Soviet Union, however, and piecemeal reform has been under way. Interestingly, the trend of reform in the 1970s has been to take the defense sector as a model for the rest of the economy. At the Twenty-Fourth Party Congress in 1971 Brezhnev declared that

> taking into account the high scientific-technical level of defence industry, the transmission of its experience, inventions and discoveries to all spheres of our economy acquires the highest importance.[20]

In the 1970s certain organizational features and management techniques—especially in the area of technological innovation—have been borrowed from the defense sector and applied in civilian industry.[21] This marks an attempt to use the defense sector as a model or dynamo of technological progress in the economy as a whole.

The priority of military production is a matter not only of central decisions, but also of the structure of industry and the attitudes of workers and managers. This was clearly illustrated by an article in *Literaturnaya Gazeta* in 1972 and the correspondence it provoked. The author of the article pointed out that in numerous ways—in prestige, in the priority given by other ministries (for example, in construction projects), in wages, in cultural and housing facilities, in labor turnover—light industry fared worse than heavy industry.[22] One of the correspondents wrote that

> the best conditions are given to the so-called "leading" branches. Then we have the remaining enterprises in Group A/heavy industry. Last in line are the Group B enterprises. Naturally the most highly skilled cadres—workers, engineers or technicians—find jobs or try to find them where the pay is highest, so they are concentrated in the "leading" branches of industry. What is more, these branches receive the best materials, the most ad-

> vanced technology, the latest equipment etc. etc. . . . Even at the same machine-building enterprise, in the production of "prestige" output and Group B output, there is no comparison in quality and in the attitude to the categories of output (in terms of technology, design work, management, pay, etc.).[23]

There is little doubt that within heavy industry the defense sector occupies the position of highest prestige, and therefore shows these features to the highest degree.

The Soviet system of economic planning and administration has not been altered fundamentally since it was first established. It remains a relatively effective mechanism for extracting resources from the economy and directing them to the goals set by the political leaders, and one of the most important of these goals has been the creation of military power. The defense sector occupies a key—and in some respects, a privileged—position in this system, not only in terms of central priorities, but also in terms of the organization of industry and the attitudes of workers and managers. The debates about economic reform have resulted in partial and piecemeal changes rather than in a fundamental transformation of the system. There has been a tendency over the last ten years to use the defense sector as a model for the rest of industry. In terms of the militarization of the Soviet economy, this is an ambiguous development. On the one hand, it testifies to a political concern about the performance of civilian industry; on the other, it highlights the special position and performance of the defense sector.

The Armed Forces and the Rationales for Military Power

There is little evidence of opposition inside the Soviet Union to Soviet military policy. Since 1965 there have been few if any indications of disagreement in the Party leadership about the level of military expenditure. This contrasts with the Khrushchev period, when military outlays did provide a focus of political argument. And in the dissident *samizdat* literature, although sharp criticism has been made of many features of

Soviet life, few voices have been raised against the military policy of the Soviet state. Almost the only exception is the warnings which Andrei Sakharov has given the West of the growing military power of the Soviet Union; and Sakharov's background in nuclear weapons development makes him in this instance a very special case. Thus the situation is rather different from that in the United States, where militarism and racism formed the chief targets of protest in the 1960s and 1970s. There are many reasons for this difference, but the chief one appears to be that inside the Soviet Union the Soviet military effort is widely seen as legitimate and as pursuing legitimate goals. This is in spite of the fact that the burden of military expenditure is greater than in the NATO countries and that there are many competing claims for the resources which are devoted to defense.

One of the main reasons for the acceptance of Soviet military policy is no doubt that for the last thirty to thirty-five years the Soviet Union has enjoyed a period of peace and internal stability which stands in sharp contrast to the wars and upheavals of the first half of the century. The Soviet armed forces have seen very little combat since 1945—certainly nothing to compare with the military role of the American, British, and French forces. The Soviet claim that Soviet military strength is conducive to peace does not, therefore, fly directly in the face of reality. This is one reason why there has been, in the Soviet view, no contradiction between the processes of political detente and the growth of Soviet military power. Soviet military power is regarded as a crucial element in detente because it makes it impossible for the West to deal with the Soviet Union from a position of strength or to use its armed forces in an unfettered way throughout the world.[24]

Although Soviet forces have been engaged in relatively little combat since 1945, military power is certainly regarded by the Soviet leaders as contributing to their political purposes. The main object of that policy has been to prevent the West from conducting offensive actions—whether military or political—against the Soviet Union and its allies. Soviet military aid to third world countries is to be seen in the same context. Since the 1960s the Soviet Union has come to use its military power—in the form of advisers and arms transfers—more frequently as a way of gaining influence and undermining Western power. (There may now be an economic element in Soviet arms transfers: excess production can be exchanged—in some instances—for hard currency. But the primary rationale is still political.[25])

But military power has also been a major factor in Soviet relations with socialist states. The Soviet Union used military force in Hungary in 1956 and in Czechoslovakia in 1968 in order to maintain its dominant position in Eastern Europe. That position is underpinned by the ever-present threat of military force, even though that threat is not voiced openly. In the 1960s the confrontation with China assumed a military form with the build-up of forces along the Chinese frontier. Thus apart from deterring offensive policies directed against the Soviet Union and helping to destroy Western domination in different parts of the world, Soviet military power has been used as an instrument to create and sustain Soviet domination over other states. Moreover, as Soviet military strength has grown, new roles have been found for it, particularly in the projection of power outside the Soviet frontiers. The intervention in Afghanistan illustrates the Soviet Union's growing ability to use its military power in this way, and—more important—its willingness to do so.

In the late 1960s the Soviet Union attained strategic parity with the United States and on that basis entered into negotiations to limit strategic arms.

Of course, it remains extremely difficult to say what constitutes parity or equality (does it mean equality with one particular state or with all potential enemies combined?), and acceptance of the principle still leaves great scope for disagreement both within and between the negotiating states. Moreover, the principle of parity provides a basis for negotiation between the Soviet Union and the United States only because they have so many more nuclear weapons than other states that even the other nuclear powers can be left largely out of account. But does every state have the right to parity? Obviously not, since the Non-Proliferation Treaty represents a commitment of a kind to stop the spread of nuclear weapons. Negotiations between the superpowers on the basis of parity goes along with the attempt to prevent other states from attaining that status. Precisely because the Soviet Union and the United States are using arms control negotiations in this double-edged way, they are likely to stimulate other states to acquire nuclear weapons of their own. Consequently arms control negotiations on the basis of parity are by no means the foundation for a process of radical demilitarization.

In spite of the acceptance of parity as the basis for negotiations to limit strategic arms, it remains true that there are major differences between Soviet and American strategic thought. American thinking has laid particular emphasis on the ability, under all circumstances, to inflict widespread destruction on the enemy's society. Soviet thinking, on the other hand, has been concerned to limit the damage to Soviet society in the event of nuclear war. Even in a relationship of parity Soviet policy has been directed toward limiting the vulnerability of the Soviet Union to nuclear attack and ensuring the viability of Soviet society in war-time. Whether this can be achieved seems very doubtful (even though viability is a relative term), but it does appear to be the rationale behind important elements of Soviet military, military-economic, and civil defense policies, and it does have important implications for the militarization of Soviet society.

The main bulk of the Soviet forces is made up of the five branches of service: the Strategic Rocket Forces, the National Air Defence Forces, the Air Forces, the Ground Forces, and the Navy. There are also special forces which sometimes engage in civilian work. The Construction Troops carry out construction work for the armed forces and on high-priority civilian projects; the Academic City near Novosibiirsk, for example, where the Siberian Division of the Academy of Sciences is based, was built by them. The Railroad and Road Troops play an important part in building and maintaining the Soviet rail and road communications system. These are quite natural offshoots of the Soviet armed forces. But there are three elements of the

Soviet military system which are of greater interest from the point of view of the militarization of Soviet society. These are the civil defense organization, DOSAAF (*Dobrovol'noe obshchestvo sodeistviya armii, aviatsii i flotu*—the Voluntary Society for Cooperation with the Army, Aviation, and the Navy), and the system of military-patriotic education. All are designed to strengthen the ability of the Soviet Union to defend itself, and all have political functions beyond that goal.

Soviet civil defense has three major objects: to provide protection for the population against weapons of mass destruction; to ensure stable operation of the economy in war-time; and to eliminate the effects of enemy use of weapons of mass destruction.[26] Civil defense organizations may also take part in disaster relief operations. The effectiveness of the civil defense effort is very difficult to judge because it would depend so much on the way in which nuclear war was initiated. It could not prevent widespread destruction, although it could reduce its scale. It has been estimated that about 100,000 full-time personnel are engaged in civil defense work at all levels of the government and economic structure.[27] There is an extensive program of education and training which is designed to enable the population to carry out civil defense measures should the need arise.

DOSAAF has as its main aim the strengthening of the Soviet Union's defense capability by training the Soviet people for the defense of the socialist fatherland.[28] DOSAAF is open to all Soviet citizens over the age of fourteen and has about 80 million members. Its main activities are: military-patriotic education; training of young people for service in the armed forces; training in technical skills; dissemination of military-technical knowledge; direction of sports which have military-technical significance. DOSAAF has clubs and sports facilities and is organized at factories, farms, educational institutions, and so on. It seems clear that DOSAAF's activities are of substantial help to the armed forces in providing recruits with skills which will be useful during military service, and also in raising the physical and technical level of the Soviet population. For the same reasons its work is useful to Soviet industry. Much of what DOSAAF does is done by nonmilitary organizations in the West. It is nevertheless significant that in the Soviet Union it is the goals of military preparedness and defense capability that provide the justification and the driving force for activities of this kind. Here again the importance of the military factor as a modernizing force in Soviet society is evident.

Both civil defense and DOSAAF contribute to the Soviet Union's ability to defend itself; they also contribute to the more diffuse process of military-patriotic education.

> Military-patriotic education is called upon to instil a readiness to perform military duty, responsibility for strengthening the defence capability of the country, respect for the Soviet armed forces, pride in the Motherland and the ambition to preserve and increase the heroic traditions of the Soviet people. Military-patriotic education is carried out in the teaching process in secondary and higher educational establishments, in the system of political education, by means of propaganda in the press, on radio and television, and with the help of various forms of mass-political work and of artistic and literary works. Of great significance for military-patriotic education is the mastery of basic military and military-technical skills which young people acquire in secondary schools, technical schools, higher educational establishments, in studies at the houses of defence and technical creativity, aero, auto motor and radio clubs, at the young technicians' stations, in military-patriotic schools, defence circles, at points of pre-induction training, in civil defence formations. Physical training with an applied military bent presupposes the development of qualities of will, courage, hardiness, strength, speed of reaction, and helps to raise psychological stability, trains the sight, hearing etc.[29]

Military-patriotic education is directed not only toward satisfying the practical needs of the armed forces but also toward increasing support for, and loyalty to, the Party and the Soviet state. It represents a fusion of community, nationalist, and military appeals. The Great Patriotic War occupies a key position in the program of military-patriotic education as the source of examples and illustrations of the desired qualities. This, as we have noted, was a time when Party and people were most closely united in a common purpose, and military-patriotic education is evidently an effort to recapture and reinforce that bond by tapping a source of strong sentiment in the Soviet people. In this context it can be seen as a response to the problems of legitimation that the Soviet state has faced in the post-Stalin period.

This military-patriotic education does not amount to a glorification of war and should therefore be distinguished from Fascist militarism. Indeed, the Party's peace policy (the effectiveness of which is seen to rest on Soviet military power) is an essential component of the program of education. Moreover, one might wonder just how effective the program is in instilling the desired qualities into a population that seems very far from matching the ideal of the "new Soviet man." But quite clearly military-patriotic education will help to instil acceptance of the Party's military policy and belief in the importance of military power. In this way it will help to sustain the Soviet military effort and the special position which the defense sector and the armed forces enjoy in Soviet society.

A Military-Industrial State?

As a major instrument of Soviet external policy the armed forces naturally enjoy an important position in the Party-state apparatus. The Ministry of Defence and the General Staff are overwhelmingly staffed by professional officers who have spent all their careers in the armed forces. Since 1945 the post of Minister has, more often than not, been held by a professional soldier, although the present minister, Ustinov, has spent most of his life in the defense industry. The chief functions of the Ministry and the General Staff are those of similar institutions in other countries: to draw up plans, develop strategy and tactics, gather and evaluate intelligence about potential enemies, educate and train the troops, and administer the whole network of military institutions. The Soviet Union, unlike the United States, does not have an extensive network of civilian institutions conducting research into military operations; operational analysis is done very largely within the armed forces.

The existence of a large military establishment within the state might be thought to pose difficult problems of civil-military relations and to threaten the Party's dominant position in Soviet society. It is true that there have been elements of conflict and tension in Party-military relations, but the principle of Party supremacy has never seriously been threatened. Special mechanisms of control exist in the armed forces, the most important being the Main Political Administration, which is both an administration of the Ministry of Defence and a department of the Central Committee. Some Western observers have seen in this organization an institutionalized Party distrust of the military.[30] But in fact this view is mistaken and the Main Political Administration should more properly be seen as a bridge between the Party and the armed forces, symbolizing their unity and the assumptions that they share about the importance of military power for the Soviet state.[31]

The Soviet Union embodies the apparent paradox of a militarized social system in which the military, while an important political force, are not the dominant one. This is not to say, however, that the armed forces—or, more particularly, members of the High Command—have played no role in the political crises of the post-Stalin period. In each case of leadership change—Beria's arrest and execution in 1953, Malenkov's defeat by Khrushchev in 1955, the defeat of the "anti-Party group" in 1957, and Khrushchev's fall in 1964—members of the High Command played some role. But military support was one factor among others, and probably not the decisive one. Moreover, Marshal Zhukov's disgrace in 1957, only months after he had helped Khrushchev to defeat the "anti-Party group" in the Central Committee, shows that engaging in leadership politics can be a risky business for soldiers. The spectre of Bonapartism was conjured up by Khrushchev as a major justification for Zhukov's removal from office. Even though it appears to have been a contrived justification, it underlined the determination of the Party leadership to retain its supremacy over the armed forces. Military involvement has been made possible only by splits in the Party leadership, and on no occasion has it resulted in a conflict in which Party leaders were ranged on one side and the military on the other; the High Command has had its own internal politics and divisions.

The political quiescence of the armed forces is to be explained by reference not so much to the formal mechanisms of Party and secret police control as to the way in which military interests have been given priority in Party policy. To say this is not to minimize Stalin's brutal treatment of the armed forces or to deny that Khrushchev often pursued policies that were to the distaste of the High Command. But by stressing the importance of international conflict and national solidarity the Party has provided an ideological framework which gives a clear meaning to the armed forces' existence. Party policy has also given the officer corps a privileged material position and a high status in Soviet society. Finally, the professional interests of the officer corps have been generally well served, especially in the allocation of resources to defense and in the opportunities for career advancement.

Since Stalin's death in 1953, and more particularly since Khrushchev's fall from power in 1964, officers have been given considerable freedom to discuss questions of military policy and a greater voice in the policy-making process. This has resulted from the general diffusion of power at the center of the Soviet state and has parallels in other areas of Soviet life where vigorous debates have been conducted about matters of policy. The Brezhnev Politburo has placed great emphasis on "scientific" policy-making and on expert and technically competent advice.

The diffusion of power has created what some writers refer to as "institutional pluralism."[32] Like all pluralism, however, it is imperfect in the sense that some groups and institutions have more power than others. In this respect the armed forces and the defense industry occupy a special position. The armed forces enjoy wide prestige as the embodiment of national power and integrity—a prestige which is enhanced by the extensive program of military-patriotic education. The Ministry of Defence and General Staff are institutions of undoubted competence, with a monopoly of expertise in military affairs; there are no civilian institutions able to challenge this expertise. The high priority given to the defense sector remains embedded in the system of economic planning and administration. The defense industry has been in the forefront of Soviet technological progress and is seen by the Party leaders as something to be emulated rather than restricted in the age of the "scientific-technical revolution." Finally, key aspects of military policy are shrouded in secrecy, and this limits criticism of the priority given to defense in resource allocation and of the way in which those resources are used.

This is not to suggest that the military policy of the Soviet state has been pursued against the wishes of the Party leadership. The final decisions on military policy rest with the Politburo and with the Defence Council, which comprises several leading Politburo members under Brezhnev's chairmanship. All the evidence points to a set of shared assumptions among the leaders about military power and military expenditure. There are differences of view, no doubt, but these appear to be marginal, and the overall policy seems to rest on a broad consensus.[33] It is, however, possible that this state of affairs will change in the post-Brezhnev leadership and that the level of military effort will become a contentious issue as it was under Khrushchev. Then the institutional power of the armed forces and the defense industry might be important in determining the outcome of the argument.

Can we speak then of a Soviet "military-industrial complex"? It is true that there is a large military establishment and a large defense industry. But the term itself often carries theoretical connotations that make it inapplicable to the Soviet Union. Sometimes it suggests a degenerate pluralism in which the balanced interplay of interests has been undermined by links between the armed forces and industry; in this sense it seems not to be appropriate because it implies too great a degree of pluralism—and it implies pluralism as a norm—for the Soviet Union. Sometimes it is implied that the driving force of arms policies is the pursuit of profit by capitalist enterprises; this too would be inappropriate, and for this reason Garaudy has argued that the Soviet Union has a "bureaucratic-military complex"—that is, a military-industrial complex without the economic driving-force.[34] An objection of a different kind is summarized in the statement that the Soviet Union does not *have* a military-industrial complex, but *is* such a complex. This is too sweeping a statement, but it does make the point that the history of the Soviet Union is so bound up with military power that it seems wrong to speak of a separate military-industrial complex acting within the state.

Whether or not we say the armed forces and the defense industry constitute a military-industrial complex in the Soviet Union matters less than the fact that they exhibit many features that are identified as a characteristic of such a complex. Because of the way in which the Soviet economic system is organized it does not exhibit these features in the same way, or to the same degree, as the American defense sector; but it does share them nevertheless. For example, competition is to be found in the weapons development process between offensive and defensive systems, with new technology in one area stimulating innovation in another. This may happen without any direct stimulus from outside. Second, the military R and D system shows considerable inertia in its operations, thus generating strong pressure for follow-on systems. Third, the R and D system does not appear to have a strong innovative dynamic of its own. Intervention by the political leadership is required for major innovations; but because the Party leaders have devoted so much attention to this area, such intervention is often forthcoming. Further, the military R and D system is not especially conducive to the cross-fertilization of technologies to produce new weapons, but this may happen as designers search for ways of meeting new requirements. Finally, the steadiness of Soviet arms policies may be accounted for, in part, by the planning to which weapons development and production are subject.

The Soviet military effort, which was created in the course of international rivalry, is now rooted in the structure of the Soviet state. This is not to say, of course, that the external stimuli have vanished. It is clear that foreign actions do impinge on Soviet arms policies and this can be seen both in the histories of specific weapons systems and in the direction of overall policy.[35] The advanced capitalist powers have set the pace in making major weapons innovations, and this has served to stimulate Soviet military technology. Of course it must be borne in mind that military power rests not only on the quality of military technology, but also on its quantity and on the way in which the troops are trained to use it. The arms competition between East and West consists of both qualitative and quantitative elements; although the balance of the two may change, the arms race has never been a question of one of these elements to the exclusion of the other. Western military technology has spurred Soviet weapons development, but has often been justified in terms of superior Soviet numbers.

It would be wrong therefore to deny the effects of foreign actions of Soviet arms policies. But it would be equally mistaken to see Soviet policy as merely a reaction to Western actions. Foreign influences are refracted through the Soviet policy-making process, in which Soviet perceptions, military doctrine, foreign policy objectives, and domestic influences and constraints come into play. The effect of foreign actions on Soviet policy is complex and not at all automatic. In many cases the foreign influences combine with domestic factors to speed up the internal dynamic of Soviet arms policies.[36] The very existence of large armed forces, a powerful defense industry, and an extensive network of military R and D establishments generates internal pressures for weapons development and production. The interplay of demands and invention gives rise to proposals for new and improved weapons. As a system progresses from conception to development, military and design bureau interests become attached to it, building up pressure for production. If it passes into production—and here a decision by the Party leadership is required for major systems—enterprise managers are likely to favor long production runs.

Dieter Senghaas has pointed to two principles which are important in understanding military-industrial complexes and which can be applied in the Soviet case.[37] The first of these is the principle of "configurative causality," which states that the overall configuration of the complex can be seen to give rise to pressures for arms production, even though these pressures may vary from case to case and cannot be identified in every specific instance. The second principle is that of "overdetermination" or "redundant causation"; to remove one cause or set of causes is not to eliminate the policies themselves, since other causes remain sufficient. This principle lies behind the argument that it is not enough to tackle the international causes of the East-West arms competition; the domestic roots too must be eradicated. These principles are both helpful in understanding Soviet arms policies. Although much of Soviet military policy-making is shrouded in secrecy, enough is known about the structures of the military-industrial-scientific complex to suggest that internal pressures are generated and considerable inertia built up in the military effort. It seems clear too that the removal of external stimuli, while it might alter Soviet arms policies in some important respects (for example, make it less technologically innovative), would not eliminate its driving-force entirely, because much of that force is derived from domestic sources. (Nor could one say that military power would wither away because it had no role: it has been noted already that as Soviet military power has expanded it has acquired new roles.) The question then is: How are these domestic sources to be weakened?

Conclusion

This essay has tried to outline in general terms the domestic sources of the Soviet military effort. It has suggested that these sources are deeply embedded in Russian and Soviet history. Disarmament and demilitarization would involve therefore more than the surgical removal of some element of the Soviet state; it would have far-reaching effects throughout the whole society. Indeed, complete disarmament and demilitarization could come about only with the destruction of the international state system (and would not necessarily happen then).

And although the "withering away of the state" is one of the anticipated consequences of communist construction, the Soviet Union has one of the most powerful and extensive state apparatuses in the world. Yet, although the sources of Soviet militarism are strong, this essay has tried not to present them as absolute, or to suggest that there is no scope for initiatives for demilitarization. There are some developments in the Soviet Union today which suggest that a change of direction is possible. It would be a serious error to overestimate their importance or the degree to which they can be influenced from outside the Soviet Union. But it would be an even greater mistake to suppose that no change is possible or that its direction could not be influenced from afar.

Soviet military policy contains several contradictions which may, with time, become more apparent and exert an influence on Soviet politics. Having attained equality of superpower status with the United States, the Soviet Union is now faced with a new set of questions about military power and the direction of its policy. The Soviet leaders have said that they are not striving for superiority, but they have made it clear that they will not fall behind the United States in military power. The Soviet Union has thus locked itself into a relationship of parity with the United States. At one level the maintenance of parity—along with the arms control negotiations which it underpins—provides the justification for Soviet military policy. At another level, however, the attainment of parity has meant that the Soviet Union has come to share full responsibility for the continuing arms competition. This has had a subtle, yet profound effect on the attitude of many people in the West to Soviet military policy. Many of those sympathetic to Soviet policy deemed it legitimate for the leading socialist state to catch up with the leading capitalist power; but sharing responsibility for the arms race is not regarded so favorably, especially in view of the danger of nuclear war. In a similar way, the continuation of a high level of military effort, even after parity has been attained, may help to breed opposition inside the Soviet Union to the amasssing of more military power. It is possible, for example, that Soviet militarism may emerge as a more important focus for dissident criticism, though the strength of nationalist sentiment (including dissident Russian nationalism) and the deep roots of legitimation should not be forgotten.

The Soviet Union shares with the United States the contradiction that growing military power does not bring greater security, even for superpowers. The accumulation of military power may only spur other governments to increase their own forces, thus nullifying the original gain. It is true that military power can further foreign policy, but it cannot ensure complete security in the nuclear age. The "Soviet military build-up" of the 1960s and 1970s has brought the Soviet Union political gains, but it has also helped to stimulate countervailing actions, and it is highly doubtful whether, in the last analysis, Soviet security is more assured now than it was fifteen years ago. Moreover, the extension of Soviet military power throughout the world increases the risk that the Soviet Union will become embroiled in a military adventure which will arouse opposition at home, just as the American war in Vietnam did, or the Russo-Japanese war of 1904–05. The failure of military power to ensure security should, in principle, provide the opportunity of pressing the importance of pursuing nonmilitary cooperative arrangements for security rather than seeking to provide one's own security at the expense of others'.

These contradictions would be of little importance if there were no possibility of giving them political significance. The last fifteen years have been a period of consolidation and conservative reform in the Soviet Union. But beneath the stable surface changes have been taking place which could result in major shifts of direction in Soviet policy. The rate of economic growth has been declining, thus increasing the prospect that pressure for far-reaching reform will reemerge. Agricultural performance has improved greatly, but at a very high cost, again raising the prospect of reform. Other pressures exist for changing the priorities of resource allocation—for example, in order to speed up development of Siberia or to raise living standards. The cumulative effect of such pressures might be to weaken the position of the defense sector or to involve it more deeply in nonmilitary functions. But it is not only the economic system that has been the focus of debate; discussion has also been taking place about the Soviet Union's proper relationship to the rest of the world. Some have pressed for as great a degree of autarky and isolation as possible; others have argued for a more outward-looking approach which would recognize that the world faces many problems which can be solved only by common and concerted action.[38] With the impending change of leadership these various factors may combine to create a turning-point in Soviet politics. The present leadership, as has been seen, has given immense importance to military power. It is as yet unclear how the next generation, which will not have been marked so deeply by the war, will view military power.

In pointing to these developments one should not forget the militarizing pressures that were analyzed earlier in this paper. Nor should one suppose that a change of course undertaken by a Soviet leadership would amount to radical disarmament or demilitarization. But the possibility for some change does exist and it should be the aim of the peace movement to try to influence that change in the desired direction. There are considerable difficulties in seeking to influence Soviet policy from the outside, for the political system is very impermeable, both in physical and cultural terms: it is hard to gain access to the policy-making process, and foreign attempts to influence policy will automatically be viewed with suspicion.

There are, nevertheless, two courses to be pursued. The first of these is directed at Western governments and should aim at ensuring that they do not foreclose, through their own policies, the possibility of Soviet moves toward disarmament and demilitarization. This course is a natural concomitant of efforts to press Western governments in that direction too. But some attempt is needed to take the Soviet dimension consciously into account, and this means that the causes of Soviet militarism, and the ways in which pressure on Western governments can also serve to influence the Soviet Union, need to be analyzed. Such influence need not necessarily be directed solely at disarmament, but could try to draw the Soviet Union into cooperative efforts to solve such problems as the world food supply.

This might make it easier subsequently to work out cooperative, nonmilitary security arrangements.

The second course is directed at the Soviet Union and should try to engage people there in a dialogue about the problems of disarmament and demilitarization. Such a dialogue should be as extensive as possible, and should not be confined to officials and representatives of officially approved bodies on the one hand, or to dissidents (whether in the Soviet Union or abroad) on the other. The variety of political views and currents in the Soviet Union is very wide, and dissident and official views overlap and shade into each other; there are, for example, strong nationalist tendencies in both official and dissident thinking, and dissident reformist views find an echo in official circles as well.[39]

The importance of this course is that vigorous debates about Russia's destiny and the proper path of Soviet development are taking place inside the Soviet Union and among Soviet emigrés; in Eastern Europe too there is such argument about the future of state socialism. But the issues of disarmament and demilitarization—which are important for everyone's future—scarcely figure at all in these discussions, even though militarism and the lack of democracy are linked in the Soviet case. If these issues could be injected into the discussions, they would then be subject to a great deal of creative political thinking—and thinking, moreover, that is more attuned to the specific problems and conditions of the Soviet Union. Besides, it has been seen that the military burden in the Soviet Union is very heavy, but that its legitimation is also strong. Debate and discussion about the problems of Soviet militarism might help to weaken that legitimation.

It should not be supposed that everyone will welcome such discussion, and the attempt to generate it may well be regarded as unwarranted interference in the internal affairs of the Soviet Union. But in the nuclear age we are all affected by the military policies of the superpowers, and hence we surely have the right to try to influence them.

Notes

1. The figures available on arms production and force levels give only the roughest indication of Soviet military production. They show no very sharp fluctuations since 1950, but they are too crude to register any but the most massive changes. The late 1950s and early 1960s appear to be the period of lowest effort. Western estimates of Soviet defense spending as a proportion of GNP seem to fit this pattern, with the Khrushchev years as the period when the proportion was lowest. Most estimates, derived by whatever means, fall into the range of 8 to 14 percent, with the lower estimates for the late 1950s and early 1960s. See, for example, the following: A. S. Becker, *Soviet National Income 1958–64* (Berkeley and Los Angeles, 1969), chapter 7; F. D. Holzman, *Financial Checks on Soviet Defense Expenditures* (Lexington, Mass., Toronto, and London, 1975); H. Block, in Joint Economic Committee, U.S. Congress, *Soviet Economic Prospects for the Seventies* (Washington, D.C., 1973), pp. 175–204; W. T. Lee, *The Estimation of Soviet Defense Expenditures 1955–75* (New York, 1977).
2. *The Military Balance* (IISS, London) each year gives a figure for the manpower in the Soviet Armed Forces. In 1979 that figure is 3-6 million (*The Military Balance 1979–1980*, p. 9). This does not include approximately 400,000 KGB and MVD troops. On top of these figures there are the 400,000 troops who engage in construction, railroad, farm, and medical work. See M. Feshback and S. Rapawy, in Joint Economic Committee, U.S. Congress, *Soviet Economy in a New Perspective* (Washington, D.C., 1976), pp. 144–52.
3. Defence Minister Ustinov has declared that "service in the Soviet armed forces is a wonderful school of labour and martial training, of moral purity and courage, of patriotism and comradeship" (*Pravda*, November 8, 1979, p. 2). See T. Rakowska-Harmstone, "The Soviet Army as the Instrument of National Integration," in John Erickson and E. J. Feuchtwanger, eds., *Soviet Military Power and Performance* (London, 1979), pp. 129–54.
4. See, for example, *Markizm-Leninizm o voine i armii* (Moscow, 1968), chapter 5.
5. See in particular Dieter Senghaas, *Rüstung und Militarismus* (Frankfurt am Main, 1972).
6. J. Gould and W. L. Kolb, eds., *A Dictionary of the Social Sciences* (London, 1964), pp. 429–30.

7. William E. Odom, "The Militarization of Soviet Society," *Problems of Communism*, no. 5 (1976), pp. 34–51.
8. *Ibid.*, p. 51.
9. E. P. Thompson, "Detente and Dissent," in Ken Coates, ed., *Detente and Socialist Democracy* (Nottingham, 1975), pp. 123–25.
10. On these early debates see John Erickson, *The Soviet High Command 1918–1941* (London, 1962), pp. 113–213; I. V. Berkhin, *Voennaya reforma v SSSR (1924–25 gg)* (Moscow, 1958).
11. E. H. Carr, *Socialism in One Country, 1924–1926*, Vol. 2 (Harmondsworth, 1970), p. 59.
12. J. V. Stalin, *Problems of Leninism* (Moscow, 1947), p. 356.
13. This is not to deny that there was opposition to the Soviet state during the war; but the memory of the war is very potent. See, for example, Chapter 12 of Hedrick Smith, *The Russians* (London, 1976).
14. On this period of Khrushchev's rule see especially Michel Tatu, *Power in the Kremlin* (London, 1969).
15. It is also possible to trace the "Soviet military build-up" to the Central Committee resolution "On the Defence of the Country" in 1929. But the present phase has its roots in the "revolution in military affairs" which was the subject of much discussion in the early 1960s.
16. For a discussion of the organization and functioning of the defense sector, see my "Soviet Military R & D: Managing the Research-Production Cycle," in J. Thomas and U. Kruse-Vancienne, eds., *Soviet Science and Technology* (Washington, D.C.: George Washington University for the National Science Foundation, 1977), pp. 179–229; for a more detailed discussion, see my two chapters in R. Amann and J. Cooper, eds., *Innovation in Soviet Industry* (forthcoming).
17. See my paper "The Soviet Style of Military R & D," in F. A. Long and J. Reppy, eds., *The Genesis of New Weapons. Decision-Making for Military R & D* (forthcoming).
18. *Markizm-Leninizm o voine i armii* (Moscow, 1968), pp. 258–59.
19. *Pravda*, April 26, 1963; Tatu, *Power in the Kremlin*, pp. 343–44.
20. *Materialy XXIV s"yezda KPSS* (Moscow, 1971), p. 46.
21. See especially Julian Cooper, *Innovation for Innovation in Soviet Industry*, Center for Russian and East European Studies, University of Birmingham, Discussion Paper, Series RCB/11, 1979, pp. 87–92.
22. A Levikov, "'A'; 'B,'" in *Literaturnaya Gazeta*, November 15, 1972, p. 11.

23. *Literaturnaya Gazeta*, February 7, 1973, p. 10.
24. See, for example, S. Tynshkevich, "Sootnoshenie sil v mire i faktory predotyrashcheniya voiny," *Kommunist vooruzhennykh sil*, no. 10 (1974), p. 16; N. A. Kosolapov, "Sotsialno-psikhologicheskie aspekty razryadki," *Voprosy filosofii*, no. 4 (1974), pp. 36–37; V. M. Kulish, ed., *Voennaya sila i mezhdunarodnye otnosheniya* (Moscow, 1972), chapter 1.
25. See *World Armaments and Disarmament. SIPRI Yearbook 1979* (London), pp. 172–73; G. Ofer, "Soviet Military Aid to the Middle East," Joint Economic Committee, U.S. Congress, *Soviet Economy in a New Perspective* (Washington, D.C., 1976), pp. 216–39.
26. See the article on civil defense in *Sovetskaya Voennaya Entsiklopedia*, 3 (Moscow, 1977), pp. 23–25.
27. CIA: *Soviet Civil Defense*, NI 78–10003, Washington, D.C., July 1978, p. 2.
28. See Odom, "Militarization,'" pp. 44–47; *Sovetskaya Voennaya Entsiklopedia*, 3 (Moscow, 1977), pp. 255–57.
29. *Sovetskaya Voennaya Entsiklopedia*, 2 (Moscow, 1976), p. 245.
30. This has been a very widespread view, advanced most thoroughly in R. Kolkowicz, *The Soviet Military and the Communist Party* (Princeton, 1967).
31. T. Colton, *Commanders, Commisars and Civilian Authority* (Cambridge, Mass., 1979) argues that the Main Political Administration in effect identifies with the military. See also R. Fritsch-Bournazel, "Les Forces Armées et al 'société socialiste avancée,'" *Pouvoirs*, no. 6 (1978), pp. 55–64.
32. "The Soviet System: Petrification or Pluralism," in J. Hough, *The Soviet Union and Social Science Theory* (Cambridge, Mass., 1977), pp. 19–48.
33. For a discussion of marginal shifts of resources, see J. Hardt, "Military-Economic Implications of Soviet Regional Policy," prepared for Colloquium at NATO Economic Directorate, Brussels, April 1979.
34. R. Garaudy, *The Turning-Point of Socialism* (London, 1970), p. 138.
35. A very clear example is Soviet atomic bomb development. See my *Entering the Nuclear Arms Race: The Soviet Decision to Build the Atomic Bomb*, Working Paper No. 9, International Security Studies Program, Wilson Center, Washington, D.C., 1979.
36. See my "Research Note: Soviet Thermonuclear Research," *International Security*, Winter 1979/80.

37. Senghaas, *Rüsting und Militarismus*, pp. 361–64.
38. For a discussion of the different trends, see W. Clemens, Jr., *The USSR and Global Interdependence* (Washington, D.C., 1978).
39. See, for example, the discussion in R. Medvedev, *On Socialist Democracy* (London, 1975), chapters 3 and 4.

4
The American Arms Boom
Emma Rothschild

The United States may buy itself two things with its $1 trillion defense budget of 1981 to 1985. The first is an economic decline of the sort the comes about once or twice in a century. The second is a nuclear war.

This country is in the early years—not, despite the new shine of the Carter Doctrine, at the very beginning—of the most expensive military boom in history. In the process, the distinction between the military and the nonmilitary modes of the American economy is being suppressed. So is the distinction between nuclear and non-nuclear war. The continuum of money and destruction is being projected, through investment in military research and development, into the far future.

The expansion in military science and technology is the most ominous component of a defense budget that is dense with the ghosts of past and future wars.[1] The new defense boom has been welcomed—in the U.S. Congress, for example—as a response to recent events in Southwest Asia and elsewhere. But its main focus, instead, is on nuclear conflict.

The greatest increase in any major category within the 1981 budget is for "research, development, test, and evaluation," or "RDTE." Spending on strategic and other nuclear weapons increases particularly fast, as does futuristic research at the "leading edge" of military technology. With the money it spends to buy and keep scientists and engineers, the Defense Department is designing the weapon of ten and twenty years from now. With its research boom, it is defining a revised American doctrine of science-intensive war.

This effort is not new, and it is scheduled to persist for the balance of the five-year defense plan. The proportion of

---

*This essay was first published in *The New York Review of Books* under the title "Boom or Bust." It is reprinted here with permission from *The New York Review of Books*. Copyright © 1965–81.

defense spending devoted to research and the procurement of new weapons has increased steadily since 1976. This constitutes, as the Report shows, the first sustained boom in U.S. military investment—investment in Southeast Asia aside—since 1960–63.

The RDTE budget for 1981 is $16.5 billion. The MX missile—the race track of Ozymandias—is its most expensive item. The MX is allocated $1.5 billion in research money: this is more than the combined R and D budgets for the United States Department of Labor, the Department of Education, the Department of Transportation, the Environmental Protection Agency, the Federal Drug Administration, and the Center for Disease Control; over 140 percent of the R and D budget of the National Science Foundation.[2]

This allocation for the MX is only part of a build-up in research on nuclear, antinuclear, and postnuclear weapons systems. The "science and technology" program ("advanced research," "technology opportunities," and so forth) receives special commendation from Defense Secretary Brown, who presided as Director of Defense Research and Engineering in 1961–65 over the first great boom in strategic research, and is now concerned to "overcome the effects of reduced funding during the 1965–75 period." It is as though the years of obscurity, of the bargain-basement, low-technology Vietnam war were over; as though military scientists can now step out into the clear light of particle beams, space optics, and blue-green lasers.

The military doctrine that Brown outlines is suited to the epoch of innovative war. He returns again and again to concepts of flexibility, precision, "selective and measured" attack, and calibrated retaliation. Even the hopes and dreams of Russian leaders are measured; to the calibration of retaliation is added a calculus of values, in which the utility of certain "political control targets" exceeds that of, let us say, the entire city of Gorky, with missile sightings adjusted accordingly. Is there to be a further role for social scientists and moral philosophers in the teams of savants who are nourished by Sea Launched Ballistic Missiles?

The notion of "flexibility" is a leading piety of American strategic doctrine. Nor is there anything new about the idea of a "continuum" of nuclear weapons. But it is elevated by Brown into the writing on the wall of future destruction, from bazookas to particle weapons. "A continuum of deterrence," and "unbroken continuum" from "conventional to intercontinental forces": the word occurs five times in a brief discussion of so-called theater nuclear weapons, for use within one region such as Europe. At one extreme is the American first strike. "Even supposing a U.S. first strike," Brown muses at one point in the report, the Russians would have many surviving weapons.

This exercise in the use of the conditional is not likely to reassure those, such as the authors of the most recent SIPRI *World Armaments and Disarmament Yearbook*, who see in the MX missile system and in the latest antisubmarine technologies a refinement of the U.S. ability to strike first at its enemies.[3] Next in the continuum come the varieties of intercontinental retaliation dictated by the doctrine of "countervailing" force. Here again the emphasis is on precision, on choosing frequently among military and political targets, on "retaining an assured destruction capability" for the weeks of burning cities, social destruction, and ionizing radiation which would follow a limited "exchange."[4]

From here to the long-range "theater" nuclear weapons—such as the Pershing II and cruise missiles which will be able to strike from Western Europe into the Soviet Union—is a mere nudge along Brown's continuum. Thence to the array of "battlefield" and other nuclear warheads, of which the United States maintains some 7,000 in Europe alone, and "many thousands more" elsewhere. "Conventional" weapons, too, are to be found in the rainbow of modern war, often, indeed, launched from "dual purpose" nuclear or non-nuclear artillery, missiles, planes, and ships. At the end of the continuum, chemical weapons, of which the "deterrent stockpile" is to be maintained in 1981, which feature ("lethal chemical munitions concepts") in the Army's 1981 research budget, and for which "a facility that will have the capability to build binary chemical bombs, warheads and projectiles is being designed."

What is most remarkable about the doctrine of the continuum from non-nuclear to nuclear conflict is the cool and precise rhetoric in which it is described. Brown notes that "we have no more illusions than our predecessors that a nuclear war could be closely and surgically controlled." But the Report returns obsessively to the promise of such illusions: to "increased NATO options for restrained and controlled nuclear responses," to the "effectiveness and versatility" of nuclear-armed destroyers in the Indian Ocean.

This is the banalization of the nuclear epoch. We no longer find the pious disclaimers, the epithets ("of course, terrible") which earlier defense secretaries once appended to the words describing nuclear war. Nor are there frequent references to "the limited utility of nuclear weapons" (Donald Rumsfeld in the last Republican Defense Budget). The phrase "total war" is used casually in a discussion of defense spending. The unthinkable is being thought, ignored, presumed upon.

The Report puts forward three sorts of arguments in favor of increased defense spending. The first, and most familiar, suggests that because the Soviet Union is spending much more than the United States on its military effort, the United States must now re-arm. The Report is full of speculation on Russian intentions: the fact that their forces in Eastern Eruope are "much too offensively oriented," and that their positions in the Far East are "apparently designed for offensive operations"; their curious propensity to "take more seriously than we have done, at least in our public discourse, the possibility that a nuclear war might actually be fought." But the argument relies in general upon the simple reiteration of relative expenditures.

The shortcomings of such comparisons are well known, as the Report itself comes close to acknowledging. They are selective, in that they sometimes measure the Soviet Union against the United States and sometimes NATO against the Warsaw Treaty Organization. They pass lightly over the proportion of Russian military efforts which is directed not against NATO but against China. They move even more expeditiously past the sharp qualitative advantages enjoyed by the U.S., such as the "rather startling asymmetries" which SIPRI detects in U.S. and Russian strategic submarines.[5]

The comparisons of dollar costs are even more misleading. They are measured, the Report explains, "by what it would cost to buy Soviet programs (including personnel) in the U.S. economy." Estimates are thus arrived at for such quantities as "Soviet resources devoted to RDT & E." One has only to imagine the reverse to see the tenuousness of such calculations. A Russian "estimate" of American military research would start, to be sure, with the published budget figure of $16.5 billion. To this it would add the $1.3 billion which the Department of Energy will spend on nuclear weapons and other defense research and a sizeable part of NASA's $5.6 billion R and D budget. The Russian economists next need to calculate what portion of R and D spending by American business supports the military effort, notably in two industries, aircraft and communications equipment, which are called by the government "Defense product industries."

At this point, they might decide what it would cost "to buy" this science and technology in the Soviet Union—to reproduce the utility of Hewlett-Packard's basic research, or of such military contractors as Penn State University.[6] Do they multiply by two? Or three? Or is Penn State unreproducible? All that remains for our diligent academicians is to head, charts in hand, for the Armed Services Committees of Mr. Smirnov and Mr. Ustinov and the other titans of the Soviet Union's military-industrial complex.[7]

This exercise is not frivolous. Some such sequence may indeed have helped to determine the present arms race. We can assume that the Soviet Union reacted to the American military build-up of the late 1960s—an effort directed in large part at Southeast Asia—by investing in military research. The weapons that the Russians are building now are the products of that research. The Americans in turn react by increasing their own research, which will produce the arms race of the early 1990s; such are the dynamics of comparative weaponry.

The second argument in favor of the military boom suggests that the "growth in international turbulence" in Afghanistan,

Africa, the Caribbean, Thailand, and elsewhere makes such an effort essential. One may question whether the times are, indeed, notably turbulent. There are relatively few wars under way, and revolution is distinctly on the retreat. It is even more questionable whether acquiring the capacity to construct particle beam weapons in the 1990s is likely to reduce turbulence in the third world in 1980. One of the major new projects, the CX airlift plane, is recommended for "contingencies outside of Europe," yet it is some years from being deployed. The strategy of knowledge-intensive war suggests that the United States will look for precision and measured responses in its worldwide military efforts: in other words, the use of tactical nuclear weapons. Is this what the Carter Doctrine requires? Is this what Congress is buying with its bucks?

Brown's report, meanwhile, demonstrates a far more muscular attitude to U.S. military intervention outside Europe than has been seen for some years. "Our defense establishment could be faced with an almost unprecedented number of demands," Brown writes. We are not far from Henry Kissinger's recent thoughts, when after considering whether U.S. troops would be welcome in Oman he said:

> The immediate crisis shouldn't deflect us from other areas of potential danger. The situation in Turkey requires our urgent attention. Thailand could be a dangerous situation. Morocco remains under attack from adversaries armed with Soviet weapons. Central America is in turmoil. We may yet be needed in Southern Africa.[8]

The third argument is the murkiest. It suggests that "perceptual problems" are critical, that the United States must increase its military spending lest it "lost, not from war, but from changes in perceptions about the balance of nuclear power." Even those who accept this argument—I do not—should ask themselves whether the United States is buying the right power and the right perceptions with its new defense dollars. Must it sell the far future with blue-green lasers? Is the Brown Doctrine of science-intensive war the best standard under which to fight the battle of perceptions? It should be added that the Report's calculus of "perceptual" costs and benefits is bizarre. Thus we learn that "the aura of great U.S. military power" is "a legacy of World War II, Korea, the Cuban missile crisis, and even (up to a point) Southeast Asia . . . ," that "the mining of Haiphong Harbor demonstrated the deterrent effect of mines. . . ."

The Brown position is based on a view of the American economy and American society as organized around knowledge and science. The Report contrasts the "manpower-intensive Soviet economy" with the "more capital-intensive and technologically advanced American economy." The obvious strategy, thus, is to lead from strength or from comparative advantage; to prepare to fight an automated and innovative war. This choice has the further advantage of appealing to the apparent preferences of the Congress for hardware and for clean wars.* Yet even on these terms, the strategy is perilous. The Report is full of allusions to "problems with materiel readiness, in part because of the advanced equipment coming into the forces." We learn, in passing, of production problems in constructing nuclear attack submarines, of "shore processing software, computer loading and array reliability problems" with Navy sensor systems; that the Air Force finds it difficult to maintain "their increasingly complex equipment," given "maintenance backlogs" and "increases in our accident rates"; that the Army's "telephone switches in Europe are obsolete, require continuous costly maintenance, and often break down," and will be replaced by German digital switches.

We are not far from the more familiar problems of the civilian economy: from subway systems whose sensors break down, and hospitals in which electronic hardware surpasses medical software, from the maintenance problems of DC-10s (the Federal Aviation Administration's budget for civilian R and D is less than that allocated to one Navy aircraft). The military has conventionally assumed that because it can afford the most elaborately redundant controls, and because its operations are isolated from the messiness of real-life clinics and sewage tunnels, it is thereby free from such tribulations. Even this may no longer be the case.

There is a related and deeper contradiction in the notion of knowledge-intensive war. The United States is practising a variety of "*la guerre savante*," the stylized struggle which has dominated European wars since the sixteenth century. But as Fernand Braudel shows in his *Les Temps du Monde*, such struggle is only possible when it is practised by both sides at once; the veterans of Flanders campaigns who brought their learned battle formations to Oran in the 1590s and to Brazil in the 1630s found opponents who were playing in a different game.[10] The United States cannot expect that the Soviet Union will continue to join in its high science game, as this game becomes ever more idiosyncratic and ever more indulgent. The American military is choosing those weapons systems which are, in Robert Oppenheimer's phrase, "technically sweet." But this sweetness seems increasingly determined by the most introspective of scientific cultures. Are the random dashes and dummy missiles of the MX "sweet" to Russian probability theorists and computer scientists? The arms race implicit in the new military boom requires the most precise coordination of national scientific emotions, as the United States and the Soviet Union move together toward the MX, to "invulnerable" missiles for the Russians, pressure on SALT, new missile defenses, pressure on the ABM Treaty, laser weapons, even more pressure to abrogate the ABM Treaty, warfare in space.

The epigraph to Brown's Report is a remark made by Abraham Lincoln, in 1861: "I think the necessity of being *ready* increases—look to it." That America's leaders should choose, now, to evoke the last war fought in this country is itself awesome. The insignia to the Defense Budget would be not what Lincoln said on the eve of the Civil War, but rather what he said at its end: "It is sure that I have not controlled events, events have controlled me."[11]

The last, striking contradiction of the doctrine has to do with its economic costs. These, too, are determined by the technology-intensive character of the projected boom. Yet they have been to an extraordinary extent forgotten in discussions of the Defense Budget. Just as it is assumed that investment in lasers will somehow encourage the loyal Pathans, that the incantation of numbers (4 percent real growth in defense spending) is itself useful, so too are the economic consequences of the boom ignored.

The Budget was greeted with enthusiasm: "Defense Stocks Lead Market Up," and a survey of business opinion in the *Wall Street Journal* to the effect that "we're in a war economy." There seemed nothing, as in 1950 and 1966, that could so fortify business confidence as a vigorous defense effort. The recession of 1980, it seemed, was "postponed." Yet this optimism is founded on a profound misunderstanding of the changes that have taken place in the American economy since 1970 and thus of the likely benefits of the defense boom.

Even the most rosy expectation does not deny that military spending will stimulate inflation. Previous arms booms began in years of moderate price increases (consumer prices increased 1 percent in 1950 and 2.9 percent in 1966); United States inflation early in 1980 reached an annual rate of 16 percent. This tendency is likely to be exacerbated because many engineers, skilled workers, and high-technology components are in short supply; the chairman of General Dynamics (the contractor for the Navy's troublesome attack submarines) looks forward to "some type of priority system" favoring defense contractors.[12]

It is much less likely that the boom will provide extensive new employment for American workers. In the first place, the character of defense spending is, following Brown's dictum and the exigencies of the times, increasingly capital-intensive. If a billion dollars in the 1960s could procure a sizeable arsenal of General Motors rifles for Vietnam, it will not now pay General Dynamics for a single Trident submarine. Secondly, by cutting into other government programs, military spending may jeopardize the most precarious of existing jobs.

One mysterious aspect of the economic crisis of the 1970s in the United States is the extent to which employment has continued to increase. This is in part because manufacturing industry there—far more than in France or West Germany—has maintained jobs. But it is also because employment in social and public services, particularly health services, has multiplied. Thus of the nine million jobs created in the U.S. economy from 1973 to 1978, one-half were in services and state and local government (a further quarter were in retail trade). These jobs, often temporary or part-time, are peculiarly at risk in a recession; it is worth recalling that the last great surge in service employment in the United States was in the late 1920s, and was brought to an end by the Depression.[13] Will the overpaid aeronautical engineers of 1981 spend their disposable income on nursing home services? Or will the Carter administration, cutting government civilian programs to limit inflation and balance the budget, begin a new crisis of lay-offs in social services?

There is one problem of the U.S. economy which the military boom may be expected to alleviate. This is the decline in rates of growth of labor productivity in the 1970s, with an actual reduction in 1974 and 1979. It seems likely that shifts in the economy away from the production of goods for military consumption and toward the production of social services have reduced growth in productivity. Many industries that are dependent on defense enjoy high levels and high rates of growth of productivity. They buy components, intermediate inputs, from other equally vigorous sectors. The service industries, by contrast, tend to buy paper, construction, other services.[14] Yet even here the stimulus of procurement may be limited. Perhaps modern defense contractors behave, economically speaking, like business services or technology consultants.

U.S. military expenditures started to increase in the mid-1970s. Military contracts for goods and services—what the Defense Department comptroller calls "procurement," which includes spending for maintenance goods and for foreign military sales—increased from $45.8 billion in 1976 to $55.6 billion in 1977 and $69.0 billion in 1979.[15] Yet this boomlet has done little for productivity growth. The Soviet economy, of course, is a poor example of the economic benefits of militarization. The Defense Department Report is generous with its estimates of Soviet economic growth in the 1980s. How can an elemental enemy be at the same time a pitiful and impoverished giant. Recent figures show, however, that the Soviet economy grew in

1979 at 2 percent as against a planned 4.3 percent, and industrial productivity 2.4 percent against 4.7 percent, with productivity in agriculture and transport falling.[16]

What, in these circumstances, are we to make of the military-induced boom in "business confidence"? It is perhaps the most ominous of the ghoulish economic indications of the past several weeks, not only for what it reveals about the perversity of capitalist economies. Business optimism, now, is evidence of a keening desire by American industry to return to the old economic and technological patterns of the 1940s, 1950s, and 1960s. The economic changes of the period since 1970 have amounted to a vast, if unintended and perhaps unwanted, transformation of the American economy toward the provision of social security. There has even, within this metamorphosis, been some conversion of scientific and technical efforts toward secular society; some social innovation. Now, every instinct of the American political economy seems to be crying retreat, to be crying war.

If one considers the history of the American economy in the twentieth century, it seems possible that military industries have functioned as a "leading sector"—in the economist Joseph Schumpeter's sense of a dominant industry—during the long expansion of the 1940s to the 1970s. One does not have to believe in specific explanations of economic cycles such as Kondratieff's to see that modern economic growth is characterized by long periods of expansion, more or less associated with a given "locus" of innovation. Such periods include, for the world economy, 1848 to 1873 and 1895 to 1920, as well as the post-World War II boom that ended in the early 1970s.[17]

There has been no undisputed leader during the U.S. expansion of the postwar years. Instead, some theorists of economic cycles point to an assortment of leading industries, including electronics, consumer electrical goods, and air travel. What seems possible is that the military industries themselves have constituted such a focus. They do not function as a single or multiple industrial sector, as did the railroads and the automobile and electricity businesses in earlier booms, but rather as a cluster of industries joined by a common objective and a common customer. Their role in the war-time and postwar American expansion would certainly fit Schumpeter's criterion for the longest waves of the economic cycles as "breaking up old and creating new positions of power, civilizations, valuations, beliefs and policies," as well as creating new ways of organizing scientific research and innovation.[18]

If this speculation is plausible, what we should have seen in the 1970s was the elaboration and decline of military innovation in the United States. The obsolescence is what Mary Kaldor calls "baroque technology."[19] Is it to be glimpsed within the optimism of Harold Brown's knowledge-intensive budget? Will the $200 million to be spent on Very High Speed Integrated Circuits produce some pale imitation of the past triumphs of military electronics and its civilian spin-off? Is the MX the residual monstrosity of the long expansion led by the military, and does it portend the decline not of the auto-industrial but of the military-industrial age, the Edsel and the Vega writ as large as the deserts of Utah?

The defense boom and the business confidence it inspires are from this perspective deeply disturbing. They suggest an instinctive return to the industrial and scientific culture of an obsolete expansion, the power of what Veblen, writing of the British railroad industry in the 1890s, called "the inertia of use and wont."[20] Such a reversion can only make the long cyclical decline of military industries more painful and more dangerous.

The United States in 1970—after the first decline in military spending for Vietnam—consecrated a fifth of its engineers, a fourth of its physicists, a fifth of its mathematicians, almost half of its aeronautical engineers to defense-related employment.[21] Estimates in the Rumsfeld defense budget suggest that the proportion did not fall during the Republican defense recession and may have increased since.[22] At the trough of the recession in military research, the United States devoted 28 percent of its national research and development effort to defense, as compared to 7 percent in West Germany, 19 percent in France, and 4 percent in Japan.[23] An economy in the throes of decline cannot afford to lose this portion of its knowledge, of its education system, of its future to old industries and to destruction.

There is now, as not often in the world since Nagasaki, the intuitive possibility of nuclear war. There is also the possibility of a remilitarized world economy which will make this prospect more imminent, year after year, as the research boom becomes a boom in procurement, in strategic doctrine and in military culture. Very little is more important, as we enter the 1980s, than to act against the one and against the other.

Notes

1. *Department of Defense Annual Report*, Fiscal Year 1981, Harold Brown, Secretary of Defense, Department of Defense, January 29, 1980.
2. *Special Analyses, Budget of the United States Government*, Fiscal Year 1981, pp. 303–33.
3. Stockholm International Peace Research Institute (SIPRI), *World Armaments and Disarmament. SIPRI Yearbook 1979* (London: Taylor & Francis), p. 449.
4. Kevin N. Lewis, "The Prompt and Delayed Effects of Nuclear War," *Scientific American*, July 1979.
5. *SIPRI Yearbook 1979*, p. 417.
6. "ARL, Penn State University," is listed as one of the contractors of the Navy's "Advanced ASW (Antisubmarine Warfare) Torpedo," Department of Defense, *Program Acquisition Costs by Weapon Systems*, Fiscal Year 1981.
7. See Mary Kaldor and Alexander Cockburn, "The Defense Confidence Game," *The New York Review*, June 13, 1974.
8. Interview with Henry Kissinger, *Wall Street Journal*, January 21, 1980.
9. Deborah Shapley, "Arms Control as a Regulator of Military Technology," *Daedalus*, Winter 1980.
10. Fernand Braudel, *Les Temps du Monde (Civilisation matérielle, économie et capitalisme*, Vol. III) (Paris: Armand Collin, 1979), pp. 44–47.
11. Quoted by Hans Morgenthau, in D. Carlton and C. Schaerf, eds., *Arms Control and Technological Innovation* (London: Croom Helm, 1977), p. 262.

12. *Wall Street Journal*, February 1, 1980.
13. Edward Denison, "Service Industries—Trends and Prospects," *Survey of Current Business*, January 1945.
14. Wassily Leontief and Marvin Hoffenberg, "The Economic Effects of Disarmament," *Scientific American*, April 1961; "The Input-Output Structure of the U.S. Economy, 1972," *Survey of Current Business*, February 1979.
15. "Procurement" in this sense is different from and larger than "procurement" of weapons in the budget sense. Procurement for foreign military sales accounted for $5.4 billion of the total in 1979.
16. *Le Monde*, January 27–28, 1980.
17. See Eric Hobsbawm, "The Development of the World Economy," *Cambridge Journal of Economics*, September 1979.
18. Joseph Schumpeter, *Business Cycles*, Vol. II (New York: McGraw-Hill, 1939), p. 696.
19. Mary Kaldor in *Arms Control and Technological Innovation*, p. 331.
20. Thorstein Veblen, *Imperial Germany and the Industrial Revolution* (Ann Arbor: University of Michigan Press, 1966).
21. Estimated in Richard Dempsey and Douglas Schmude, "Occupational Impact of Defense Expenditures," *Monthly Labor Review*, December 1971.
22. Donald Rumsfeld, *Annual Defense Department Report*, Fiscal Year 1979, p. 102. A recent study of American physicists confirms this tendency. E. L. Woolett, "Physics and Modern Warfare: The Awkward Silence," *Am. J. Phys.* 48 no. 2, February 1980.
23. Figures for 1975 from Bernard Delapalme et al., *Science and Technology in the New Socio-Economic Context* (Paris: OECD, 1980).

5
The Arms Race and Nuclear War: An Interview
George Kistiakowsky

Kistiakowsky: My life is divided into four equal periods. The first twenty years I was growing up and experiencing war firsthand. The second twenty years were exclusively chemistry, which gets us to 1940. The next twenty years were half and half—chemistry and weapon building. I was still successful in chemistry and very successful in weapons. The last twenty years I have been trying mostly to undo the nuclear weapons—and this has been the least successful.

Q: It is probably the most difficult.

Kistiakowsky: Oh yes. This last change, it was gradual. You have to be aware that I come from a liberal, academic family. My father, a sociologist, was very unusual at the turn of the century. His writings were largely concerned with questions of human rights, which was an unpopular subject in Russia in those days. Nobody was really interested. The main question was whether you were a Marxist or not, something very different from concern for human rights. That was the atmosphere in which I grew up.

I joined the anti-Bolshevik cause because I saw the Bolsheviks as completely authoritarian and, I felt then, allied with the German Empire. I went into war work in 1940 because I was violently against Nazism. After World War II, I was foolish enough to swallow hook, line, and sinker the intense Washington propaganda that the Soviet Union was ready to conquer the world. Of course, Stalin was primarily concerned in building a belt—a protective belt—around the USSR. This was a reaction

---

*This interview, conducted by *Chemical and Engineering News*, was first published in and is reprinted with permission from *Chemical and Engineering News*, February 2, 1981.

to the invasions of Russia which had been occurring every century from long, long ago. Going beyond that, such as in Greece and Iran, Stalin was very cautious. Even minor threats of military action caused him to pull back. He was, of course, very ugly about the blockade of Berlin, but again he was damn cautious. He really didn't interfere with our support of Berlin. In the Korean years he was cautious again about involving the Soviet Union.

But it took me a little time for all this to sink in. And then I began to see all of the lies, such as the so-called missile gap. I knew there was no missile gap, because our U-2 reconnaissance flights over the Soviet Union could not find any missile deployment. This was 1958—after the U-2s began flying. We put a lot of effort into detecting possible deployment sites. And we could find only one, north of Moscow. This was really a test site. It wasn't really an operational site. Those first ICBMs were so huge that you couldn't hide them.

Q: They weren't in silos?

Kistiakowsky: They were in hangars and then lifted upright. They were readied in the horizontal position and then lifted upright to be launched over a huge pit. Even by December 1960 there were only about six that were operational.

At this time, the late 1950s, I was near the Cabinet level—I was on the level with deputy secretaries. I attended all the National Security Council meetings, by orders of the President. I began to realize that the policy was being formed in a way which really was quite questionable. It was being formed by people who didn't really know the facts and didn't have time to learn them because of bureaucratic preoccupation. Some of them were intellectually below me. I am an arrogant enough person to say so. I am not going to give names.

Q: You don't include President Eisenhower in this?

Kistiakowsky: No. For Eisenhower I acquired a great liking and admiration. He had a clear mind. He had some problems of speech, but his thinking was very clear. And his heart was in the right place. He talked to me about his fear of the military-industrial complex, as he called it in his farewell speech as President. That was very much his concern. He felt that the military was much too aggressive. He felt it was interfering, for instance, with his [Eisenhower's] efforts to get a nuclear test ban. He sent me to the headquarters of the Strategic Air Command in the fall of 1960. As he said in a National Security Council meeting, "I distrust those generals and I am sending George to find out what they are up to."

Then came Kennedy and I began to realize that he was not interested in arms control. I continued as a member of the President's Science Advisory Committee for several years. Then I was also on the general advisory committee of the Arms Control and Disarmament Agency. It was perfectly obvious to me that the chairman of this committee was as uninterested in real arms control as anybody. He was just going through the motions. That was the general attitude in Washington.

I could see these growing armaments—the U.S. acquiring an overkill, the Soviets acquiring an overkill, beyond all concepts of common sense militarily. And then my final break came because I was foolish enough to think that I could do something about slowing down the Vietnam war.

Q: The formal break came in 1970?

Kistiakowsky: No, I resigned my job in January 1968.

Q: You were resigning from what?

Kistiakowsky: From my jobs in the government—my military connections, on advisory committees and so on. I wrote a letter to the Secretary of Defense. It was blunt.

Q: The tendency today is for an even higher percentage of our research and development effort to go into the military.

Kistiakowsky: I think more than 50 percent. It certainly will reach this level, especially with Reagan coming in.

Q: In C&EN (Chemical and Engineering News) *we recently asked the Presidential candidates a series of questions. Reagan certainly indicated further increases for military R and D. And even President Carter said the ratio for federal R and D spend-*

ing was today roughly 45 percent defense, 55 percent civilian. But he said it was going to go to about a 50–50 split.

Kistiakowsky: I object to you using the word *even* Carter. Because I think Carter is virtually undistinguishable from Reagan.

Q: In the latter stages.

Kistiakowsky: Yes, in the latter stages of his Administration. Because here we are dealing with a man—and you can put that in print—who certainly sees his personal interest, in that case re-election, as supreme because he identifies his own welfare apparently with the welfare of the country. It is a tragic attitude to have. And it is an attitude that was quite appropriate to the seventeenth and eighteenth century of absolute monarchs.

Q: The state, it is I.

Kistiakowsky: That's right. I have recently read a fascinating book about Peter the Great. And that's it—he was Russia. And I am afraid that Carter had a little bit of that feeling.

Q: It's not unknown among Presidents.

Kistiakowsky: No, it's not unknown. But here it was less moderated by other considerations. I am very upset about this militarization of the country. I think as Eisenhower said in his farewell address—it is destroying our democracy. Look at what we have seen lately—this fantastic, cancerous growth of neo-conservatives, militarists, and their affiliation with the quasi-Christian preachers on television. This all stems from our military emphasis. I don't know if you are aware, I also believe that there is a close correlation between the magnitude of involvement in military affairs and the economic welfare of a nation. After World War II the countries that have had the lowest economic success are the U.S. and the Soviet Union.

Q: Maybe Britain too?

Kistiakowsky: Britain was the third country which after the war was very heavily committed to military expenditures. It simply ran out of steam. I don't know what is happening to the

U.S. now or how it will end. We are beginning to imitate England. One recession follows another.

Q: Do you have any comments on the composition of the Reagan transition team for science and technology?

Kistiakowsky: I think it is really funny. It would be screamingly funny if it weren't so sad for the country.

Q: In that it does seem to be rather closely related to the military-industrial complex?

Kistiakowsky: That's right. It is the military-industrial complex. Even more interesting, my old friend Simon Ramo, whom I have known for twenty-seven years, is a co-chairman of this committee. He is the par-excellence member of the military-industrial complex. In fact, he is a founding member of it. He is supposed to have said that science will now have to be directed toward strengthening our military capability.

Q: Looking at the next ten years, we are going to deploy Trident submarines. Trident I missiles are coming in now. More advanced Trident II missiles will probably come in the next 10 years. We presumably will get the MX intercontinental ballistic missile (ICBM). We are upgrading our Minuteman III missiles. We also will have the air-launched cruise missiles. We are almost certain to get a new bomber. We will get the Pershing II intermediate-range ballistic missile. We will get ground-launched cruise missiles and a sea-launched version. We also may see a revival of antimissile missiles (ABMs). Do you see all this as reaction to—to use one of your phrases—another Pentagon nightmare?

Kistiakowsky: Yes, I think so. Let's put it this way. There is no doubt about it that the Soviet Union has been technically progressing toward our level. Right after World War II it was much more behind technologically than it is now.

The Soviets undoubtedly are progressing. They are putting an enormous effort into their military, and numerically they are ahead of us. They are draining their talent in that direction. But qualitatively they are still behind us by several years.

And this lag of about five years seems now to have been almost stabilized.

As you look back at the history of the strategic nuclear arms race, you will find that our military has fed the populace, the taxpayers, and Congress with a sequence of false leaks—the bomber gap, the missile gap, the civil defense gap, the anti-missile missile gap. Now we have the missile accuracy gap—the latest one. We also had the MIRV (multiple independently targetable re-entry vehicles) gap.

Q: We were always ahead in MIRVs, weren't we?

Kistiakowsky: Of course. But the Pentagon was saying in the late 1960s that the Soviets already were deploying MIRVs. Actually what they were deploying were multiple, but not independently targetable, warheads—buckshot. Now for the past couple of years, I think because the other things have been sort of exhausted, we are dealing with an accuracy gap.

Q: Would you analyze that for us?

Kistiakowsky: I know enough about these things to feel rather confident about what we can do with so-called national technical means of verification.

Q: Satellites, monitoring, and spying.

Kistiakowsky: Yes, but not Mata Haris. What we can do is to assert that Soviet missiles cannot be any more accurate than so and so.

Q: What do you mean by so and so?

Kistiakowsky: Whatever the figure is—tenth of a mile.

Q: But can one get to one-tenth of a mile? Can missiles really travel, say, 7000 miles and have their many warheads hit within one-tenth of a mile of their targets?

Kistiakowsky: Why not? The Pentagon characters say we already have a tenth of a mile.

Q: But with your background, do you think this is feasible and believable?

Kistiakowsky: Yes. I think so, with very sophisticated guidance and supersonic re-entry vehicles.

Q: I believe you are saying then that the perceived threat Soviet ICBMs pose to our ICBM silos is a real one, from a technical standpoint.

Kistiakowsky: No, I am saying that this threat is enormously exaggerated by the Pentagon. I don't trust them when they say specifically that this, say one-tenth of a mile, is the accuracy of Soviet missiles. All they can really assert, if they are honest, is that the accuracy of Soviet missiles is no better than this number. But it may be worse.

But even supposing a given Soviet missile in a test firing does have the accuracy that the Pentagon gives the Soviets credit for, there are so many other factors involved in being able to destroy 1000 of our missiles in a single attack. For instance, there is the ability of the bus (the postboost vehicle which carries the warheads) to determine reliably where it is in space and impart the correct direction and velocity as it releases the warheads. Also, in an attack, the missiles would have to fly on a trajectory essentially over the North Pole. No missiles have been fired along this route. Therefore the gavitational anomalies, which affect accuracy, are not completely known.

Q: Haven't these been measured to some extent with satellites?

Kistiakowsky: Maybe.

Q: Could you explain fratricide?

Kistiakowsky: Yes, that's another uncertainty. In the early 1960s when there were a lot of nuclear warhead tests in the atmosphere it was discovered that a one megaton warhead exploded on the ground will lift into the mushroom something on the order of 1 million tons of dirt. This contains a hell of a lot of rocks—pieces of concrete and so on. These rocks have to come down. For minutes there is a colossal column of crap that is very dangerous for re-entry vehicles, which are not designed to withstand this. It is essentially a barrier, it prevents another warhead from coming in. Re-entry vehicles are built to overcome the heating in the atmoshphere but don't have the armor to withstand the impact of rocks, etc. The ablating layer will be damaged and once that happens the damn things will burn up.

Q: What do you feel then would be a more appropriate military response over the next ten years? Presumably we don't look in favor on the very extensive program to modernize the U.S. strategic nuclear arsenal.

Kistiakowsky: No, I think one should modernize the forces. But I think one has to be extremely cautious in building provocative weapons. And I think some weapons are exceedingly provocative from the point of view of the Soviets. Trident II and MX—regardless of how they are deployed, and particularly if they are deployed without concealment—clearly become weapons for first strike. The only justification for building a missile such as MX, for which the Pentagon claims extraordinary accuracy as well as quite large warheads, is to be extremely effective against Soviet ICBM silos. There is no point in destroying empty silos. Therefore, clearly we are talking about a first strike, before the Soviets have launched their ICBMs.

Q: As we are going to have all these new weapons systems, the Soviets are going to respond, probably with mobile ICBMs.

Kistiakowsky: If we go through with our plans, yes, that's, of course, what they will do. So gradually as time goes on the chance for real arms control becomes lower and lower. Before the end of this century the probability of nuclear weapons use, somewhere in the world, is very high. And the probability of escalation into a holocaust is far from zero.

Q: You obviously see an extremely dangerous and unstable situation developing in the next decade.

Kistiakowsky: Yes. I am just editing for publication a speech I gave at the New York symposium in September on the medical effects of nuclear war. In it I say that probably before the end of this century we will have quite a few more nuclear powers around the world. And the way the politics are developing, most of them will be governed by autocrats, military dictators, generals, and admirals for whom war is a normal extension of foreign policy. These people have absolutely no concept of the fact that nuclear weapons have completely changed the whole nature of war.

Q: We are going to put all this effort into weapons—scientific talent is of course the primary resource going into it. The Soviets are going to do the same. If we are lucky and haven't had a war by 1990, all we will have done is proceed from a dangerous situation to a very dangerous situation. It does all get rather pessimistic, doesn't it?

Kistiakowsky: Yes. That's why I keep telling my audiences that I am so old that I probably will not see it, but most of you will probably be involved in nuclear war.

Q: You presumably feel that failure to ratify the SALT treaty has been a mistake.

Kistiakowsky: It is really a tragedy. SALT II was exceedingly advantageous to us for a number of very important reasons. It limited the number of MIRV warheads on the very large Soviet missiles to ten. They can carry as many as thirty and they undoubtedly will once the lid is off. That is a cheap and easy way to increase their fire power, and the Soviets will probably do it. Also, the Soviets had to reduce their total number of delivery systems about 250 under the treaty.

Q: SALT II also set a limit on the total number of MIRVed ICBMs.

Kistiakowsky: That's right. A very important number. It set a limit—not more than 300 of the very heavy missiles, SS-18s. And—something I consider of the highest importance—both sides agreed not to interfere with the so-called national technical means of verification, not even by camouflage. Certainly the ability to know what goes on on the other side is terribly important. I know, because of the experiences we had in the White House in the late fifties when we began to get the first information back from the U-2 flights. The information, compared to today's, was piddling. Even so, it made an enormous difference to the feeling of confidence we had.

Q: *I assume you have no doubt that the SALT II treaty was verifiable. As you remember, this was a big political issue in this country.*

Kistiakowsky: Yes it was verifiable. I have complete confidence. Also, the former head of the Central Intelligence Agency, William Colby, said that flatly to a group of Senators when the Council for a Livable World gave a seminar.

Q: *What do you know from your contacts, about the charges that the Soviets have violated SALT in various ways?*

Kistiakowsky: That's the standard technique in Washington. But I have talked with an erstwhile friend of mine who was the U.S. co-chairman of the standing committee that was set up after SALT I. The committee is half Soviets, half Americans.

Q: *That was one of the provisions of SALT I.*

Kistiakowsky: That's right. The standing committee constantly meets to discuss infractions of the treaty. And his statement to me—and he is not a peacenik, anything but—was that there just weren't any infractions of any great significance. He said a few minor matters were pointed out to the Soviets and they corrected them. The Soviets pointed out to us similar, minor infractions and we corrected them.

We could have had SALT II agreement three years ago. It was delayed completely by the Carter Administration.

Q: *Can it be said, he came in with rather ambitious plans?*

Kistiakowsky: He came in completely naive—a Georgian red neck. And the tragedy was that mission of Cyrus Vance—who was completely out of this business until he became Secretary of State—in January 1977. Carter sent him on a mission to Moscow in March with a proposal that I understand was largely engineered by the enemies of an agreement. That proposal superficially looked very sensible.

Q: It was for real reductions.

Kistiakowsky: Yes, but the reductions were of the large ICBMs.

Q: Which only the Soviets have.

Kistiakowsky: The idea was to replace them more or less with submarine-based missiles. But for the Soviet Union, the submarines are basically very insecure. If you ask yourself where can they be based, there are only two places. One is near Murmansk, and the other is in the Soviet Far East. Neither place is very satisfactory because as the subs leave these ports they can be very easily followed by our forces.

Q: Basically the point you are making is that Soviet submarine-based missiles are relatively a secondary weapon for them.

Kistiakowsky: Yes. And as you know, they have only seven or eight of them operating at any one time in the open ocean, against maybe twenty or thirty of ours.

Q: So you feel that this was a kind of a trap that the Carter Administration let itself into?

Kistiakowsky: That seems to be the way the Soviets felt about it.

Q: The information we get from the Pentagon is that there is a certain momentum to the Soviet nuclear arms buildup. This is certainly true over the past fifteen years or so. And it is also true that this is a period when basically they were catching up. But this momentum is said to be continuing beyond equivalence, to a Soviet superiority. Do you think that the Soviets would taper off their arms effort and be satisfied with an equivalence situation?

Kistiakowsky: They agreed in SALT I, which was in 1972, to stop adding to their strategic forces, numerically. And they did so. It is now eight years, and before that they had been adding enormous numbers of missiles at a rate of something like 300 ICBM silos per year. They brought it up to about 1400 silos.

Q: And this has not increased since then?

Kistiakowsky: No, they have stuck by that agreement. So I have a feeling they would have been willing to stick by SALT II. From their point of view that would still have been consistent with their invasion of Afghanistan. Regardless of how outrageous it appears to the rest of the world, including me, they see it as a securing of their borders—like the belt they created in the West after World War II.

Q: What realistically do you see the scientific community doing—is there a way it can get itself more seriously into this arms race issue?

Kistiakowsky: I think the science community owes it to the public to do something about it. Some of us are doing it, for instance, the Federation of Atomic Scientists, the Pugwash Group, the Union of Concerned Scientists, and so on. Trying to do it, at any rate. Other scientists have an indifferent point of view. And, of course, those that go and work for the military by and large are on the other side of the fence, unfortunately. You cannot work on weapons if you are in principle against their deployment and in favor of limitations. It doesn't work that way.

Among the activities of the Council for a Livable World, I am very encouraged by this joint venture in which the council's education fund is involved with the Physicians for Social Responsibility (PSR). Because, you see, American people have a great trust in experts.

Q: Maybe misguided at times, but true.

Kistiakowsky: Sure, but they have it. When I, as a civilian, talk to an audience about militarism and weapons and so on, people are skeptical because I am not a military person. The military is the expert on those things. Its word is believed. And, as you know, the Pentagon has a very large public relations effort. It is not keeping silent.

But by the same token people have a very great respect for physicians. They are the ones who know about health and illness, life and death. When physicians talk at our joint symposia about the medical effects of nuclear war, people listen. Our symposia are usually started by Dean Howard Hiatt of the Harvard School of Public Health. He is also a professor of medicine at Harvard Medical School. As he puts it, nuclear war is the last epidemic that human beings will be exposed to. There is no medical way of dealing with it, except to prevent it from happening.

Q: That first meeting, the one up here in Cambridge, had a lot of impact.

Kistiakowsky: Yes, that's right. The council was not officially involved in that one. But I was one of the speakers. There were also other speakers from the council including Bernard Feld [Massachusetts Institute of Technology physicist and editor of the *Bulletin of the Atomic Scientists*]. At another time we have had Cyrus Vance as a speaker. In fact, we are very respectable—practically establishment (ha ha).

Q: You see this as a route to develop eventually a broader grass-roots understanding of what the whole arms race is about. Eventually it will become a political issue.

Kistiakowsky: Yes, the population will then put the pressure on Congress and will elect better people to Congress than the collection of Neanderthal characters that got into the Senate this time.

Q: I assume it was a very disappointing Senate race for the council.

Kistiakowsky: Yes, we supported fourteen candidates.

Q: Did they all lose?

Kistiakowsky: No, seven got through. So in the balance we didn't do very badly, considering the total election results.

Q: Let us get back to this effort the council is making with the physicians. You are apparently saying that any broad public review of the arms race is going to have to come from a grass-roots, political realization of what is happening and what it means. And you feel that the physicians with their credibility represent a very useful route to start such a serious debate and to bring to the public just what is involved. And scientists then can piggyback on this effort. Is that how you perceive it?

Kistiakowsky: Exactly. The council has the role of helping the physicians by describing the physical effects of nuclear explosions. At our joint meetings everybody who talks about physical characteristics is a council speaker. The medical effects are covered by PSR speakers. But then we also put together a last section which has the purpose of explaining to the people that you can't prevent nuclear war by continuing the arms race. Sooner or later that will lead to a war.

Q: How long will it take to get this wide public debate?

Kistiakowsky: It is a battle against enormous odds.

Q: Is it an enormous public awareness effort, a sort of super Earth Day?

Kistiakowsky: I see ourselves as a sort of pygmy David planning to fight . . . a giant. Whom did David fight?

Q: Goliath. Is there a parallel to the initial environmental movement—those involved probably felt that way also when they started.

Kistiakowsky: That's right. In the fifties there was a real mass movement to stop nuclear weapons.

Q: I remember, the ban-the-bomb movement. Whatever happened to that?

Kistiakowsky: It was the partial test ban, that banned nuclear tests in the atmosphere, that destroyed it.

Q: How did that happen?

Kistiakowsky: Fallout from nuclear tests was built up in public consciousness as a big, crucial issue. It is the fact that you are being exposed to an unknown and maybe lethal energy—your children as well as you. And that you have no control over it. You didn't know it was coming, you couldn't tell it was there.

Q: This is the same as the fear of nuclear power plants?

Kistiakowsky: Yes, the fear of nuclear plants is very similar. And we have problems in trying to redirect the public fear of nuclear plants into fear of nuclear war. When you get emotional about nuclear plants and don't care about nuclear war, it's worrying about a pimple on your cheek when you have a goodly case of cancer.

6
Danger: Nuclear War
Jonathan A. Leonard

After a long hiatus, nuclear issues are again the rage—and the tone is bellicose. The energy crisis, Iran, Afghanistan, and the recession have struck home. Like Samson unaccountably shorn, we feel threatened. The result is understandable. Many now want to intimidate the Russians, think about limited nuclear war, build better atomic weapons, "win" the nuclear arms race, and so regain some of our lost influence over an unruly and dangerous world.

Of course, all these wants raise important questions. For instance, will we intimidate or merely incite the Russians? Can a "limited" nuclear war be contained? Will an arms build-up further encourage other countries to make nuclear weapons? Can we really expect to win the race? And what are the chances of unleashing a nuclear Armageddon?

Faced with these questions, all three of this year's presidential contenders responded passively, like leaves in a fast-moving stream. They knew that these and related questions needed airing: each said as much from time to time. They were perfectly aware that an irate public should be reminded periodically of the risks inherent in strong action. But their campaigns were generally geared to flow with the current, not against it. So anything they did to remind people about nuclear risks was relatively mild.

Partly for this reason, in 1980 a big share of that "reminding" job has fallen to a group of doctors calling themselves Physicians for Social Responsibility (PSR). They have provided forums for the nation's leading advocates of arms control. They have bent the ears of national leaders. They have staged meetings, lectures, conferences, television interviews, and press

---

*This article first appeared in *Harvard Magazine*, November–December 1980.

briefings across the country. They have marshaled an array of arguments that command respect. And they have been told by many—including both Jimmy Carter and Leonid Brezhnev—that their work has helped reduce the threat of war.

This is no mean feat for an organization only roused out of hibernation in March 1979 by a few Harvard and other Boston-area physicians. True, PSR had once been prominent: in the early sixties it drew up a report assessing the medical impact of a large nuclear blast on Boston, and this helped convince the Kennedy administration that bomb shelters would be futile. But PSR had done little in many years. So it seems reasonable to ask: What changed it from a mere band of doctors into a leading force on the neglected side of a great international debate?

That transformation can be traced to one event. In late 1979, PSR persuaded the Harvard and Tufts medical schools to sponsor a two-day symposium entitled "The Medical Consequences of Nuclear Weapons and Nuclear War." The symposium, held at Harvard's Science Center on February 9 and 10, 1980, brought together some of the nation's most respected proponents of arms control. They set out to tell the media and an overflow audience of about six hundred what the medical dangers of nuclear war were and what the effects of such a war would be. Never before had this been done carefully at a well-announced public gathering.

Howard Hiatt, dean of the Harvard School of Public Health, explained in his introductory remarks why the grim exercise was important.

> What purpose, I wondered initially, to describe such almost unthinkable conditions? But the conditions are not unthinkable—rather, they are infrequently thought about. As Professor Victor Weisskopf points out in the current *Bulletin of the Atomic Scientists* [February 1980], it is "surprising and most depressing that the public and most of the interested scientists rarely discuss . . . the danger of nuclear war."
>
> Among the painful results of silence are the continuing proliferation of nuclear weapons and the failure to reject nuclear war out of hand as a "viable option" in the management of world problems. Incredible as it may seem to any reasonable

> person, we hear with increasing frequency proposals that we consider launching limited nuclear attacks and even suggestions that we might "win" a nuclear war. We have come together to break the silence on the issue.

That silence was indeed broken. A few speakers addressed related matters, like leukemias and other cancers arising from bomb tests and weapons manufacture. But most aimed their remarks directly at nuclear war.

A principal speaker, Harvard Professor of Chemistry Emeritus George Kistiakowsky, former head of the Manhattan Project's explosives division and scientific adviser to presidents Eisenhower, Kennedy, and Johnson, examined the dangers of international politics and nuclear proliferation. Kistiakowsky summed up the prospects for nuclear war as follows:

> I think that with the kind of political leaders we have in the world ... nuclear weapons will proliferate. ... I personally think that the likelihood for an initial use of nuclear warheads is really quite great between now and the end of this century, which is only twenty years hence. My own estimate, since I am almost eighty years old, [is that] I will probably die from some other cause. But looking around at all these young people [in the audience], I am sorry to say I think a lot of you may die from nuclear war.

Another prominent speaker, J. Carson Mark, former head of the theoretical-physics division at the Los Alamos Scientific Laboratory, explained what would happen if Boston were struck with a single one-megaton device. That bomb would be strictly standard fare by modern standards. We and the Russians have thousands like it. But it would release the explosive force of a million tons of TNT, a force more than fifty times greater than the 1945 blast that flattened Hiroshima.

If such a bomb exploded, say, three thousand feet over Boston Common, it would saturate the downtown area with deadly ionizing radiation. A huge shock wave would descend like a giant hand, snapping skyscrapers like match-sticks and turning everything in its path into an evenly distributed pile of rubble over a four-mile radius extending out to and beyond Harvard Yard. Even farther out, if the day were clear, searing heat from the downtown inferno would inflict severe or fatal burns.

That could be only the beginning. As at Hiroshima, fires would burn out of control. Such fires might heat air over a large area and cause that air to rise, making cooler air rush in at greater speed from the sides. This inrush of air, fanning the flames like a bellows, could create a city wide firestorm that would exhaust the oxygen supply, asphyxiate people in bomb shelters, turn those shelters into ovens, and kill everyone within reach of the flames. This is precisely the sort of storm created by conventional bombings of Dresden and Hamburg, Germany, in the Second World War and by the lone Hiroshima bomb in 1945.

Or suppose the bomb went off at ground level instead of at three thousand feet. Then the partly blocked shock wave and heat would be a little less destructive. But the bomb would dig a crater a few hundred feet deep and up to a half-mile across. Particles of dirt, dust, and debris from the crater—containing radioactive by-products of the blast—would rise into the air and slowly fall to earth. Wherever they touched down, they would expose victims to dangerous and often lethal doses of radiation. According to M.I.T. Physics Professor Bernard Feld, editor of the prestigious *Bulletin of the Atomic Scientists,* it has been "conservatively" estimated that a one-megaton ground burst of this kind would produce lethal fallout over something like a thousand square miles.

Where would the fallout go? That would depend on the speed and direction of the wind. But even a twenty-mile-an-hour breeze could carry lethal fallout hundreds of miles and would make vast downwind reaches hazardously radioactive for weeks, months, or even years after the blast.

Everyone seemed to agree that civil defense, except in ideal circumstances, would prove trivial. Evacuation plans would depend on timely advance warning—which is unlikely, at best. And bomb shelters would save relatively few, since the costs and complexities of effective sheltering are huge. Even without firestorms, strong shelters would be destroyed by large or nearby blasts. Radioactive fallout would find victims in any shelters that did not filter the air. Starvation would stalk shelter-dwellers lacking enough food and water to endure weeks or months of radioactive peril. And emerging survivors would find themselves the impoverished refugees of a dead city.

What could medicine do about all this? Participating physicians, including leading experts on radiology and radiation sickness, felt the right answer was "Not much." Quite aside from those killed outright, the injured in moderately to severely damaged areas would find most doctors and medical workers incapacitated, most hospitals and clinics destroyed. Even if people and equipment could be mustered, streets blocked with debris from fallen buildings would keep most of the injured beyond reach. And even if some magic wand should clear the streets, all the nation's hospitals could not hold more than a fraction of those suffering from severe burns, chest wounds, ruptured internal organs, compound fractures, and radiation sickness. So, as in the aftermath of Hiroshima, the injured would have to fend pretty much for themselves.

How many would in fact survive is a good question. An old but still highly regarded PSR report—published in the *New England Journal of Medicine* in 1962 and cited at the meeting—assumed that a single twenty-megaton bomb was exploded over Boston. This was about the megatonnage the U.S. Government then felt would be targeted upon that city in a war. The dire forecast: 2.1 of the 2.9 million people living in Greater Boston would die (half instantly and half of injuries), some 500,000 would be maimed or disabled, and fewer than 300,000 would escape immediate crippling effects.

Of course, there is no reason to assume Boston would be the only city struck. Much has been said about accidental nuclear strikes and other kinds of "limited" attacks, some involving only one bomb. But nobody knows whether the party struck would choose a limited response. Cries of "Remember the Alamo!" and "Remember the Maine!" suggest such restraint may be unnatural. As Yale Psychiatry Professor Robert Lifton said bluntly, it is absurd to think that leaders can reach a rational agreement about limited bombing ("I'll go so far, I'll drop this weapon, you drop your weapon, and then we'll stop"), because people under stress simply don't behave that way. It seems far more likely, as former Admiral and Pentagon planner Gene LaRocque claimed, that a limited or accidental attack would sow confusion and invite massive retaliation.

LaRocque, a strong critic of defense policy and director of the private Center for Defense Information in Washington, had other worrisome things to say about military strategy. Among them: We now have thirty thousand assorted nuclear weapons and the Russians have twenty thousand. We have placed nuclear devices on 70 percent of our warships, and we have doled them out to virtually all our "conventional" air wings and ground divisions. The result: Not only is the potential for accidental launch significant, but "there is no way to fight a war between U.S. and Soviet troops without involving nuclear weapons. . . . They are so organic, so built into the training of our officers and men, that their use will be natural once we get into a fighting situation."

As for long-range missiles, LaRocque added:

> We have such sophisticated weapon systems that war is only thirty minutes away. Thirty minutes' flight time from the Soviet Union—or fifteen minutes from the submarines sitting off the coast right now with nuclear weapons aimed at Boston and New York. And there is no defense against Soviet missiles, absolutely none. There is also no control over a nuclear war once it starts. Some people suggest that if we improved our command and control we'd be able to fight a controlled nuclear war. It only takes one nation to start a nuclear war, but it takes at least two to agree to stop. No matter how good our control is, we have no way to stop a nuclear war once it starts.

All this raises ominous questions about whether the United States as a whole could survive a large attack. Most of those at the meeting felt there would be survivors, but that those survivors' prospects for enjoying life and sustaining an advanced culture were very slim.

Suppose, for example, that possible damage to the ozone layer, climatic changes, and worldwide radioactive contamination could be discounted. And suppose further that the Russians merely wanted to reduce our retaliatory might. Unable to do much about our nuclear submarines, they would presumably shoot most of their weapons at bomber bases and ICBMs (intercontinental ballistic missiles) in "hard" silos scattered through the West.

This is precisely the kind of "counterforce" attack our government now plans to use against the Soviet Union in the event of war. Against either country, such a strike would kill relatively few people directly. But large bombs would need to go off at ground level to destroy the hardened silos, and that would produce massive fallout.

According to Bernard Feld:

> [A] counterforce exchange between the United States and Soviets would involve something like five thousand megatons on each side. . . . This would create lethal fallout. And since the U.S. sites are spread over the west, and the prevailing winds blow mainly from west to east, it would cause lethal fallout over an area of about five million square miles. That is, roughly speaking, the area of the United States. There would be a fair amount of overlap, so you can't say the entire United States would be absolutely 100-percent covered. But a reasonably large fraction of the United States east of the Rockies would be covered with lethal fallout.

Or else, what would happen if, by accident or intent, the U.S. launched its weapons first? With our missile silos empty, the Russians might tell their remaining missiles, airborne bombers, and invulnerable submarines to hit industrial targets. They would strike factories, areas for food processing and storage, transport systems, oil refineries, power plants, and so forth. Such an attack was described by M.I.T. Physics Professor Henry Way Kendall, chairman of the board of the Union of Concerned Scientists. As Kendall noted, most industrial targets cluster around big cities. An attack on them, say, on the order of three to four thousand megatons, would probably kill most American citizens. And it would place the survivors in a race to restore their productive capacity before existing stocks of goods ran out.

> It is obviously impossible [Kendall said] to make secure predictions of what the prospects would be in this grim race. But it is likely, if not overwhelmingly likely, that the race would be lost,

> that the survivors could not re-establish an industrial society, and that as things got worse and worse they would drop to the economic equivalent of something like the Middle Ages—scattered bands probably competing for resources, conflicts further aggravating the waste and destruction. What this amounts to is that civilization would simply stop functioning and, although there would be biological survival, the prospects for re-establishing anything that had the form or shape of the United States—or even a small industrial microfacsimile of the United States—would be gone, and in that sense the United States is obliterated and survival is not possible.

Against this somber backdrop, physicians discussed what they should do. All felt that preventive measures offered the best hope. As Dean Hiatt put it:

> [T]here is in fact no reason to consider the consequences of nuclear war in strictly medical terms. But if we do, we must pay heed to the inescapable lesson of contemporary medicine: Where treatment of a given disease is ineffective or where costs are insupportable, attention must be given to prevention. Both conditions apply to the effects of nuclear war. Treatment programs would be useless and the costs would be staggering. Can any stronger arguments be marshaled for a preventive strategy?

Bernard Lown, professor of cardiology at the Harvard School of Public Health, went further, insisting that physicians, "charged with responsibility for the lives of patients and the health of the community, must commit themselves to a new area of preventive medicine—the prevention of thermonuclear war."

But the strongest call to action came from Nobel laureate Salvador Luria, director of M.I.T.'s Center for Cancer Research. Said Luria: "One cannot spend one's life trying to cure a few people and not be aware and active in the struggle to eliminate weapons that may destroy most of humanity. So I hope out of this conference will begin to emerge a national movement whose clear purpose is to fight the use, the preparation, and the existence of nuclear weapons in our own and other countries." That hope may bear fruit, for in the months since the symposium there have been signs that such a national movement has begun to stir.

What did the symposium conclude? Perhaps its conclusions were best summed up by a formal statement released at the end of the meeting, on February 10. Three weeks later, on March 2, that same statement appeared as a full-page open letter in the *New York Times*. Signed by an imposing array of medical leaders, the letter was addressed to "President Carter and Chairman Brezhnev." It reviewed the dangers brought out at the symposium, asked that the threat posed by the two countries' nuclear arsenals be recognized, and urged that a start be made in having those arsenals dismantled. The message drew high-level and widespread acclaim.

PSR member Eric Chivian (Harvard '64, M.D. '68), the M.I.T. staff psychiatrist who conceived and organized the symposium, explained the rationale behind both the *Times* advertisement and the doctors' current work. He said: "The real problem is lack of information and misinformation at all levels. Many people believe nuclear war is going to happen and are so terrified they don't talk about it. But everyone wants to do something. The man in the street doesn't want his kids blown up. And that sentiment can be mobilized."

To help mobilize it and keep it mobilized, PSR has kept busy. Besides arranging multitudes of talks, interviews, and so forth, last April it organized a smaller symposium in Washington, and on September 27 and 28 it staged another major one in New York. The latter, sponsored by Columbia's College of Physicians and Surgeons and Yeshiva's Albert Einstein College of Medicine, was modeled after the Harvard-Tufts affair. It drew many of last February's speakers; it also drew other important participants, the two best known being chief SALT II negotiator Paul Warnke and former Secretary of State (and former Deputy Secretary of Defense) Cyrus Vance.

Such "mobilizing" work is impressive. Nevertheless, it sometimes seems to beg the old question of whether anything really concrete can be done. Specifically, what about our well-founded distrust of the Russians? And even if they could be trusted, aren't they simply too aggressive and well armed for any U.S. peace initiative to succeed?

Many now feel this to be so. But throughout history, distrust has characterized the relations between great powers. That has not prevented arms races from being fit topics for negotiation, especially in hindsight. And offering to negotiate reduction of a nuclear stockpile easily capable of crushing the Russians several times over—even if they strike first—is a bit like a small boy with a thousand snowballs offering to throw ten away. It is hard to see how this could do much harm.

Nor is there any compelling reason to believe that Russia has foisted the nuclear arms race upon us. On the contrary, America invented the atom bomb, produced the first hydrogen bomb, developed the first strategic bombers, deployed the first armed ICBMs, launched the first nuclear submarines, deployed the first submarine-based missiles, and invented the first MIRVs (multiple individually targeted re-entry vehicles), which permit one missile to deliver many bombs. More recently, we have been deferring ratification of the SALT II treaty, pressing the Europeans to accept missiles able to strike the Soviet Union, and developing MX and cruise-missile systems that will advance the nuclear arms race another notch. As George Kistiakowsky said last February, referring to that race, "Let's not for a moment believe that we are angels, that we are for peace and the other side is bloodthirsty. The thing is pretty even." So there is every reason for thinking the United States could exert a powerful influence to contain or cut back the arms race if it chose.

On the other hand, it takes two to slow an arms race, just as it takes two to end a nuclear war. That is why virtually all the February speakers appeared to reject unilateral disarmament out of hand, why the *Times* letter went to both Carter and Brezhnev, and why, as Kistiakowsky put it, "this appeal has to be made to both sides."

So far, both sides have expressed interest. Carter and Brezhnev sent encouraging replies to the Times letter. Brezhnev, citing the awesome consequences of nuclear war, promised the doctors Soviet "understanding and support." And Carter, welcoming the doctors' "service to the cause of nuclear sanity and to public understanding of this vital subject," termed arms limitation "crucial."

Beyond that, the Soviets promised to publicize the letter

widely in their country, a pledge they have since kept. And White House special counsel Lloyd Cutler, meeting with a PSR delegation in Washington, encouraged further action. Should Congress reconsider the SALT II treaty, he suggested, physicians' testimony might improve its ratification prospects.

Meanwhile, both governments are supporting plans to hold a March 1981 colloquium of American, Soviet, and Japanese doctors on the medical consequences of nuclear weapons. This meeting was the brainchild of two Harvard professors—cardiologist Lown, inventor of the defibrillator and a world expert on sudden cardiac death; and cardiologist James Muller, assistant professor of medicine at the Harvard Medical School. Together with Herbert Abrams, chairman of the Harvard Medical School's department of radiology, and symposium coordinator Chivian, they recently set up a new organization called International Physicians for the Prevention of Nuclear War, to direct international attention at the weapons problem and bring the colloquium into being.

It is now expected that this gathering will bring together prominent Japanese doctors with experience derived from the Hiroshima and Nagasaki bombings and a host of U.S. and Soviet medical luminaries. Among the latter: Jonas Salk, perfecter of the first polio vaccine; Lewis Thomas, chancellor of the Sloan-Kettering Cancer Center, David Hamburg, president of the U.S. National Academy of Sciences' Medical Institute; and Evgenii Chazov, Soviet deputy minister of health, director general of the USSR National Cardiology Research Center, and Leonid Brezhnev's personal physician.

No gathering of this kind has ever been held before. The nearest to it have been meetings of the so-called Pugwash Movement, a series of scientific conferences in the 1960s that encouraged the nuclear-test-ban and nonproliferation treaties and helped keep international communication going during such tense times as the Cuban missile crisis. Consciously modeled on those Pugwash meetings, the colloquium is accordingly viewed as the first in a series of annual events. Later meetings, the doctors hope, may include participants from other countries that possess nuclear weapons.

Naturally, there is no way to tell in advance how the March plans will fare. But they have received strong support. They have prompted many top medical leaders to say they will attend. And they could provide a good vehicle for projecting international concern. So right now, like some newly emergent butterfly, they seem the fragile embodiment of an idea whose time has come.

Dr. Chivian feels that all this shows how much more physicians can sometimes do than they might think. "Doctors," he says, "especially prominent ones, have a unique opportunity to convince people about the true nature of nuclear war. Their credibility as medical and scientific experts is quite high, so they have a definite chance to do something important."

But Chivian is no wide-eyed optimist. He feels that people are "frighteningly" adapted to the possibility of nuclear war, and that, for the time being, the tide is running the wrong way. There is no comfort in recalling that when the Japanese ran short of oil four decades back, they decided forthwith to invade their neighbors. And jibes like "Nuke the Ayatollah," even when not seriously intended, show how many of us feel. Certainly, as far as the dangers of nuclear war and the prospects for arms limitation go, the times are dark.

That probably accounts for much of the recent action. Robert Lifton, quoting a line from poet Theodore Roethke, suggested at the February symposium that "in a dark time, the eye begins to see." But to see truly, the threatened eye must be awake, its owner summoned from sleep by some alarm. And that alarm should be convincing. This presumably explains why so many powerful minds are now willing, even eager, to help rouse the public eye from sleep—by continuing, as Dean Hiatt said, "to break the silence."

7
The Bureaucratization of Homicide

Henry T. Nash

Men in blue, green, and khaki tunics and others in three-button business suits sit in pastel offices and plan complex operations in which thousands of distant human beings will die.

Richard J. Barnet

During the 1950s and 1960s, the hot years of the Cold War, I held several jobs with the Department of Defense (DOD). I remember most vividly my job with the Air Targets Division of the Air Force where I worked as an intelligence analyst. Here I helped select targets in the Soviet Union at which, in the event of war, Air Force officers would fire nuclear warheads.

As an analyst in the Political and Economics Section of the Air Targets Division my responsibility was to "nominate" as targets buildings indentified as Communist Party headquarters located in various Soviet cities. In order for a nominated target to win its way into the Bombing Encyclopedia (the official Secret Air Force catalogue of strategic targets in each communist country), a Significant Summary Statement was prepared which briefly (roughly fifty words or less) described each target and its strategic importance. While I worked at selecting and justifying political targets, fellow-analysts in other offices were busy identifying different types of strategic targets—petroleum depots, airfields, or industrial centers. Each of us made nominations for the integrated Air Force strategic target list and we each hoped our targets would be chosen for a DOD strategic plan of nuclear attack designed to bring about a rapid,

---

unconditional surrender of Soviet forces. Like myself, my colleagues were graduates of liberal arts colleges and many were taking evening graduate courses in fields such as international relations or economic theory. Most of us had vague hopes of a college teaching job some day but, meanwhile, taking courses meant improving our professional credentials and this made it easier to live with the more mundane aspects of our nine-to-five life.

Today, as a professor in a small liberal arts college, I am frequently visited by haunting memories of my work with Air Targets. I'm surprised how clear these memories are; the details of my work, the faces and names of my colleagues, and the atmosphere of the place where I worked—a gray, creaking two-story temporary barracks-like building, anchored to Constitution Avenue by the weight of a large heavy windowless cinderblock room in which classified documents were read and filed. But the haunting memories are tied less to people and place than to a nagging and disturbing question: What was it about work with Air Targets that made me insensitive to its homicidal implications? I and my colleagues, with whom I shared a large office, drank coffee, and ate lunch, never experienced guilt or self-criticism. Our office behavior was no different from that of men and women who might work for a bank or insurance company. What enabled us calmly to plan to incinerate vast numbers of unknown human beings without any sense of moral revulsion? At least no signs of moral revulsion surfaced when we were having an extra martini or two at lunch to celebrate the inclusion of some of our government control centers in a Joint Chiefs list of prime Soviet targets.

The Cold War made selecting targets for attack in the Soviet Union seem respectable. Within the Defense Department one was struck by the atmosphere of a war to be waged and won. Crisis conditions made targeting seem imperative, which, in turn, made it morally acceptable.

Another factor was that the complex vastness of the Defense Department prevented any intelligence analyst from determining how his work might be used by higher-ranking officials. The relationship between cause and effect was obscured. Because of the size of the Defense bureaucracy, managerial efficiency called for the compartmentalization of work and, within our intelligence operation, one basis for compartmentalization was the "need to know." This meant that analysts were permitted to know something only if it were needed to complete an assigned task. Without a need to know, access was prohibited. Thus, in the case of the Air Targets Division, I had access to targeting information pertaining to Soviet government control centers but I did not have access to data concerning other categories of targets, such as Soviet petroleum depots or air bases. Working on tasks of limited yet clearly defined scope appealed to analysts who might otherwise have felt at sea in the vastness of the bureaucracy. Need to know, initially designed to help reduce intelligence leaks, restricted each analyst's appreciation of the larger context of which his job was a small part. Obscuring the "big picture" helped promote peace of mind.

While some administrative arrangements prevented analysts from grasping how all the parts fit together, others helped analysts achieve a sense of professional security and personal gratification. For example, analysts usually worked as members of a committee, team, or task force. Although this groupthink process often blunted the expression of individual insights and diluted strong conclusions, it offered something of value to individual team players. A well-received team product provided reinforcement through shared, mutual congratulations while, in the case of a negative or critical reaction, the individual player could absolve himself from personal responsibility by blaming less insightful team members or by joining fellow-teammates in blaming the unappreciative system. The team made it possible to savor the gratification of praise and muted the unappealing impact of criticism.

It was not only the protective structure of the team that shielded the individual analyst from serious challenges or the ignominy of being proven wrong; the broad theoretical or conjectural context within which research was carried on offered security as well. The fact that most study requirements were cast in terms of long-range predictions ("The Stability and Cohesion of the Soviet Government Control System: 1985–

90," for example, or "Sources of Soviet Petroleum in the Year 2000") provided protection. It was difficult if not impossible for any potential critic to prove that a colleague was incorrect, or put him on the spot, if the study consisted of speculative generalizations about probable future developments concerning a broad, complex subject. Analysts were cognizant of this invulnerability and liked it.

Another facet of DOD research was the practice of developing reports in terms of the so-called worst-case situation. With regard to assessments of Soviet military capabilities, for example, analysts strained to depict the most extreme and threatening dimensions of the Soviet Union's ability to develop the full resources of its military potential. The worst-case approach to "research" was encouraged by the Department of Defense since, to the extent that Soviet military potenialities were described in their most horrendous dimensions, the Department strengthened its chances to motivate Congress to provide increased defense funds. Furthermore, the worst-case approach imposed no constraints on the analyst's imaginative freedom to estimate future levels of enemy weaponry. Again, under these circumstances an analyst's conclusions were less susceptible to effective challenge. Further immunity from criticism was assured by the fact that each analyst's conclusions, or those of his team, would be immediately classified and access to the finished product restricted to those who held proper clearances and the need to know.

Ascertaining enemy capabilities in terms of the worst case disposed analysts to perceive relations among nations as being hostile, combative, and consequently threatening. This encouraged the view that America's interests were best protected through superiority in arms. Thus, what was initially only an approach to intelligence research (the worst case) came to color the analyst's world-view, an outlook that was buttressed by compatible attitudes in the Defense environment. The worst case inevitably disposed Defense analysts to concentrate on assessing enemy capabilities, primarily military, without ascertaining what enemy intentions might be. Worst-case thinking implied that enemy intentions were known (maximum aggressiveness) and that a concentrated effort to list enemy capabilities was required. Worst case rendered legitimate the ideological conviction that stressed the critical importance of "standing up to the Russians." This could be best done through the acquisition of more weapons since, of course, the only thing the Russians respected was force.

What all of this fostered in the workaday concerns of Defense analysts was a persistent preoccupation with the state of military technology—the numbers game. Assembling, or at least being familiar with, lists, tables, and catalogues of the estimated number and characteristics of enemy weapons was an essential part of being a respected intelligence analyst. As the arms race continued and the United States and the Soviet Union acquired more and more weapons, there were more and more items to count and describe. The strong technological and quantitative orientation of these tasks held the attention of analysts and the relationship of weapons to human life was an incidental consideration. During a NATO war game I remember the surprise expressed by an Air Force colonel when he was informed of the number of casualties that resulted from his striking an "enemy" urban center with a one-megaton weapon. It took the simulated reality of a war game to bring home the human dimensions of this act. The colonel quickly regained his composure, reassuring himself that this was, after all, only a game.

In retrospect, in the anxious atmosphere of the Cold War, and in the setting of the Department of Defense where arms were considered the means of survival, thinking about the social characteristics of an enemy society constituted an unrewarding, almost irresponsible pursuit. How useful was it to grasp the intricate dynamics of another society if you were the most powerful nation in the world and had already decided to seek security through military intimidation? The significance of military power in determining the behavior of government officials was illustrated by remarks made by Pham Van Dong, Premier of North Vietnam, and Henry Kissinger, then President Nixon's national security affairs adviser. These remarks enabled Richard Barnet to contrast the capacities of the leaders of North Vietnam and America to comprehend each other's political motivations.

> I was struck by how well the Vietnamese politician understood Nixon's character and situation as well as the pressures that operated on him. The Premier had the ability to put himself in Nixon's place. Kissinger, on the other hand, while evidencing respect and even a little admiration for his adversary's skill, seemed to have no genuine understanding of what motivated him. In Hanoi, Nixon was a human being, not liked, but seriously considered. In the White House, Pham Van Dong was a chessboard figure. Those with power easily convince themselves that they do not need to understand their adversaries. Those without power know they cannot afford not to understand.[1]

A circular three-step form of logic offered comfort to Defense bureaucrats. Superior military power disposed defense planners not to take the trouble to comprehend their victims. Not knowing whom one was planning to kill made the somber prospect of using weapons much less onerous. Therefore, it was possible to think of arms superiority as the best means of achieving national security.

Also contributing to the atmosphere of intelligence work was the stress given to security clearances. Every analyst was required to have a security clearance and with a clearance was granted access to documents bearing security classifications up through Top Secret. Clearance usually required a six- to twelve-month probe of an applicant's past—where he had lived and worked, whom he knew, and organizations he had joined. I can recall how we criticized the clearance process, pointing out how subjective the process was because of the weight given to impressions of neighbors and casual acquaintances. Despite the many critical comments about clearances, I also had the impression that being cleared had its rewards. These were personal and had to do with being confronted with a screening process, passing a test, and then enjoying final acceptance. Being cleared represented a flattering experience sharpened by the quality of selectivity, not unlike the feeling accompanying acceptance by a fraternity or country club. You knew you were chosen. Being included confirmed that you had been found worthy by those unseen and unnamed officials somewhere in the upper reaches of the bureaucracy who managed America's security needs. It was a perverse gratification in a way—to feel rewarded simply for things one refrained from doing in the past—but most analysts quietly savored the fact that someone had considered them fit to share vital national secrets in the cause of security.

Among those finally cleared for work at Defense there were some upon whom was bestowed a higher, more selective, *special* clearance. Special clearance meant that one was granted access to unique intelligence acquired by means of highly secret techniques, such as electronic sensors used to intercept another nation's official communications or specially trained deep-cover agents in high places. When I was "chosen" for a special clearance, my immediate feeling was one of achievement and pleasure. I also remember the earlier feeling when I was not cleared for special intelligence and how important it seemed to me to be one of the three or four who were cleared among the twenty or so analysts in the Political and Economics Section. With subdued envy I would watch those chosen few leave our office several times a day to check the "take" in the "back room," the guarded, windowless cinderblock cubicle filled with combination safes. These special people would periodically read over my work to see if some fact or point of emphasis should be altered on the basis of what they were privileged to see and I was not. Intelligence community decorum made it inappropriate to question any changes made by this select few. One simply exhibited a silent respect for superior knowledge.

Thinking back on DOD security practices, I realize that levels of clearance represent just another dimension of information fragmentation. When I was denied access to special information I felt that I was not as fully informed as others and, because of this, I was not as fully a part of, or as responsible for, the ongoing work. If nuclear weapons were being assigned to a section of Kiev or Kharkov, I imagined that someone else was more responsible than I.

Along with Civil Service grade and job experience, special

intelligence clearances also helped establish a hierarchy within the office. Hierarchical relationships, wherever they exist, create a distraction of their own by causing one to think about where one stands in relation to others. Within the intelligence community, not everyone had the special clearance and, largely because of this fact, one came to want it. If this sign of more complete acceptance was not extended, one wondered why. Yet there was no way to determine why, nor was there any way to correct the situation. Doubts and hopes were generated which distracted attention from the substance of one's work. A preoccupation with the structure, process, and mechanics of day-to-day existence was encouraged by the atmosphere of the Department of Defense, and one quickly became absorbed by these concerns. What was done with the end product of work assumed a secondary importance.

If, on the other hand, a moment arose when one's thoughts happened to fasten on the human consequences of developing and using arms, there was consolation to be found in the Defense environment. The unsavory aspects of such ruminations were blunted by the reminder that America's victims deserved their fate and that it was the victims who were responsible for bringing a nuclear holocaust down on their own heads. Describing the Soviet leadership as evil, corrupt, immoral, sadistic, power-mad, and inhuman—plus being communists—provided at least a partial justification for their elimination. Vilifying the enemy, describing him in demeaning terms, is a longstanding government practice intended to legitimize the killing of others. In World War II, the enemies were Nazi pigs, and yellow-bellied Japs. During the Cold War referring to communists as Red Fascists helped to link them with legitimate victims of World War II. Later, in the Vietnam war, the North Vietnamese were seen as aggressive communists and were therefore evil. Killing them was further facilitated by depicting them as "slants" and "gooks." Since gooks were only half human, their eradication was "no big deal." Besides, if the Vietnamese were seen as caring less than Americans about this temporal life, if they didn't mind dying all that much, killing them became a less traumatic experience.

Finally, the language of the Defense world deserves attention. As America emerged in the 1950s as a world power committed to the use of military capabilities for national security, a variety of new words became part of the language of the foreign affairs bureaucracy. Beyond its usual function of facilitating communication, language in Defense, and in the intelligence community in general, helped to obscure the reality of what the work was all about—to distract attention from the homicidal reality and give a brighter hue to the ominous. Presumably certain words and expressions "took hold" because civil servants felt comfortable with them. Certain words helped link Defense work with familiar and positive experiences of each individual's past and thereby reinforce the innocuous quality of ongoing projects. Some examples of Defense language can help clarify these observations.

Changing the name of the War Department to the Defense Department, Strike Command to Readiness Command, and the Air Force's use of the maxim "peace is our profession" are examples of this. Impressions of the benign were strengthened by the careful construction of acronyms, such as PAL (Permissive Action Link), an electronically controlled DOD system of interconnected locks used to prevent the unauthorized launching of an intercontinental ballistic missile.

The vocabulary of Defense, to the extent that phrases such as "power vacuum" and "power equilibrium" could be used, had the ring of respected and predictable laws of the physical sciences that had nothing to do with such things as war and annihilation. Weapons were called military "hard-ware," thereby evoking impressions of something familiar, useful, and available in a neighborhood store. I recall the time in the late 1950s when the term "baby H-bomb" was commonly used in referring to low yield, small tactical nuclear weapons suitable for use in limited wars. This image of the lovable "baby" bomb helped to make a typical question in war planning such as "should we deliver ten or fifteen baby nukes on the Irkutsk Party headquarters?" seem like an innocent inquiry. Adding further to the impression that weapons were part of warm household relations was a 1968 Air Force *Fact Sheet* statement that described the Minuteman III missiles as "... the newest member of the ICBM family." The practice of referring to nuclear weapons by terms conventionally used to suggest everyday human experiences was evident with America's first use of atomic bombs in Japan—the Hiroshima bomb was named "Little Boy" and it was the weight of "Fat Man" that fell on Nagasaki.

As America's involvement in the Vietnam war grew deeper, the Defense vocabulary expanded and displayed an even greater imaginative and anaesthetizing flair. Bombing raids became "surgical strikes" and the forced movement and impounding of Vietnamese citizens were part of America's "pacification program"—terms suggesting images of the hospital operating room or a Quaker meeting. The enemy was not killed, but, instead, was "taken out," "wasted," or "blown away" as a consequence of "executive action" or a "protective reaction" foray. A military ground offensive was termed "aggressive defense" and spraying an area with machine-gun fire was nothing more than "reconnaissance by fire." James C. Thompson, sensitive to the contribution of bureaucratic jargon to the development of professional callousness, wrote:

> In Washington the semantics of the military muted the reality of war for the civilian policy-makers. In quiet, air-conditioned, thick-carpeted rooms, such terms as "systematic pressure," "armed reconnaissance," "targets of opportunity," and even "body count" seemed to breed a sort of games-theory detachment. Most memorable to me was a moment in the late 1964 target planning when the question under discussion was how heavy our bombing should be, and how extensive our strafing. . . . An Assistant Secretary of State resolved the point in the following words: "It seems to me that our orchestration should be mainly violins, but with periodic touches of brass."[3]

Americans are no longer fighting in Vietnam but the use of language for political purposes continues. Recent examples are the efforts by Defense planners to make the controversial neutron bomb, a small nuclear warhead (or nuclear "device") that produces twice the radiation of ordinary nuclear bombs, seem both appealing and palatable by referring to it as a "radiation enhancement weapon." Since the neutron bomb is designed to kill people while sparing buildings, some prefer to suggest a certain kitchen-cosiness by calling it the "cookie cutter."

I have been back to Washington a number of times to talk with old friends. Each time I visit the Pentagon or wait in the visitor's lobby at CIA headquarters in Langley, Virginia (where the grounds are called "the campus"), I catch myself staring at the men and women who pass by. I overhear snatches of conversations and am struck by the amount of laughter. It's all very much as I remember it—people whose speech and behavior suggest their sociability, but also their strong conviction that they are doing what needs to be done and it is therefore right. Nothing in the air seems sinister or hints of guilt. There is still the working atmosphere of a bank or insurance company.

In her book *Eichmann in Jerusalem*, Hannah Arendt analyzes why few Nazis or Germans were able to express a sense of guilt for the monstrous crimes they committed in the final solution to the Jewish question. Arendt's explanation was that the Nazi bureaucracy provided mechanisms for establishing distance between the individual and the reality of genocide. It was important for those who did the actual killing to know that they were not responsible for the planning. And those who planned never had to kill. The Nazi state was administered by ordinary men and women performing routine acts no one of which seemed, in itself, unacceptably sinister. This aspect of the holocaust is suggested by Arendt's statement that her study of Adolf Eichmann is a "report on the *banality* of evil."

What I look for when I return to Washington and talk to former colleagues is the reassurance that things have changed. It does seem that the tensions of the Cold War have lessened. Public statements coming from the highest level of government indicate that this is the case. The American-Soviet dialogue is less shrill. But within the heart of the bureaucracy, among the career civil servants of ten or twenty years, there is a holding back from the risks of detente and I wonder if things have really changed. I fear that my memories of the Air Targets Division are more relevant than I wish to believe.

My memories of my experiences in the intelligence community would become less relevant if analysts today were able to stand back from their day-to-day activities and begin to examine the implications of their work with more objectivity. Thought can sensitize men and women to the implications of their actions and this could impose new inhibitions on the behavior of the foreign affairs bureacracy. One wonders:

> . . . could the activity of thinking as such, the habit of examining whatever happens to come to pass or to attract attention, regardless of results and specific content, could this activity be among the conditions that make men abstain from evil-doing or even actually "condition" them against it.[3]

There are, as I have indicated, forces within the system that work against such self-examination but the tentative move toward a policy of detente offers a setting within which this could begin to happen. Referring once again to Arendt, to the extent that critical self-examination does not occur, the individuals comprising the bureaucracy are abandoning a human undertaking which she considers to be of the highest value, the activity of thinking. Many of the tragedies of the past are attributable less to the evil or stupidity of man than to his thoughtlessness.

Notes

1. Richard J. Barnet, *Roots of War* (Harmondsworth and Baltimore: Penguin Books, 1973), p. 60.
2. James C. Thompson, Jr., "How Could Vietnam Happen? An Autopsy," in Stephen L. Spiegel, ed., *At Issue* (New York: St. Martin's Press, 1977), p. 384.
3. Quoted by Richard J. Bernstein in a review of Hannah Arendt's *The Life of the Mind*, *New York Times Book Review*, May 28, 1978, p. 1.

PART III Disarmament and Peace

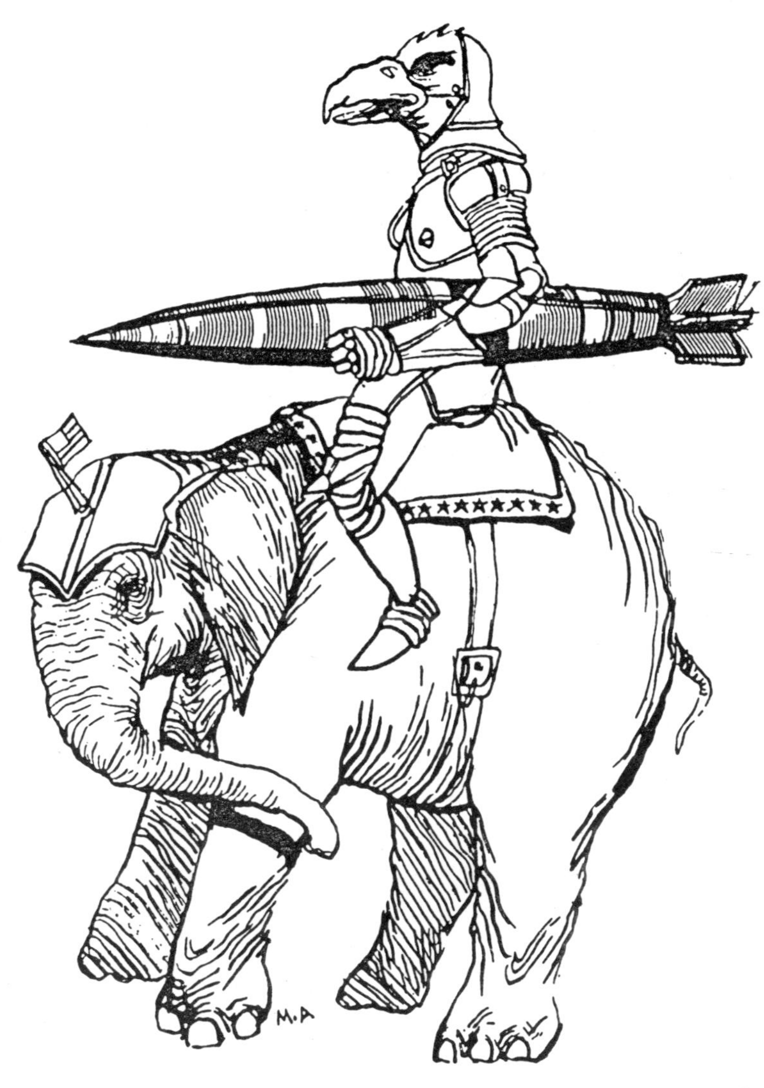

8
Appeal for European Nuclear Disarmament

Launched on April 28, 1980

We are entering the most dangerous decade in human history. A third world war is merely possible, but increasingly likely. Economic and social difficulties in advanced industrial countries, crisis, militarism, and war in the third world compound the political tensions that fuel a demented arms race. In Europe, the main geographical state for the East-West confrontation, new generations of even more deadly nuclear weapons are appearing.

For at least twenty-five years, the forces of both the North Atlantic and the Warsaw alliance have each had sufficient nuclear weapons to annihilate their opponents, and at the same time to endanger the very basis of civilized life. But with each passing year, competition in nuclear armaments has multiplied their numbers, increasing the probability of some devastating accident or miscalculation.

As each side tries to prove its readiness to use nuclear weapons, in order to prevent their use by the other side, new, more "usable" nuclear weapons are designed and the idea of "limited" nuclear war is made to sound more and more plausible. So much so that this paradoxical process can logically only lead to the actual use of nuclear weapons.

Neither of the major powers is now in any moral position to influence smaller countries to forgo the acquisition of nuclear armament. The increasing spread of nuclear reactors and the growth of the industry that installs them, reinforce the likelihood of world wide proliferation of nuclear weapons, thereby multiplying the risks of nuclear exchanges.

Over the years, public opinion has pressed for nuclear disarmament and detente between the contending military blocs. This pressure has failed. An increasing proportion of world resources is expended on weapons, even though mutual extermination is already amply guaranteed. This economic burden, in both East and West, contributes to growing social and political strain, setting in motion a vicious circle in which the arms race feeds upon the instability of the world economy and vice versa: a deathly dialectic.

We are now in great danger. Generations have been born beneath the shadow of nuclear war, and have become habituated to the threat. Concern has given way to apathy. Meanwhile, in a world living always under menace, fear extends through both halves of the European continent. The powers of the military and of internal security forces are enlarged, limitations are placed upon free exchanges of ideas and between persons, and civil rights of independent-minded individuals are threatened, in the West as well as the East.

We do not wish to apportion guilt between the political and military leaders of East and West. Guilt lies squarely upon both parties. Both parties have adopted menacing postures and committed aggressive actions in different parts of the world.

The remedy lies in our own hands. We must act together to free the entire territory of Europe, from Poland to Portugal, from nuclear weapons, air and submarine bases, and from all institutions engaged in research into or manufacture of nuclear weapons. We ask the two superpowers to withdraw all nuclear weapons from European territory. In particular, we ask the Soviet Union to halt production of SS-20 medium-range missiles and we ask the United States not to implement the decision to develop cruise missiles and Pershing II missiles for deployment in Western Europe. We also urge the ratification of the SALT II agreement, as a necessary step toward the renewal of effective negotiations on general and complete disarmament.

At the same time, we must defend and extend the right of all citizens, East or West, to take part in this common movement and to engage in every kind of exchange.

We appeal to our friends in Europe, of every faith and persuasion, to consider urgently the ways in which we can work together for these common objectives. We envisage a European-wide campaign, in which every kind of exchange takes place; in which representatives of different nations and opinions confer and coordinate their activities; and in which less formal exchanges, between universities, churches, women's organizations, trade unions, youth organizations, professional groups, and individuals, take place with the object of promoting a common object: to free all of Europe from nuclear weapons.

We must commence to act as if a united, neutral, and pacific Europe already exits. We must learn to be loyal, not to "East" or "West," but to each other, and we must disregard the prohibitions and limitations imposed by any national state.

It will be the responsibility of the people of each nation to agitate for the expulsion of nuclear weapons and bases from European soil and territorial waters, and to decide upon its own means and strategy, concerning its own territory. These will differ from one country to another, and we do not suggest that any single strategy should be imposed. But this must be part of a transcontinental movement in which every kind of exchange takes place.

We must resist any attempt by the statesmen of East or West to manipulate this movement to their own advantage. We offer no advantage to either NATO or the Warsaw alliance. Our objectives must be to free Europe from confrontation, to enforce detente between the United States and the Soviet Union, and, ultimately, to dissolve both great power alliances.

In appealing to fellow-Europeans, we are not turning our backs on the world. In working for the peace of Europe we are working for peace of the world. Twice in this century Europe has disgraced its claims to civilization by engendering world war. This time we must repay our debts to the world by engendering peace.

This appeal will achieve nothing if it is not supported by determined and inventive action, to win more people to support it. We need to mount an irresistible pressure for a Europe free of nuclear weapons.

We do not wish to impose any uniformity on the movement nor to preempt the consultations and decisions of those many organizations already exercising their influence for disarmament and peace. But the situation is urgent. The dangers steadily advance. We invite your support for this common objective, and we shall welcome both your help and advice.

9
By What Right?
W. H. Ferry

PEACE SUNDAY SERMON: April 13, 1980
Jefferson Unitarian Church, Golden, Colorado

Multiply by ten the combined atrocities of Attila the Hun, Tamburlaine, Genghis Khan, the barbarities of the Dark Ages, and Adolf Hitler—and you will not begin to match the crime against mankind that we Americans are plotting.

Hitler saw to the slaughter of six to seven million Jews, gypsies, Poles, and Russians. All were innocent of any offense. Hitler's Final Solution, until now the metaphor of unimaginable cruelty and brutality, resulted only in mountains of skeletons, rivers of blood, tons of human cinders. Thus he became history's archcriminal.

We Americans are good people. Yet we are preparing to commit the most hideous crime in the annals of mankind.

Where Hitler murdered millions, we are ready to annihilate hundreds of millions. Where he despoiled thousands of acres of precious earth, we shall render sterile and useless vast areas of continents. Where he bombed out dozens of cathedrals, libraries, schools, and hospitals, we shall at a stroke do away with entire civilizations—including our own.

Only the most crazed advocates of preparation for thermonuclear war argue that such a war will end with winners and losers. There is a hint of divine retribution in this arrangement—that the archcriminals of all history should perish by their own devices. For make no mistake about it, we are the archcriminals.

We are ready for thermonuclear war and every day we are feverishly getting more ready. Let no one suppose that we are incapable of it: we are the only nation that has ever unleashed atomic bombs against an adversary. We have been considering atomic warfare in one place or another ever since: Korea, China, Cuba, Laos, Berlin, and Vietnam. We came within a few minutes of launching a thermonuclear war in 1962. President Kennedy decided that he would press the button if a Russian freighter crossed a certain line in the Atlantic en route to Cuba. The President knew full well what he was about. He knew that he was about to ignite history's greatest cataclysm. But somehow—I shall never be able to imagine why—he was convinced that the situation called for it. American planes were circling in readiness to take off to Russian targets; crews in bomb silos across the country awaited sleeplessly the order to insert the keys that would send hundreds of ICBMs on their way. Kennedy knew we were doomed the moment he pressed the button. He knew also that there was no way in which he could defend us from extinction. Yet he thought he had no other option, and his finger was flickering above the button when word came, thirteen minutes before deadline, that the freighter had turned back. We were that close—less than a quarter of an hour—to the extinction of our world.

There is one significant difference between Germany in the thirties and forties and the United States in 1980. To this day, the "ordinary Germans" alive in the Hitler years protest that they did not know about the gas ovens, the slavery, and the starvation that were essential components of the Final Solution. They were not, they assert, co-conspirators in such infamy because Hitler was careful not to publicize it.

We, however, are active co-conspirators in plans for extermination of tens of millions. We rejoice to learn of advances in the exotica of annihilation. The American budget for warmaking is virtually sacrosanct. The American budget for the enhancement of life—for health, education, welfare, transport—is made to give way when the Department of War demands more submarines, bombs, deployment forces, cruise missiles, and laser guns. Whatever the military can dream up that promises more effective ways of massacring and maiming human beings is voted for with enthusiasm by our representatives in Washington. They would not vote that way unless a great majority of us wanted them to. A substantial minority disagrees with these policies but does nothing. A tiny minority protests passionately but is not heard. We are told that these criminal proceedings are "reality." Our leaders would not threaten to strike first with thermonuclear weapons unless Americans wanted them to.

At the heart of this monstrous folly there is, I believe, a religious vision. It is the vision of a secular religion, to be sure, yet one unthinkingly embraced by more Americans than accept the conventional religions of the land.

The central doctrine of this religion is Manifest Destiny. The first official appearance of this idea occurred in 1846, when a Massachusetts Congressman declared "the right of our manifest destiny to spread over this whole continent."

This Manifest Destiny proved its worth in remarkably few years.

But the idea did not subside after we conquered the wilderness. It was assimilated into the American ethos, and has now taken on world-encompassing dimensions. We now believe that it is Manifest Destiny that we be pre-eminent on the globe. We have come to consider our right—our destiny in the world—to be first, to be most influential, to have our own way in all important matters, to assert universal validity for our democratic, social, and economic credos.

And since the continent of the United States has not been attacked in more than 150 years, but instead has flowered, we have taken this a a mark of special approval of Manifest Destiny—when it is only a mark of geographical good luck. We are here below, the doctrine appears to say, to lead the world in all ways. We were always to be the country of happy endings.

Belief in Manifest Destiny is burned into every American from childhood on. One witnesses the faith at work in small and large ways. Here are the [1980 Olympic] Lake Placid crowds sticking up their forefingers and chanting, "We're Number One!" when the American hockey team wins. We hear it in the assertion that the Soviets are threatening "our oil" in the Middle East. President Carter said in his State of the Union address, "I am determined that the U.S. will remain the strongest of all nations." Manifest Destiny is the yeast steadily working in the debate over Iran and Afghanistan.

Nevertheless, on Peace Sunday 1980, this religion is clearly in distress. Vietnam, Watergate, and OPEC harshly dented our peerlessness. America seems thwarted everywhere. Our economy is out of gear and slipping backward. Upstart nations challenge our dignity and decide not to go our way. Third world countries don't care to become our clients. We begin to put up tariff barriers against micro-electronics, television sets, automobiles, and other things which Manifest Destiny said were ours without rival. We who gloried in invulnerability discover we are vulnerable on many sides.

Here, in the widespread rejection of America's leadership of the planet, can be seen, I believe, the source of the frustration, confusion, cynicism, and general malaise that are the prevailing temper. Our secular religion is failing us. The vision of a forever triumphant United States of America is chipped and fading.

But there is still one right which we cannot be denied. It is the right to blow up the world—or a large part of it—and degrade civilization. So we come to the most important question of all: *Quo warranto?* By what authority do we come to have this right? Only if we think God's right name is Satan can we believe it is conferred by any heavenly authority. When President Kennedy was poised to start thermonuclear war, his brother the attorney general asked him to consider whether the American government or any government had the moral right to initiate thermonuclear war. The President said he had no time to consider theories. He said that the country's manhood demanded what he was about to do, though he knew that there would be little left of our country or its manhood when he did.

We simply have no right in this matter. Twenty years ago, I heard an Air Force general declare that we had a moral right and obligation to use thermonuclear weapons. I have heard a few such declarations since, but with no supporting argument. What I have heard in superabundance concerns our capability for limitless destruction if we feel called upon to use it. But nowhere have I heard a single moral justification for our preparations for thermonuclear war. Nevertheless, it is certain that at this very moment, and also in celebration of Peace Sunday 1980, a good many sermons are being preached on the wickedness of our adversaries and the necessity to remain armed to the teeth and beyond.

Some wise men think we have already passed the invisible line and are being remorselessly crowded by technology and wornout ideas of power and leadership into war. I agree. The chances of averting war are in my opinion about one in a hundred. Optimists think that talking about impending doom is disloyal and hopeless. It is not disloyal to try to save the nation from fatal error. I often despair as I see the tides of war rising, but I am not despairing. My hope is that some argument or some event short of nuclear war will bring Americans to their senses, and that a radical redirection of national policy will result.

The fundamental problem is that the nuclear physicists have summarily thrust us into a completely changed world. Everything is new. The rules of the game must be drastically revised. Yet, as Einstein said, everything has changed except the way we think.

What has changed most is that great nations can no longer afford the luxury of enemies. Russia is our toughest adversary, but it is not our enemy. Our mortal enemy is war, war itself. Unless we learn this lesson promptly and thoroughly, thermonuclear war is a certainty. We have come close too often to have the slightest confidence that it cannot happen.

I conclude with some speculations about an as-yet-unborn technology that might save the world from the ultimate horror.

Technology means an assembly of ways and means to reach a desired end. The desired end is peace and the as-yet-unexplored technology is that of nonviolence. This subject has seldom been considered by our leaders except in the most perfunctory ways, and has been left to do-gooders and pacifists. But now there is no choice except to discover the technology of nonviolence and put it to work. It is frighteningly evident that no major industrial nation can any longer further its aims by violence. Consider, by way of current example, the hapless hostages in Teheran and the fragile oil fields of the Persian Gulf. If violence no longer can be the method of resolving arguments between great powers, nonviolence has to be the answer. Though this seems self-evident, it is surely not evident to anyone in Washington. Candidates are taking loyalty oaths to greater and greater war budgets all over the country for more and more weaponry, almost never being asked the central question: By what right?

The discovery and practice of nonviolence is the first order of everybody's business today, especially Washington's business. Of what might this new technology consist? This is terra incognita for all of us. It is really to think about the unthinkable, for no such machinery has ever been considered. It will surely include a complexity of institutions not yet known, and a remaking of international organs already in place—the United Nations and its related agencies, for example. If it is argued that these organizations have not proved their effectuality, the answer has to be that they have never been given a proper chance by the major powers. Now there is no choice. It is either thermonuclear disaster or a nonviolent alternative.

The UN and a host of other international arrangements yet to be invented must be given the responsibility for gradually bringing the world back from the nuclear precipice. The late Grenville Clark contributed many useful directions in his book *World Peace through World Law*. Putting together the machinery for so unprecedented an assignment will be a massive, but not impossible, task. If we were to devote the brains, money, and energy that yearly go into preparations for war into figuring out how the great nations can get along together without war, we would have a good chance of averting universal destruction.

A governance of nonviolence will stress cooperation and de-emphasize competition. Areas of great need will jostle for the attention they are not now getting—the development of renewable energy sources like wave and solar power, the recovery of depleted farmlands and reforestation of deserts, and provision of food and health care. This is not a mere litany of pressing problems, but a catalogue of the disparities that every day divide the world into more roiling factions.

Most of our preconceptions of ourselves, of our adversaries, and much of our sovereignty would disappear under a regime of nonviolence. Other countries would similarly have to abandon cherished attitudes. The resulting edifice would be monumentally bureaucratic, though surely no more bureaucratic than the trillion-dollar-a-year bureaucracies now running the international arms competition. But I cannot think of any other effective substitute for nuclear war. For better or worse, it is a real moral equivalent to modern war.

Devising a nonviolent structure to replace the machines of archcriminality is the supreme challenge of our time. As things stand, the great likelihood is that we shall fail to meet it. But we must try.

I close with Deuteronomy:

> I have set before you life and death, blessing and cursing: therefore choose life, that both thou and thy seed may live.

10
Disarmament: The Armament Process in Reverse
Mary Kaldor

Stopping cruise missiles is not just a matter of convincing the politicians. Time and time again, the statesmen of the world have met together in international fora and expressed lofty and commendable ambitions for peace and disarmament. Yet hardly anything of practical value has ever been achieved. New and more deadly kinds of weapons continue to be acquired; war and militarism continue to characterize international relations. It appears as though disarmament, which is viewed as an international act of will, is quite unrelated to armament, which is a national process involving people, money, and institutions deeply embedded in the fabric of our society.

If the campaign for European nuclear disarmament is to succeed, we need to see it, not just as a campaign to change the political will of Europeans—important as that is—but, more profoundly, as the first step in a process which reverses the process of armament. The aim would be to undermine the ideas and institutions which foster the arms race, to rechannel the energies which are currently devoted to militarization into other new directions, and create, so to speak, a vested interest in socially productive as opposed to destructive ends. The act of will that is currently thought of as disarmament would present the final blow to a crumbling military-industrial edifice, the last and perhaps least act in a series of events which totally transforms the current political, social, and economic environment of armaments.

Every armament process has its time and place. The culture which invented the stirrup was quite different from the one which developed the gun. The capitalist armament process and what is more or less its mirror image in the centrally planned economies has its own unique properties. This essay is an attempt to sketch out these properties and to see what they imply for disarmament.

The Armament Process

Modern armed forces both East and West are dominated by armaments: what one might call the fixed capital of warfare. In countries like the United States, Britain, or France which are major arms producers, the procurement of arms accounts for about half the military budget and the same is probably true of the Soviet Union. Moreover, the procurement budget is dominated by a few major weapon systems, i.e. warships, aircraft, or armored fighting vehicles, that combine a weapons platform, a weapon (gun, missile, torpedo), and the means of command and communication. In the U.S., for example, the Trident submarine, the new nuclear-powered aircraft carrier, and a handful of guided missile destroyers and frigates, account for about two-thirds of the naval procurement budget. The MX missile, together with the latest Air Force fighters F-15 and F-16, is equally important to the Air Force, while the new XM-1 battle tank accounts for a major share of the Army budget. The same is true in Britain and France. In Britain, the Multi-Role Combat Aircraft (MRCA) Tornado accounts for around 40 percent of the Royal Air Force (RAF) budget: the three antisumbarine warfare cruisers, which are actually small aircraft carriers with their associated escort and support ships, probably account for a fifth to a quarter of the British naval procurement budget.

The concept of the weapon system can be said to have originated in the first prolonged period of high peace-time military spending, namely the Anglo-German naval arms race before World War I. Socially, the rise of the concept may be likened to the replacement of tools by machines. Whereas formerly the weapon was the instrument of man, now it appears that man is the instrument of the weapon system. A weapon system demands a rigid technical division of labor that admits little variation in the social organization of the men who operate it.

Equally, the weapon system, like the machine, guarantees the existence of certain types of industry for its manufacture.

Although in almost all industrialized countries armed forces have been pruned and centralized since the war, they remain functionally organized around the weapon system. Hence, navies are organized by ship, with groups of ships organized hierarchically into task forces. At the apex of the American surface Navy is the aircraft carrier, requiring destroyers and a submarine or two for protection, aircraft to fly from its deck, and supply ships of various kinds for replenishment. The bomber and the battle tank have a similar role in the Air Force and Army. The Air Force is divided into bomber, fighter, and transport commands. The Army is made up of armor, artillery, parachute, or infantry units, but the armored units are the core of the combined arms team. The functional autonomy of individual services or military units is achieved through independent strategies associated with particular weapon systems. This would explain why strategic bombing is so central to the U.S. Air Force or why the British Navy remains committed to an ocean-going role associated with carriers long after the abandonment of overseas commitments. In the Soviet Union, for example, land-based medium- and long-range ballistic missiles constitute the basis for a separate service, the Strategic Rocket Forces.

The strategic doctrine of any particular military unit can thus be expressed in the military specifications for a particular weapon system; that is to say, in a set of specified performance characteristics. These, in turn, are the product of the manufacturing capabilities of a particular enterprise. Hence, the weapon system is the link between the enterprise and military unit, the embodiment of a persistent military-industrial alliance.

Western Countries

In the West, the design, development, and production of weapon systems is, by and large, undertaken by a few large companies known as prime contractors. In general, the prime contractors are the manufacturers of weapon platforms-aircraft, shipbuilding, automobile, or engineering companies; they assemble the complete weapon system, subcontracting subsystems, like the weapons, the engine, and the electronics, and components in such a way as to create an independent network of big and small companies. The prime contractors tend to specialize in particular types of weapon systems: Boeing and Rockwell are bomber enterprises; Dassault in France and British Aerospace make combat aircraft, Westland Aircraft makes helicopters; Electric Boat (now part of General Dynamics) and Vickers Barrow (now part of British Shipbuilders) make submarines.

The prime contractors are among the world's largest companies. Since World War II, between forty and fifty U.S. companies have regularly appeared on Fortune's list of the top 100 companies and on the Pentagon's list of the 100 companies receiving the highest prime contract awards. Their stability, in both America and Europe, has been widely noted. Firms have been amalgamated or nationalized, especially in Europe, but basically there has been very little rationalization. The plants which receive prime contracts from major weapon systems have remained much the same, under different names, for thirty years. There has been more specialization and an increased amount of subcontract work both among the prime contractors and the outside firms, especially in the electronics industry. Also, the composition of subcontractors has varied enormously along with changes in technology and the business cycle—thousands of subcontractors regularly go bankrupt during recession. But among the prime contractors, there have been few, if any, actual closures in the postwar period. Equally, there have been no new entries into the major weapons markets. The consequence is that a specific mix of skills and physical equipment, and a specific set of relationships with customers (the military units) and suppliers (the subcontractors), has been preserved—in effect, a specific manufacturing experience which corresponds to a specific military experience.

Although several of the big arms manufacturers in Europe

have been nationalized, the prime contractors operate according to the principles of private enterprise. They need to maintain their independent viability and this, in practice, means the constant search to find new markets, and to maintain or increase profit margins. Frequently, U.S. defense contractors testify to the intensity of competition—"a continuous life and death struggle to obtain defense contracts."[1] The fact that this competition takes a technological rather than price form has to do with the peculiarity of the arms market—the government as sole customer. Firms put more emphasis on the ability to offer improvements to the product than on the ability to reduce the cost of production—in the end, the government pays.

In essence, then, the Western armament process is characterized by a contradictory combination of stability and competition. The armament sector could be described as a semiplanned sector. On the supply side, it is monopolistic, i.e., has one customer, and on the demand side, it is oligopolistic, i.e., has a few competitive suppliers. On the demand side can be found all the complex mathematical techniques that are typical of a centrally planned system and, on the supply side, can be found the preoccupation with profit margins, contracts, markets, etc., that are the hallmark of private enterprise. Inevitably, these two aspects are reflected in the final product, the weapon system.

In a planned system, unless there is some overriding objective like victory in war, a plan tends to reflect the objectives of the institutions that participate in the plan, to express the various interests of the plan's constituencies. In other words, consumer sovereignty in a planned system is rare because the people who draw up the plan are strongly influenced by the people who carry it out. In peace-time, without external stimulus of war, decisions about what is "needed" for defense tend to be taken by the "experts," generally those who have gained their formative experience in the armament sector. Such decisions tend to be "autistic"—the outcome of the institutional interests of user and producers. Because the Soviet Union has always lagged behind the United States technologically, the need for any particular weapon system has been assessed against an idea of what the Soviet Union might possess when the weapon system eventually, five or ten years later, enters operational service. This idea owes more to the subjective imagination of the designers than to any hard knowledge about what is happening in the Soviet Union.

The designers are the products of their military-industrial environment. The *competition* between prime contractors propels technology forward as each corporation attempts to offer something better than its competitor and something the military, at least in the U.S. can justify to Congress. And yet this technology dynamism is confined within certain limits—limits that are defined by the *stability* of military and industrial institutions, a stability which is guaranteed by the planning system. The result is an entirely introverted form of technological change, something which has been described as "trend" or "routinized" innovation.[2]

Trend innovation has found its characteristic form in the follow-on imperative.[3] The form and function of the weapon system have not changed much since 1945. Technical change has largely consisted of improvements to a given set of performance characteristics. Submarines are faster, quieter, bigger, and have longer ranges. Aircraft have greater speed, more powerful thrust, and bigger payloads. All weapon systems have more destructive weapons, particularly missiles, and greatly improved capabilities for communication, navigation, detection, identification, and weapon guidance. Each contractor has designed, developed, and produced one weapon system after another, each representing an incremental improvement on the last. For Boeing, the Minuteman Intercontinental Ballistic Missile followed the B-52 strategic bomber, which followed the B-47. Between 1952 and 1979, Newport News's yards have produced no fewer than nine aircraft carriers, each bigger, and better than the last, bow to stern in the best follow-on tradition. And in Europe, Dassault has produced the famous series of Mirage fighters; Westland has manufactured one helicopter after another; and the submarine which the British propose to construct in order to launch the American Trident missile is likely to continue a tradition at Vickers Barrow that goes back, with interruptions, as far as the 1890s.

The idea that each weapon system must have a follow-on has become self-perpetuating. Each corporation has a planning group whose sole function is to choose suitable successors for weapons currently being produced and which maintain close contact with consorts in the military. The planning procedure is supposed to be an exercise in prediction. In actual fact, because of the intimate relationship with the armed services it becomes a self-fulfilling prophecy. Even so the system has not worked smoothly, and it has taken periodic industrial crisis to initiate the full range of new projects. Such was the crisis which followed the winding down of the Vietnam war in the early 1970s. The pressure on the defense budget which we are now witnessing is partly the result of projects initiated during that period.

Each follow-on is bigger and "better" than its predecessor. As weapon systems approach the limits of technology, they become increasingly complex and costly. It becomes harder and harder to achieve incremental improvements to a given set of performance characteristics. Although the basic technology of the weapon platform may not have changed much, such improvements have often entailed the incorporation of very advanced technology, e.g., radical electronic innovations such as microprocessors, or nuclear power for submarines, and this has greatly increased the complexity of the weapon system as a whole. And as the weapon system becomes more complex, more labor and materials are required for development and production, greatly increasing the total cost.

The weapon systems of the 1970s represent what one might describe as a quantum leap in expense and grotesque elaboration. The monstrous MX missile with its ludicrous race-track system will cost somewhere from $33 billion (the official figure) to over $100 billion (an estimate made in April 1980).[4] It will involve the biggest construction program in the history of the United States. The obese Trident submarine, which is too big to get out of the channel where it was built, will cost much the same. The real cost of producing the British-German-Italian Multi-Role Combat Aircraft will be slightly greater than the *entire* production costs of the Spitfire before and during World War II. A recent U.S. General Accounting Office report concluded:

> The cost problem facing the US military is growing worse and no relief is in sight. The so-called "bow wave" of future procurement costs is growing beyond the point of reasonableness. Current procurement programs are estimated to total about $725 billion. If these costs are spread over the next ten years (a conservative projection) the annual average of $72.5 billion will be more than twice the current funding levels.[5]

Yet many people, and not just those who question the whole basis of modern strategy, are beginning to wonder whether the extra money will buy any real increase in military utility. A number of strategic writers have come to criticize the criteria for technical improvements to weapon systems.[6] Many of the indicators of military effectiveness are thought to be no longer relevant to modern warfare. For example, the development of naval aircraft and submarines has meant that speed is no longer important for surface ships. Likewise, aircraft speed is only of advantage in fighter roles. The cost, complexity, and size of modern weapon systems consequent upon the so-called improvements in performance characteristics may turn out to be a positive liability. In the hostile environment of the modern battlefield, where the accuracy and lethality of all munitions have greatly increased, size and vulnerability go hand in hand. Complexity greatly increases unreliability, reduces maneuverability and flexibility, and creates enormous logistic problems. The U.S. Air Force's First Tactical Air Wing, whose motto is "Readiness is our Profession," recently failed a test given by the Air Force's Tactical Command to see if it was ready to mobilize for a war in the Middle East. Only twenty-three of the sixty-six F-15 aircraft were "mission capable" because of engine and parts failure, lack of spares, shortages of skilled technicians, etc.—and these problems are not untypical of Western weapon systems in general. Likewise, cost is a disadvantage because of the high attrition rates of modern warfare and because budgetary limitations lead to savings on such essentials as ammunition, fuel, spares, military pay, training, etc. The huge support systems and the overburdened centralized command systems associated with the modern weapon system are very vulnerable and could be easily disrupted in a war. Indeed, the experience of war in Vietnam and the Middle East—the problems of vulnerability, logistics, communications, etc.—has called into question the whole future of the weapon system. Destructiveness and effectiveness are no longer synonymous—if they ever were.

The degeneracy of the weapon system is not without its effects on Western economy and society as a whole. As an object of use, the weapon system is the basis of military organization both within individual nations and within the alliance as a whole. It is, at once, a symbol of legitimacy and Western unity. The dominance of American weapon systems reflects the dominance of American strategic thinking and the American defense industry. The proposals for ground-launched cruise missiles could be interpreted as an attempt to reassert that domination. As the military rationale for such systems becomes more and more remote and rarified, so their usefulness in holding together, as it were, the Western alliance becomes more open to question.

As an object of production, the weapon system is part of modern industry and its development has to be understood as consequence and cause of broader industrial tendencies. In a capitalist system, the market mechanism ensures rapid technical change. As production processes are adapted to meet changing demands, the whole economic structure undergoes radical alterations. Companies, industries, sectors, and regions rise and fall according to the dictates of the market. As the product of a semiplanned sector, armaments can interrupt this process. In so far as they guarantee the stability of military-industrial institutions, of the major corporations, armaments can help to alleviate crises. But capitalist crises produce change. That same stability has the effect of freezing industrial structure and postponing change. In so far as armaments are themselves subject to the capitalist dynamic they can also drag the economy along their own technological cul de sac, passing on the degeneracy of overgrown trend innovation. In effect they can preserve and even extend industries that would otherwise have declined and at the same time fetter the emergence of new dynamic industries. This is one reason for the persistence of mechanical engineering and shipbuilding in Britain or the automobile and aircraft industries in the United States. The absorption of resources by these declining sectors, the distorting effects of armament-induced ways of thinking about technology on new as well as older industries, are among the factors which help to explain the backwardness of arms-intensive economies like Britain and the United States compared with, say, West Germany and Japan.

The Soviet Union

There is a remarkable parallel to be drawn with what happens in the Soviet Union. The armament sector in the Soviet Union could be described as the inverse of the Western armament sector. On the supply side, arms are produced by the same kinds of enterprises that characterize the centrally planned economy as a whole. Unlike those in the West, research institutes, design bureaus and production plants are organized as separate entities under the control of nine different defense ministries. The stability of these institutions, together with their suppliers, is guaranteed by the system of planning and budgeting. Unlike in the West, where competition, the pressure for technical advance, the winning or losing of contracts may lead to the amalgamation of design teams and prime contractors and to massive shifts in the composition of subcontractors, the various industrial organizations are assured of a steady flow of work. If the stability of the prime contractors slows down the process of industrial change in the West, then this same tendency for conservatism and continuity is typical of the Soviet economy as a whole.[7]

On the demand side, however, armaments are characterized by competitiveness (with the West). Armaments in the Soviet Union are privileged products; it is often said that the armament sector is the only sector in the Soviet system which enjoys consumer sovereignty, and this is evident in the priority system. The armament sector receives the best machinery and parts; it can commandeer scarce materials; defense employees earn higher incomes and obtain better nonmonetary benefits; requests and orders from the administration tend to be dealt with more quickly. Many commentators have remarked on the unusual degree to which the consumer can ensure that specifications are met and can overcome resistance to demand-induced changes. From time to time, the leadership has imposed new solutions for forcing technology in order to initiate such programs as nuclear weapons, jet engines, missiles, etc. In general, these programs were a response to developments in the West, which was always one technological step ahead of the Soviet Union.

Hence, because of the degree of consumer sovereignty, the armament sector can represent a mechanism for change in the Soviet system. This was certainly the case in the 1930s, when military competition with Germany could be said to have been the overriding objective of the Soviet planning system. It can be argued that it was through the armament sector that the economy was mobilized.[8] The armament sector continues to transmit new technology into the Soviet system; however, precisely because of the nature of the Western armaments, technologically induced change of this kind may prove distorting and not progressive.

Disarmament

The weapon system is the basis of modern military organization. It holds together the two great military alliances and divides East from West. And yet, paradoxically, the sector which produces the weapon system is also the conceptual *link* between the two societies. For it introduces an element of planning into the capitalist system; it thus helps to stave off crisis but, at the same time, slows down change. And it introduces an element of competition into the Soviet Union, inserting a mechanism for change.

In the past, the armament sector may have worked quite well in blunting some of the contradictions of each society. This is no longer true. The declining military effectiveness and growing cost of armament are gradually undermining the political weight of the superpowers and sapping their economic strength. The crisis of the armament sector has thrown up new forms of conflict and protest. New political and economic rivalries in the West, and consumer dissatisfaction, dissidence, and increased repression in the Soviet Union are all elements of a wider breakdown in the postwar international system of which the armament sector is a central part. The crisis has drawn a response from within the armament sector, as well as elsewhere, from soldiers ill-prepared for new forms of conflict (as in Vietnam), and from workers in the defense industry, concerned about employment. The new situation represents an opportunity for change. It entails the risk of war and of rearmament. But it could alternatively initiate a process of disarmament by channeling the new protests into positive directions.

Most disarmament efforts are aimed at the role of armaments as objects of use. To reverse effectively the armament process, we also need to undermine their role as objects of production. We need to campaign against cruise missiles. But we also need to change the military-industrial culture which created them.

Industrial conversion is one way of achieving this. In a sense, any form of economic development represents a continual process of conversion—of finding new products and phasing out old ones. The conversion from arms to peaceful production would be merely one aspect of this process. Different societies have different mechanisms for conversion. The capitalist economy depends on the market as a method of allocating resources. It involves anarchy, dislocation, structural unemployment, and periodic crisis. The alternative is the central planning mechanism of the socialist countries which leads to rigidity because biases in government reflect vested bureaucratic interests. It thus avoids crises but, at the same time, is much more resistant to change than is the capitalist system.

The conversion from war to peace needs to be seen *not* as the *technical* process of converting swords to ploughshares, but as a *social* process of finding a new mechanism for the allocation of resources. Mere technical conversion from war to peace could never be sufficient. In a sense, we have already experienced this in the nonmilitary products of the arms companies—the U.S. and Soviet space programs, Concorde and the TU-144, nuclear energy, various American rapid urban transit systems and environmental products. These have become what one might call quasi-weapon systems—similarly elaborate and expensive, with, in the end, similar economic consequences. Further, these products could never provide perfect substitutes for armaments since they do not command the same urgency. It would be difficult to justify increased expenditure on space or artificial hearts in times of economic recession.

Conversion needs to be seen as a way of creating a new economic system which would minimize those problems that create opportunities for conflict and the pressure for armaments. Such a system would combine the positive elements of planning with positive elements of free enterprise, instead of, as in the armament sector, the negative elements of both. The Western armament system, as we have seen, is characterized by planning on the demand side and competition on the supply side. The Western form of military technical change, the outcome of this system, is transferred to the Soviet Union through the consumer sovereignty that is the unique characteristic of the armament sector in the Soviet Union. What is needed is a system of consumer sovereignty in which the consumer is not a military establishment engaged in a competitive arms race but an ordinary person—in other words, planning, under democratic control. How is this to be achieved in practice?

A sturdy democracy originates in popular movement, even though such movements must eventually find an institutional expression. Already, trade unions in the defense industry in Britain, West Germany, the United States, Italy, and Sweden have begun to express interest in the idea of conversion. This interest has proceeded farthest in Britain, where the workers of Lucas Aerospace and Vickers have earned a worldwide reputation for their proposals and campaigns to achieve socially useful production.

The principle that underlies the Lucas Aerospace Corporate Plan,[9] the Vickers pamphlets,[10] and various proposals from workers in other companies, including Rolls-Royce ("Buns Before the Gutter"), BAC, and Parsons, is the simple but revolutionary idea that in a society where there are substantial unfilled needs it makes no sense to put people, who could be making products to fill those needs, on the dole or into arms manufacturing. Neither the market mechanism nor central planning has proved very efficient at marrying social need to available resources. The alternative is to propose products which emanate from direct contacts between producers and consumers. This is the basis of the various worker plans.

In developing their ideas, the unions found it necessary to develop links with unions in supplier industries and with consumer organizations. Partly, this was in order to establish technical and social feasibility. For example, proposals by Rolls-Royce workers for gas turbine propulsion for merchant ships turned out to be an oversophisticated, marginally useful suggestion. More importantly, it provides a more effective method of putting political pressure on management and the government. Many of the ideas clash with priorities currently established by the government, which tend to reflect existing vested interests. Hence the shop stewards proposed energy conservation equipment and alternative forms of energy based on wind and waves; yet official energy priorities stress North Sea oil, coal, and nuclear energy. They also proposed new kinds of rail vehicles or ways of revitalizing Britain's canal system; yet transport policy places the emphasis on roads rather than railways or canals. The workers have consequently joined forces with organizations like the antinuclear energy movement or Transport 2000, which lobbies against the unplanned growth of the automobile infrastructure. On more mundane levels, unions in British Leyland pressed their management to purchase a scrap metal baler, one of the ideas put forward by the Vickers Shop Stewards. Lucas Aerospace Shop Stewards at Burnley worked closely with the local council with the idea of meeting local needs. These informal alliances between producers and consumers could provide the basis for future planning agencies which would reflect a different sort of social priorities from those that currently hold sway.

Ideally, these links should be international, for there is always the risk that social criteria for resource allocation could turn out to be national, and hence divisive on a global scale. At both Vickers and Lucas Aerospace, some international links have been forged. Vickers workers have visited India (where they helped to establish a tank factory) and Iran (where they were shocked to hear of the way Chieftain tanks had been used). They have proposed various kinds of equipment for irrigation and for water purification. Lucas Aerospace workers have discussed the possibility of adapting a road/rail vehicle they have invented for use in Tanzania and Zambia with the governments of those countries.

The Lucas Aerospace workers have actually achieved some success in pressing their management to undertake the manufacture of socially useful products. For the first time, workers are inserting their own criteria, as both producers and consumers, into the choice of products. They are, in a sense, developing a new mechanism for conversion, which, if it spreads, could change the composition of power in existing institutions—local councils, regional development councils, the Industrial Manpower Commission, the Atomic Energy Commission, for example—and which could eventually be embodied in a new set of planning institutions which set priorities according to the social needs of consumers and which guarantee stable, although mobile, employment.

Any campaign for disarmament must join forces with workers in the defense industry in demanding conversion. Conversion—along with other more traditional disarmament issues—could build upon the growing fissures within the armament system and direct current frustrations toward disarmament rather than war. It could help to initiate a process of conversion which would *precede* disarmament. Conversion would thus be seen as a way of achieving disarmament rather than a thorny problem to be solved after the politicians had finally willed the reduction of armaments. Conversion would not just be a matter of turning swords into ploughshares. It would be a matter of creating a new mechanism for the wider process of economic conversion, matching the desperate needs of the modern world with resources that are either misused or not used at all. It could thus undermine the political and economic basis for armaments in advanced industrial countries and it would help to overcome the structural problems, weaknesses, and divisions of different economic systems. Hence it could help to remove the causes of war.

Notes

1. National Security Industrial Association, quoted in J. E. Fox, *Arming America: How the US Buys Weapons* (Cambridge, Mass.: Harvard University Press, 1974), p. 101.
2. See Morris Janowitz, *The Professional Soldier* (New York: Free Press, 1960).
3. See James Kurth, "Why We Buy the Weapons We Do," *Foreign Policy*, no. 11 (1973).
4. Science Supplement, *New York Times*, April 15, 1980.
5. *Impediments to Reducing the Costs of Weapons Systems*. Report to the Congress of the United States by the Comptroller General, PSAD-80-6, November 1979, p. 3.
6. See, for example, Stephen Canby, "The Alliance and Europe, Part IV, Military Doctrine and Technology," *Adelphi Papers*, no. 109 (London: IISS) Winter 1974–75.
7. See Alec Nove, *The Soviet Economic System* (London: Allen & Unwin, 1977).
8. See Julian Cooper, "Defence Production and the Soviet Economy, 1929–41," CREES Discussion Paper, Soviet Industrialization Project Series SIPS, no. 3, 1976.
9. Lucas Aerospace Combine Committee, *Corporate Plan* (1976).
10. Vickers National Combine Committee of Shop Stewards, *Building a Chieftain Tank and the Alternative Use of Resources* and *The ASW Cruiser: Alternative Work for Naval Shipbuilding Workers* (1978).

11
European Nuclear Disarmament
Ken Coates

Remember your humanity, and forget the rest. If you can do so, the way lies open to a new Paradise; if you cannot, there lies before you the risk of universal death.
Russell-Einstein Manifesto, 1955

The Most Dangerous Decade in History

At the end of April 1980, following some months of consultation and preparation, an appeal for European Nuclear Disarmament was launched at a press conference in the House of Commons and at meetings in a variety of European capital cities. (See Chapter 8 of this volume.)

Several hundred people, many of whom were prominent in their own field of work, had already endorsed this statement before its publication. They included over sixty British MPs from four different political parties and a number of peers, bishops, artists, composers, and university teachers. The press conference, which was addressed by Tony Benn, Eric Heffer, Mary Kaldor, Bruce Kent, Zhores Medvedev, Dan Smith, and Edward Thompson, launched a campaign for signatures to the appeal and by Hiroshima Day (August 6, the anniversary of the dropping of the first atomic bomb on Japan) influential support had been registered in many different countries. Writers such as Kurt Vonnegut, Olivia Manning, John Berger, Trevor Griffiths, J. B. Priestley, and Melvyn Bragg had joined with church leaders, political spokesmen, painters (Joan Miro, Vasarely, Josef Herman, David Tindle, Piero Dorazio), Nobel Prize winners, and thousands of men and women working in industry and the professions. British signatories included the composer

Peter Maxwell Davies, the doyen of cricket commentators, John Arlott, distinguished soldiers such as Sir John Glubb and Brigadier M. N. Harbottle, and trade union leaders (Moss Evans, Laurence Daly, Arthur Scargill, and many others). It was generally agreed that a European meeting was necessary, in order to work out means of developing the agitation, and in order to discuss all the various issues and problems which are in need of elaboration, over and beyond the text of the appeal.

The Bertrand Russell Foundation is working on the preparation of this conference. A small liaison committee has been established to coordinate the work in Great Britain, and various persons and groups have accepted the responsibility for coordinating action in particular fields of work. For instance, a group of parliamentarians will be appealing to their British colleagues, but also the MPs throughout Europe; academics will be writing to their own immediate circles, but also seeking international contacts; churches are being approached through Pax Christi; and an active trade union group has begun to develop.

"A Demented Arms Race . . ."

1980 began with an urgent and concerned discussion about rearmament. The Pope, in his New Year message, caught the predominant mood: "What can one say," he asked, "in the face of the gigantic and threatening military arsenals which especially at the close of 1979 have caught the attention of the world and especially of Europe, both East and West?"

War in Afghanistan; American hostages in Teheran and dramatic pile-ups in the Iranian deserts, as European-based American commandos failed to "spring" them; wars or threats of war in Southeast Asia, the Middle East, and Southern Africa: at first sight, all the world in turbulence, excepting only Europe. Yet in spite of itself Europe is at the fixed center of the arms race; and it is in Europe that many of the most fearsome weapons are deployed. What the Pope was recognizing at the opening of the decade was that conflicts in any other zone might easily spill back into the European theater, where they would then destroy our continent.

Numbers of statesmen have warned about this furious accumulation of weapons during the late seventies. It has been a persistent theme of such eminent neutral spokesmen as Olof Palme of Sweden or the late President Tito of Yugoslavia. Lord Mountbatten, in his last speech, warned that "the frightening facts about the arms race . . . show that we are rushing headlong towards a precipice."[1] Why has this "headlong rush" broken out? First, because of the worldwide division between what is nowadays called "North" and "South." In spite of United Nations initiatives, proposals for a new economic order which could assist economic development have not only not been implemented, but have been stalemated while conditions have even been aggravated by the oil crisis. Poverty was never morally acceptable, but it is no longer politically tolerable in a world which can speak to itself through transistors, while over and again in many areas starvation recurs. In others, millions remain on the verge of the merest subsistence. The third world is thus a zone of revolts, revolutions, interventions, and wars.

To avoid or win these, repressive leaders like the former Shah of Iran are willing to spend unheard of wealth on arms, and the arms trade paradoxically often takes the lead over all other exchanges, even in countries where malnutrition is endemic. At the same time, strategic considerations bring into play the superpowers, as "revolutionary" or "counter-revolutionary" supports. This produces some extraordinary alignments and confrontations, such as those between the Ethiopian military, and Somalia and Eritrea, where direct Cuban and Soviet intervention has been a crucial factor, even though the Eritreans have been engaged in one of the longest-running liberation struggles in all Africa; or such as the renewed Indochina war following the Vietnamese invasion of Cambodia, in which remnants of the former Cambodian communist government appear to have received support from the United States, even though it only came into existence in opposition to American secret bombing, which destroyed the physical livelihood of the country together with its social fabric. A variety of such direct and indirect interventions owes everything to geopolitical expediency, and nothing to the ideals invoked to justify them. Such processes help promote what specialists call the "horizontal" proliferation of nuclear weapons, to new, formerly non-nuclear states, at the same time that they add their pressure to the "vertical" proliferation between the superpowers.

Second, the emergence of China into the community of nations (if this phrase can nowadays be used without cynicism) complicates the old pattern of interplay between the blocs. Where yesterday there was a tug of war between the U.S. and the USSR, with each principal mobilizing its own team of supporters at its end of the rope, now there is a triangular contest, in which both of the old, established contestants may, in future, seek to play the China team. At the moment, the Chinese are most worried about the Russians, which means that the Russians will feel a constant need to augment their military readiness on their "second" front, while the Americans will seek to match Soviet preparedness overall, making no differentiation between the "theaters" against which the Russians see a need for defense. It should be noted that the Chinese Government still considers that war is "inevitable," although it has apparently changed its assessment of the source of the threat. (It is the more interesting, in this context, that the Chinese military budget for 1980 is the only one which is being substantially reduced, by $1.9 billion, or 8.5 percent.)

Third, while all these political cauldrons boil, the military-technical processes have their own logic, which is fearsome.

Stacked around the world at the beginning of the decade, there were a minimum of 50,000 nuclear warheads, belonging to the two main powers, whose combined explosive capacity exceeds by one million times the destructive power of the first atomic bomb which was dropped on Hiroshima. The number grows continually. This is "global overkill." Yet during the next decade, the U.S. and the USSR will be manufacturing a further 20,000 warheads, some of unimaginable force.

World military spending, the Brandt Report on North-South economic development estimated, ran two years ago at something approaching $450 billion a year or around $1.2 billion every day.[2] More recent estimates for last year show that global military expenditures have already passed $500 billion per annum or $1.3 billion each day. Recently both NATO and the Warsaw alliance both decided to increase their military spending annually over a period of time, by *real* increments of between 3 percent and 4.5 percent each year. That is to say, military outlays are inflation-proofed, so that weapons budgets will automatically swell to meet the depreciation of the currency and then again to provide an absolute increase. It is primarily for this reason that informed estimates show that the worldwide arms bill will be more than $600 billion per annum or $1.6 billion each day very early in the 1980s.

As a part of this process, new weapons are continuously being tested. At least fifty-three nuclear tests took place in 1979. South Africa may also have detonated a nuclear device. New missiles are being developed, in pursuit of the ever more lethal pin-pointing of targets or of even more final obliterative power. In 1980 the Chinese have announced tests of their new intercontinental missile, capable of hitting either Moscow or Los Angeles. The French have released news of their preparations to deploy the so-called neutron or enhanced radiation bomb, development of which had previously been held back by President Carter after a storm of adverse publicity. In the United States, the MX missile, weighing 190,000 pounds and capable of throwing ten independently targeted and highly accurate 350 kiloton (350,000 tons of TNT equivalent) warheads at Russia, each of which will be independently targeted, with high accuracy, is being developed. The R and D costs for this missile in 1981 will amount to $1.5 billion, even before production has started. This is more, as Emma Rothschild has complained,[3] than the combined research and development budgets of the U.S. Department of Labor, Education, and Transportation, taken together with the Environmental Protection Agency, the Federal Drug Administration, and the Center for Disease Control. The MX system, if it works (or for that matter even if it doesn't work), will run on its own sealed private railway, involving "the largest construction project in U.S. history."[4] It will, if completed, "comprise 200 missiles with

2,000 warheads, powerful and accurate enough to threaten the entire Soviet ICBM force of 1,400 missiles."[5] No doubt the Russians will think of some suitable response, at similar or greater expense. As things are, the United States defense budget from 1980–85 will amount to $1 trillion, and, such is the logic of the arms race, an equivalent weight of new weaponry will have to be mobilized from the other side, if the "balance" is to be maintained.

All this frenetic activity takes place at a time of severe economic crisis, with many western economies trapped in a crushing slump and quite unable to expand civilian production. Stagnant or shrinking production provides a poor basis for fierce rearmament, which nowadays often accompanies, indeed necessitates, cuts in social investment, schools, housing, and health. The price of putting the Trident system into Britain's arsenal will probably be outbreaks of rickets among our poorer children.

But military research takes priority over everything else, and the result is staggering. In the construction of warheads, finesse now passes any reasonable expectation. A Minuteman III MIRV will carry three warheads, and each warhead has an explosive power of 170,000 tons of TNT (170 kilotons or kt). A Minuteman weighs 220 pounds. The first atomic bomb ever used in action had an explosive force of 12kt, and it weighed four tons.

Miniaturization of megadeath bombs has made fine progress. So has the refinement of delivery systems. This is measured by the standard of Circular Error Probability (CEP), which is the radius of that circle centered on the target, within which it can be expected that 50 percent of warheads of a given type might fall. Heavy bombers of the Second World War, such as those which visited Hiroshima and Nagasaki, had a very large CEP indeed. The Minuteman III system expects to land half its projectiles within a 350-meter radius of target, having flown more than 8,000 miles to do it. The MX, if it goes according to plan, will have a CEP of only 100 meters. Such accuracy means that it will be perfectly possible to destroy enemy missile silos, however fortified these might be. The Russians are catching up, however. Their SS-18 and SS-19 missiles are already claimed to have CEPs of 450 meters.

If rocketry has advanced, so too has experimental aviation. The Americans have already tested Stealth, an airplane which "is virtually invisible to Soviet radar." Critics say that invisibility has been purchased at the cost of multiple crashes, since the new machines are fashioned into shapes which are decidedly unfunctional for flying, in order to elude detection. Stealth is a fighter, but plans have been leaked (in the course of the American elections, during which, apparently, votes are assumed to be attracted to the most bloodthirsty contender) for a similarly-wrought long-range bomber. Officials in the U.S. Defense Department insist that contorted shapes are only part of the mechanism which defeats radar detection: apparently new materials can be coated on to aircraft skins, to absorb radio waves. By such means, together with navigational advances, it may be hoped to secure even greater accuracy of weapon delivery.

Two questions remain. First, as Lord Zuckerman, the British Government's former chief scientific adviser, percipiently insists, what happens to the other 50 percent of warheads which fall outside the CEP? The military may not be interested in them, but other people are. Second, this remarkable triumph of technology is all leading to the point where someone has what is politely called a "first-strike capability." Both the Russians and the Americans will soon have this capability. But what does it *mean*? It clearly does *not* mean that one superpower has the capacity to eliminate the possibility of retaliation by the other, if only it gets its blow in first. What it does signify is the capacity to wreak such destruction as to reduce any possible response to an "acceptable" level of damage. This is a level which will clearly vary with the degree of megalomania in the respective national leaderships.

All informed commentators are very wary about "first strike capability" because with it the whole doctrine of mutually assured destruction (MAD) will no longer apply. With either or both superpowers approaching "first strike" potential, the calculations are all different. Yesterday we were assured, barring accidents, of safety of a bizarre and frightening kind: but now each new strengthening of the arsenals spells out with a terrifying rigor, a new, unprecedented danger. Preemptive war is now a growing possibility. It is therefore quite impossible to argue support for a doctrine of "deterrence" as if this could follow an unchanging pattern over the decades, irrespective of changes in the political balance in the world, and irrespective of the convolutions of military technology.

In fact, "deterrence" has already undergone fearsome mutations. Those within the great military machines who have understood this have frequently signalled their disquiet. "If a way out of the political dilemmas we now face is not negotiated," wrote Lord Zuckerman, "our leaders will quickly learn that there is no technical road to victory in the nuclear arms race."[6] "Wars cannot be fought with nuclear weapons," said Lord Mountbatten. "There are powerful voices around the world who still give credence to the old Roman precept—if you desire peace, prepare for war. This is absolute nuclear nonsense."[7]

Yet serious discussion of disarmament has come to an end. The SALT II agreements have not been ratified. The Treaty on the nonproliferation of nuclear weapons is breaking down, and the non-nuclear powers are convinced that all the nuclear weapon states are flouting it by refusing to reduce their nuclear arsenals. It is true that following the initiative of Chancellor Schmidt talks will open between Senator Muskie and Mr. Gromyko in order to discover whether negotiations can begin on the reduction of medium-range nuclear arsenals in Europe. But unless there is a huge mobilization of public protest, the outcome of such talks about talks is completely predictable.

Limited War: The End of Europe?

In spite of detente and the relatively stable relations between its two main halves during the past decade, Europe remains by far the most militaristic zone of the contemporary world.

At least 10,000, possibly 15,000, warheads are stockpiled in

Europe for what is called "tactical" or "theater" use. The Americans have installed something between 7,000 and 10,000 of these, and the Russians between 3,500 and 5,000. The yields of these weapons range, it is believed, between something less than one kiloton and up to three megatons. In terms of Hiroshima bombs, one three-megaton warhead would have the force of 250 such weapons. But nowadays—this is seen as a "theater" armament, usable in a "limited" nuclear war. "Strategic" bombs, for use in the final stages of escalation, may be as large as twenty megatons. (Although of course those destined for certain types of targets are a lot smaller. The smallest could be a "mere" thirty or forty kilotons, or two or three Hiroshimas.) Towns in Europe are not commonly far apart from one another. There exist no vast unpopulated tracts, plains, prairies, or tundras, in which to confine a nuclear war. Military installations nestle among and between busy urban centers. As Zuckerman has pointed out "the distances between villages are no greater than the radius of effect of low-yield weapons of a few kilotons; between towns and cities, say a megaton."

General Sir John Hackett, a former commander of the Northern Army Group of NATO, published in 1978 a fictional history of the Third World War.[8] In his book this was scheduled for August 1985 and culminated in the nuclear destruction of Birmingham and Minsk. At this point the Russians obligingly faced a domestic rebellion, and everyone who wasn't already dead lived happily ever after. The General, as is often the case, knows a lot about specialized military matters, but very little about the sociology of communism, and not much more about the political sociology of his own side. Of course, rebellions are very likely in every country which faces the immediate prospect of nuclear war, which is why the British Government has detailed contingency plans for the arrest of large numbers of "subversives" when such a war is about to break out. (These may be discovered, in part, by reference to the secret County War Plans which have been prepared on Government instructions, to cope with every problem from water-rationing to the burial of the uncountable dead.) But there is no good reason to imagine that subversives are harder to arrest in the USSR than they are in Britain, to put the matter very mildly. Nor is there any very good reason to think that the Soviet Union stands on the brink of revolution, or that such revolution would be facilitated by nuclear war. The contrary may be the case. General Hackett's novel has Poles tearing nonexistent communist insignia out of their national flag, and contains a variety of other foibles of the same kind: but we may assume that when it speaks of NATO, it gets things broadly right.

The General discusses the basis of NATO strategy which is known as the "Triad." This is a "combination of conventional defence, battlefield nuclear weapons and strategic nuclear action in closely coupled sequence." Ruefully, General Hackett continues "This was as fully endorsed in the United Kingdom as anywhere else in the Alliance. How far it was taken seriously anywhere is open to argument. There is little evidence that it was ever taken seriously in the UK . . . an observer of the British Army's deployment, equipment and training could scarcely fail to conclude that, whatever happened, the British did not expect to have to take part in a tactical nuclear battle at all. . . ."[9]

General Hackett's judgments here are anything but fictional ones. Lord Mountbatten, in the acutely subversive speech to which we have already referred, spoke of the development of "smaller nuclear weapons" which were "produced and deployed for use in what was assumed to be a tactical or theatre war." "The belief was," said Mountbatten "that were hostilities ever to break out in Western Europe, such weapons could be used in field warfare without triggering an all-out nuclear exchange leading to the final holocaust. I have never found this idea credible." If a former Chief of Staff and one-time Chairman of NATO's Military Committee found the idea unbelievable, this is strong evidence that General Hackett is quite right that NATO's basic strategy was indeed not "taken seriously" in the UK. Yet the doctrine of "flexible response" binds the UK while it remains in force in NATO, because it is enshrined in NATO's 1975 statement for Ministerial Guidance, in Article 4:

> The long-range defence concept supports agreed NATO strategy by calling for a balanced force structure of interdependent strategic nuclear, theatre nuclear and conventional force capabili-

> ties. Each element of this Triad performs a unique role; in combination they provide mutual support and reinforcement. No single element of the Triad can substitute for another. The concept also calls for the modernisation of both strategic and theatre nuclear capabilities; however, major emphasis is placed on maintaining and improving Alliance conventional forces.

Article 11b develops this beyond any possible ambiguity:

> . . . the purpose of the tactical nuclear capability is to enhance the deterrent and defensive effect of NATO's forces against large-scale conventional attack, and to provide a deterrent against the expansion of limited conventional attacks and the possible use of tactical nuclear weapons by the aggressor. Its aim is to convince the aggressor that any form of attack on NATO could result in very serious damage to his own forces, and to emphasise the dangers implicit in the continuance of a conflict by presenting him with the risk that such a situation could escalate beyond his control up to all-out nuclear war. Conversely, this capability should be of such a nature that control of the situation would remain in NATO hands.

Yet so jittery and mobile are military techniques, and so rapidly does their leapfrog bring both superpowers to the unleashing of ever newer devices, that the settled NATO principles of 1975 were already, in 1979, being qualified:

> All elements of the NATO Triad of strategic, theatre nuclear, and conventional forces are in flux. At the strategic level, with or without SALT, the US is modernising each component of its strategic forces. And, as will be described below, the other two legs of the Triad are being modernised as well.
>
> Integral to the doctrine of flexible response, theatre nuclear forces provide the link between US strategic power and NATO conventional forces—a link that, in the view of many, poses the ultimate deterrent against a European war.
>
> With Strategic parity codified in the recent SALT II agreement, and with major Soviet theatre deployments such as the Backfire bomber and the SS-20 missile, some have perceived a loose rung near the top of the flexible response ladder. Thus, consideration is being given to new weapons systems: Pershing II, a nuclear-armed ground launched cruise missile (GLCM), and a new mobile, medium-range ballistic missile (MRBM).[10]

This fateful decision came at the end of a long process of decisions, beginning with Richard Nixon's arrival in the United States presidency. So it was that NATO finally determined, at the end of 1979, upon the installation of nearly 600 new Pershing II and Tomahawk (cruise) missiles.[11] The cruise missiles are low-flying pilotless planes, along the lines of the "doodlebugs" which were sent against Britain in the last years of Hitler's blitzkrieg, only now refined to the highest degree, with computerized guidance which aspires to considerable accuracy. And, of course, they are each intended to take a nuclear bomb for a distance of 2,000 miles, and to deliver it within a very narrowly determined area. There is a lot of evidence that in fact they don't work in the manner intended, but this will increase no one's security, because it merely means that they will hit the wrong targets.

President Nixon first propounded the doctrine of limited nuclear war in his *State of the World* message of 1971. The U.S., he said, needed to provide itself with "alternatives appropriate to the nature and level of the provocation . . . without necessarily having to resort to mass destruction." Mountbatten, of course, is quite right to find it all incredible. "I have never been able to accept the reasons for the belief that any class of nuclear weapons can be categorised in terms of their tactical or strategic purposes," he said.

As Lord Zuckerman put it to the Pugwash Conference:

> I do not believe that nuclear weapons could be used in what is now fashionably called a "theatre war." I do not believe that any scenario exists which suggests that nuclear weapons could be used in field warfare between two nuclear states without escalation resulting. I know of several such exercises. They all lead to the opposite conclusion. There is no Marquess of Queensberry who would be holding the ring in a nuclear conflict. I cannot see teams of physicists attached to military staffs who would run to the scene of a nuclear explosion and then back to tell their local commanders that the radiation intensity of a nuclear strike by the other side was such and such, and that therefore the riposte should be only a weapon of equivalent yield. If the zone of lethal or wounding neutron radiation of a so-called neutron bomb would have, say, a radius of half a kilometre, the reply might

> well be a "dirty" bomb with the same zone of radiation, but with a much wider area of devastation due to blast and fire.[12]

Pressure from the Allies has meant that presidential statements on the issue of limited war have swung backward and forward. At times President Carter has given the impression that he is opposed to the doctrine. But the revelation of "Directive 59" in August 1980 shows that there is in fact a continuous evolution in U.S. military policy, apparently regardless of political hesitations by governments. Directive 59 is a flat-out regression to the pure Nixon doctrine. As the *New York Times* put it:

> (Defense Secretary) Brown seems to expand the very meaning of deterrence alarmingly. Typically, advocates of flexible targeting argue that it will deter a sneak attack. But Brown's speech says the new policy is also intended to deter a variety of lesser aggressions, . . . including conventional military aggression . . .

Obviously, as the *New York Times* claims, this is liable to "increase the likelihood that nuclear weapons will be used."[13]

Where would such weapons be used? That place would experience total annihilation, and in oblivion would be unable to consider the nicety of "tactical" or "strategic" destruction. If "limited" nuclear exchanges mean anything at all, the only limitation which is thinkable is their restriction to a particular zone. And that is precisely why politicians in the United States find "limited" war more tolerable than the other sort, because it leaves a hope that escalation to the total destruction of both superpowers might be a second-stage option to be deferred during the negotiations which could be undertaken while Europe burns. It does not matter whether the strategists are right in their assumptions or not. There are strong reasons why a Russian counterattack ought (within the lights of the Soviet authorities) to be directed at the U.S. as well as Europe, if Soviet military strategists are as thoughtful as we may presume. But the very fact that NATO is being programed to follow this line of action means that Europeans must awaken to understand what a sinister mutation has taken place, beneath the continuing official chatter about "deterrence."

The fact that current Soviet military planning speaks a different language does not in the least imply that Europe can escape this dilemma. If one side prepares for a "theater" war in our continent, the other will, if and when necessary, respond, whether or not it accepts the protocol which is proposed for the orderly escalation of annihilation from superpower peripheries to superpower centers. The material reality which will control events is the scope and range of the weapons deployed: and the very existence of tens of thousands of theater weapons implies, in the event of war, that there will be a "theater war." There may be a "strategic" war as well, in spite of all plans to the contrary. It will be too late for Europe to know or care.

All those missiles and bombs could never be used in Europe without causing death and destruction on a scale hitherto unprecedented and inconceivable. The continent would become a hecatomb, and in it would be buried not only tens, hundreds of millions of people, but also the remains of a civilization. If some Europeans survived, in Swiss shelters or British Government bunkers, they would emerge to a cannibal universe in which every humane instinct had been cauterized. Like the tragedy of Cambodia, only on a scale greatly wider and more profound, the tragedy of postnuclear Europe would be lived by a mutilated people, prone to the most restrictive and destructive xenophobia, ganging for support into pathetic strong-arm squads in order to club a survival for themselves out of the skulls of others, and fearful of their own shadows. The worlds which came into being in the Florentine renaissance would have been totally annulled and not only the monuments would be radioactive. On such deathly foundations "communism" may be installed, in the Cambodian manner, or some other more primary anarchies or brutalisms may maintain a hegemony of sorts. What is plain is that any and all survivors of a European theater war will look upon the days before the holocaust as a golden age, and hope will have become, quite literally, a thing of the past.

A move toward European Nuclear Disarmament may not avoid this fearful outcome. Until general nuclear disarmament has been agreed and implemented no man or woman will be able to feel safe. But such a move may break the logic of the arms race, transform the meanings of the blocs, and begin a unified and irresistible pressure on both the superpowers to reverse their engines away from war.

We Must Act Together

If the powers want to have a bit of a nuclear war, they will want to have it away from home. And if we do not wish to be their hosts for such a match, then, regardless of whether they are right or wrong in supposing that they can confine it to our "theater," we must discover a new initiative which can move us toward disarmament. New technologies will not do this, nor will introspection and conscience suddenly seize command in both superpowers at once.

We are looking for a *political* step which can open up new forms of public pressure and bring into the field of force new moral resources. Partly this is a matter of ending superpower domination of the most important negotiations.

But another part of the response must involve a multinational mobilization of public opinion. In Europe, this will not begin until people appreciate the exceptional vulnerability of their continent. One prominent statesman who has understood, and drawn attention to, this extreme exposure, is Olof Palme. During an important speech at a Helsinki Conference of the Socialist International, he issued a strong warning.

> Europe is no special zone where peace can be taken for granted. In actual fact, it is at the centre of the arms race. Granted, the general assumption seems to be that any potential military conflict between the super-powers is going to start someplace other than in Europe. But even if that were to be the case, we would have to count on one or the other party—in an effort to gain supremacy—trying to open a front on our continent, as well. As Alva Myrdal has recently pointed out, a war can simply be transported here, even though actual causes for war do not exist. Here there is a ready theatre of war. Here there have been great military forces for a long time. Here there are programmed weapons all ready for action . . .[14]

Basing himself on this recognition, Mr. Palme recalled various earlier attempts to create, in North and Central Europe, nuclear-free zones, from which, by agreement, all warheads were to be excluded. (We shall look at the history of these proposals, below.) He then drew a conclusion of historic significance, which provides the most real, and most hopeful, possibility, of generating a truly continental opposition to this continuing arms race:

> Today more than ever there is, in my opinion, every reason to go on working for a nuclear-free zone. *The ultimate objective of these efforts should be a nuclear-free Europe.* [My emphasis.] The geographical area closest at hand would naturally be Northern and Central Europe. If these areas could be free from the nuclear weapons stationed there today, the risk of total annihilation in case of a military conflict would be reduced.

Olof Palme's initiative was launched exactly a month before the United Nations Special Session on Disarmament, which gave rise to a Final Document which is a strong, if tacit, indictment of the arms race which has actually accelerated sharply since it was agreed. A World Disarmament Campaign was launched in 1980 by Lord Noel Baker and Lord Brockway and a comprehensive cross-section of voluntary peace organizations: it had the precise intention of securing the implementation of this Document. But although the goal of the UN Special Session was "general and complete disarmament," as it should have been, it is commonly not understood that this goal was deliberately coupled with a whole series of intermediate objectives, including Palme's own proposals. Article 33 of the statement reads:

> The establishment of nuclear-weapon-free zones on the basis of agreements or arrangements freely arrived at among the States of the zone concerned, and the full compliance with those agreements or arrangements, thus ensuring that the zones are genuinely free from nuclear weapons, and respect for such zones by nuclear-weapons States, constitute an important disarmament measure.

Later, the declaration goes on to spell out this commitment in considerable detail. It begins with a repetition:

> The establishment of nuclear-weapons-free zones on the basis of arrangements freely arrived at among the States of the region concerned, constitutes an important disarmament measure,

and then continues:

> The process of establishing such zones in different parts of the world should be encouraged with the ultimate objective of achieving a world entirely free of nuclear weapons. In the process of establishing such zones, the characteristics of each region should be taken into account. The States participating in such zones should undertake to comply fully with all the objectives, purposes and principles of the agreements or arrangements establishing the zones, thus ensuring that they are genuinely free from nuclear weapons.
>
> With respect to such zones, the nuclear-weapon States in turn are called upon to give undertakings, the modalities of which are to be negotiated with the competent authority of each zone, in particular: (a) to respect strictly the status of the nuclear-free zone; (b) to refrain from the use or threat of use of nuclear weapons against the States of the zone . . .
>
> States of the region should solemnly declare that they will refrain on a reciprocal basis from producing, acquiring, or in any other way, possessing nuclear explosive devices, and from permitting the stationing of nuclear weapons on their territory by any third party and agree to place all their nuclear activities under International Atomic Energy safeguards.

Article 63 of this final document schedules several areas for consideration as nuclear-free zones. They include Africa, where the Organization of African Unity has resolved upon "the denuclearization of the region," but also the Middle East and South Asia, which are listed alongside South and Central America, whose pioneering treaty offers a possible model for others to follow. This is the only populous area to have been covered by an existing agreement, which concluded with the Treaty of Tlatelolco (a suburb of Mexico City), opened for signature from February 1967.

There are other zones which are covered by more or less similar agreements. Conservationists will be pleased that they include Antarctica, the moon, outer space, and the seabed.

Two snags exist in this respect. One is that the effectiveness of the agreed arrangements is often questioned. The other is that if civilization is destroyed, the survivors may not be equipped to establish themselves comfortably in safe havens among penguins or deep-sea plants and fish, let alone upon the moon.

That is why a Martian might be surprised by the omission of Europe from the queue of continents (Africa, Near Asia, the Far East all in course of passing; and Latin America, with the exception of Cuba, already having agreed) to negotiate coverage within nuclear-free zones. If Europe is the most vulnerable region, the prime risk, with a dense concentration of population, the most developed and destructible material heritage to lose, and yet no obvious immediate reasons to go to war, why is there any hesitation at all about making Olof Palme's "ultimate objective" into an immediate and urgent demand?

If we are agreed that "it does not matter where the bombs come from," there is another question which is more pertinent. That is, where will they be sent to? Clearly, high priority targets are all locations from which response might otherwise come. There is therefore a very strong advantage for all Europe if "East" and "West," in terms of the deployment of nuclear arsenals, can literally and rigorously become coterminous with "U.S." and "USSR." This would constitute a significant pressure on the superpowers since each would thenceforward have a priority need to target on the silos of the other, and the present logic of "theater" thinking would all be reversed.

Nuclear-Free Zones in Europe

If Europe as a whole has not hitherto raised the issue of its possible denuclearization, there have been a number of efforts to sanitize smaller regions within the continent.

The idea that groups of nations in particular areas might agree to forego the manufacture or deployment of nuclear weapons, and to eschew research into their production, was first seriously mooted in the second half of the 1950s. In 1956, the USSR attempted to open discussions on the possible restriction of armaments, under inspection, and the prohibition of nuclear weapons, within both German states and some adjacent countries. The proposal was discussed in the Disarmament Sub-Committee of the United Nations, but it got no further. But afterward the foreign secretary of Poland, Adam Rapacki, took to the Twelfth Session of the UN General Assembly a plan to outlaw both the manufacturing and the harboring of nuclear arsenals in all the territories of Poland, Czechoslovakia, the German Democratic Republic, and the Federal German Republic. The Czechoslovaks and East Germans quickly endorsed this suggestion.

Rapacki's proposals would have come into force by four separate unilateral decisions of each relevant government. Enforcement would have been supervised by a commission drawn from NATO countries, Warsaw Pact adherents, and nonaligned states. Inspection posts, with a system of ground and air controls, were to be established to enable the commission to function. Subject to this supervision, neither nuclear weapons, nor installations capable of harboring or servicing them, nor missile systems, would have been permitted in the entire designated area. Nuclear powers were thereupon expected to agree not to use nuclear weapons against the denuclearized zone, and not to deploy their own atomic warheads with any of their conventional forces stationed within it.

The plan was rejected by the NATO powers, on the grounds, first, that it did nothing to secure German reunification, and second, that it failed to cover the deployment of conventional armaments. In 1958, therefore, Rapacki returned with modified proposals. Now he suggested a phased approach. In the beginning, nuclear stockpiles would be frozen at their existing levels within the zone. Later, the removal of these weapon stocks would be accompanied by controlled and mutually agreed reductions in conventional forces. This initiative, too, was rejected.

Meanwhile, in 1957, Romania proposed a similar project to denuclearize the Balkans. This plan was reiterated in 1968 and again in 1972.

In 1959, the Irish Government outlined a plan for the creation of nuclear-free zones throughout the entire planet, which were to be developed region-by-region. In the same year the Chinese People's Republic suggested that the Pacific Ocean and all Asia be constituted a nuclear-free zone, and in 1960 various African states elaborated similar proposals for an all-African agreement. (These were re-tabled again in 1965 and 1974.)

In 1962 the Polish government offered yet another variation on the Rapacki Plan, which would have maintained its later notion of phasing, but which would now have permitted other European nations to join in if they wished to extend the original designated area. In the first stage, existing levels of nuclear weaponry and rocketry would be frozen, prohibiting the creation of new bases. Then, as in the earlier version, nuclear and conventional armaments would be progressively reduced according to a negotiated timetable. The rejection of this 1962 version was the end of the Rapacki proposals, but they were followed in 1964 by the so-called Gomulka plan, which was designed to affect the same area, but which offered more restricted goals.

Although the main NATO powers displayed no real interest in all these efforts, they did arouse some real concern and sympathy in Scandinavia. As early as October 1961, the Swedish government tabled what became known as the Undén Plan (named after Sweden's foreign minister) at the First Committee of the UN General Assembly. This supported the idea of nuclear-free zones and a "non-atomic club," and advocated their general acceptance. Certain of its proposals, concerning nonproliferation and testing, were adopted by the General Assembly.

But the Undén Plan was never realized, because the U.S. and others maintained at the time that nuclear-free zones were an inappropriate approach to disarmament, which could only be agreed in a comprehensive "general and complete" decision. Over and again this most desirable end has been invoked to block any less total approach to discovering any practicable means by which it might be achieved.

In 1963, President Kekkonen of Finland called for the reopening of talks on the Undén Plan. Finland and Sweden were both neutral already, he said, while Denmark and Norway notwithstanding their membership of NATO, had no nuclear weapons of their own and deployed none of those belonging to their alliance. But although this constituted a defacto commitment, it would, he held, be notably reinforced by a deliberate collective decision to confirm it as an enduring joint policy.

The Norwegian premier responded to this demarche by calling for the inclusion of sections of the USSR in the suggested area. As long ago as 1959, Nikita Khrushchev had suggested a Nordic nuclear-free zone, but no approach was apparently made to him during 1963 to discover whether the USSR would be willing to underpin such a project with any concession to the Norwegian viewpoint. However, while this argument was unfolding, again in 1963, Khrushchev launched yet another similar proposal for a nuclear-free Mediterranean.

The fall of Khrushchev took much of the steam out of such diplomatic forays, even though new proposals continued to emerge at intervals. In May 1974, the Indian government detonated what was described as a "peaceful" nuclear explosion. This provoked renewed proposals for a nuclear-free zone in the Near East, from both Iran and the United Arab Republic, and it revived African concern with the problem. Probably the reverberations of the Indian bang were heard in New Zealand, because that nation offered up a suggestion for a South Pacific free-zone later in the same year.

Yet, while the European disarmament lobbies were stalemated, the Latin American Treaty, which is briefly discussed above, had already been concluded in 1967, and within a decade it had secured the adherence of twenty-five states. The last of the main nuclear powers to endorse it was the USSR which confirmed its general support in 1978. (Cuba withholds endorsement because it reserves its rights pending the evacuation of the Guantanamo base by the United States.) African pressures for a similar agreement are notably influenced by the threat of a South African nuclear military capacity, which is an obvious menace to neighboring Mozambique, Zimbabwe, and Angola, and a standing threat to the Organization of African Unity. In the Middle East, Israel plays a similar catalyzing role, and fear of an Israeli bomb is widespread throughout the region.

Why, then, this lag between Europe and the other continents? If the pressure for denuclearized zones began in Europe, and if the need for them, as we have seen, remains direst there, why have the peoples of the third world been, up to now, so much more effectively vocal on this issue than those of the European continent? Part of the answer surely lies in the prevalence of the nonaligned movement among the countries of the third world. Apart from a thin scatter of neutrals, Europe is the seed-bed of alignments, and the interests of the blocs as apparently disembodied entities are commonly portrayed as absolute within it. In reality, of course, the blocs are not "disembodied." Within them, in military terms, superpowers rule. They control the disposition and development of the two major "deterrents." They keep the keys and determine if and when to fire. They displace the constituent patriotisms of the member states with a kind of bloc loyalty, which solidly implies that in each bloc there is a leading state, not only in terms of military supply, but also in terms of the determination of policy. To be sure, each bloc is riven with mounting internal tension. Economic competition divides the West, which enters the latest round of the arms race in a prolonged and, for some, mortifying slump. In the East, divergent interests are not so easily expressed, but they certainly exist, and from time to time become manifest. For all this, subordinate states on either side find it very difficult to stand off from their protectors.

But stand off we all must. The logic of preparation for a war in our "theater" is remorseless, and the profound worsening of tension between the superpowers at a time of worldwide economic and social crisis all serves to speed up the gadarene race.

A Step Toward New Negotiations

Of course, the dangers which already mark the new decade are by no means restricted to the peril arising from the confrontation between the superpowers. In the past, these states shared a common, if tenuous, interest in the restriction of nuclear military capacity to a handful of countries. Once they were agreed upon a nonproliferation treaty they were able to lean upon many lesser powers to accept it.

America, the Soviet Union, and Britain tested their first successful atomic bombs in 1945, 1949, and 1952. France joined the "club" in 1960, China in 1964, and India in 1974, when it announced its "peaceful explosion." After a spectacular theft of plans from the Urenco plant in Holland, a peaceful explosion is now expected in Pakistan. Peaceful explosions in South Africa, Israel, Libya, Iraq, Brazil: all are possible, and some may be imminent.

One by-product of the Soviet invasion of Afghanistan is the resumption of supply of American weapons to Pakistan (so much for President Carter's campaign for "human rights") in spite of clear presumptions involved in the agreement on nonproliferation.

And there is worse news. The announcement of a major program of development of nuclear power stations in Britain, at a cost which commentators have assessed as £20,000 million or more, does not entail simply a headache for English environmentalists. It seems at least thinkable, indeed plausibly thinkable, that some entrepreneurs have seen the possibility of launching a new boom, supported on technological innovation, following the random exportation of nuclear power plants to the third world.

With such plants and a meccano set, together, if necessary, with some modest bribery or theft, by the end of the eighties there may be a Nigerian bomb, an Indonesian bomb, not a proliferation but a plague of deterrents.

Solemnly, we must ask ourselves the question, knowing what we know of the acute social and economic privations which beset vast regions of the world: is it even remotely likely that humanity can live through the next ten years without experiencing, somewhere, between these or the other conflicting parties, an exchange of nuclear warheads?

The moral authority of the superpowers in the rest of the

world has never been lower. Imperatives of national independence drive more and more peoples to accept that their military survival requires a nuclear component. Even if Afghanistan had never been invaded, even if NATO had not resolved to deploy its new generation of missiles, this burgeoning of destructive power would remain fearful. As things are, the superpowers intensify the terror to unimagined levels.

In this new world of horror, remedies based on national protest movements alone can never take practical effect, while governments remain locked into the cells of their own strategic assumptions. Yet something *must* be done, if only to arrest the growing possibility of holocaust by accident.

We think the answer is a new mass campaign, of petitions, marches, meetings, lobbies, and conferences. The fact that talks on disarmament are stalemated, that United Nations decisions are ignored, and that confrontation has replaced negotiation only makes it more urgent that the peoples of Europe should speak out. All over Europe the nations *can* agree, surely *must* agree, that none will house nuclear warheads of any kind. The struggle for a nuclear-free Europe can unite the continent, but it can also signal new hope to the wider world. With an example from Europe, nonproliferation will no longer be enforced (and increasingly ineffectively enforced) by crude superpower pressures, but also, for the first time, encouraged by practical moral example. A European nuclear-free zone does not necessarily imply reduction of conventional weapons, nor does it presuppose the demolition of the two major alliances. But the absence of warheads all over Europe will create a multinational zone of peaceful pressure, since the survival of the zone will be seen to depend upon the growth of detente between the powers.

No one believes that such a campaign as this can win easily, but where better than Europe to begin an act of renunciation which can reverse the desperate trend to annihilation?

Notes

1. *Apocalypse Now?* (London: Spokesman, 1980), p. 3.
2. Estimates vary markedly, because it is difficult to know what values to assign to Soviet military production costs. If budgets are taken, then Soviet expenditure is apparently greatly reduced, because under a system of central planning prices are regulated to fit social priorities (or cynics might say, Government convenience). The alternative is to cost military output on the basis of world market or United States equivalent prices, which, since the U.S. still has a much more developed economy than the USSR, would still tend to underestimate the real strain of military provision on the Soviet economy.
3. Chapter 4 of this volume.
4. Herbert Scoville, Jr., "America's Greatest Construction: Can it Work?" *New York Review of Books*, March 20, 1980, pp. 12–17.
5. "The MX system can only lead to vast uncontrolled arms competition that will undermine the security of the U.S. and increase the dangers of nuclear conflict," says Scoville.
6. *Apocalypse Now?* p. 27.
7. *Apocalypse Now?* p. 13.
8. *The Third World War* (London: Sphere Books, 1979).
9. *Ibid.*, p. 50.
10. *NATO Review*, no. 5, October 1979, p. 29.
11. The acute problems which this missile has encountered in development make an alarming story, which is told by Andrew Cockburn in *The New Statesman*, August 22, 1980.
12. F. Griffiths and J. C. Polanyi, *The Dangers of Nuclear War* (Toronto: University of Toronto Press, 1980), p. 164.
13. Editorial, August 1980.
14. This speech is reproduced in full in *European Nuclear Disarmament: A Bulletin of Work in Progress*, no. 1 (London: Bertrand Russell Peace Foundation, 1980).

Notes on Contributors

Ken Coates is a director of the Bertrand Russell Peace Foundation and co-author with Tony Topham of *Trade Unions in Britain* (1980).

Daniel Ellsberg began his career as a specialist for the Pentagon on nuclear command and control systems. His public release of the "Pentagon Papers" in 1971 marked his break with a career that spanned the administrations of four presidents. Now he devotes himself to speeches and direct action for nuclear arms limitation.

W. H. Ferry is a writer and social critic, and the American organizer for European Nuclear Disarmament (END).

David Holloway lectures in politics at the University of Edinburgh and is author of a number of essays on Soviet military questions. His thanks also to Silviu Brucan, Judith Reppy, and William Sweet for comments on an earlier draft.

Mary Kaldor is Research Fellow at the Science Policy Research Unit, University of Sussex, and author of *The Arms Trade with the Third World* (1971), *The Disintegrating West* (1978), and *The Baroque Arsenal* (to be published by Deutsch in spring 1981).

George Kistiakowsky was a key participant in the Manhattan Project to develop the first nuclear weapons. He received his Ph.D. in Chemistry at the University of Berlin in 1925. He spent four years at Princeton University before joining Harvard University's chemistry faculty in 1930. He was chairman of the department from 1947 to 1950 and has been on emeritus status since 1971. Today, at 80 and retired from active participation in science itself, he devotes all of his considerable energies to the prevention of nuclear war. To this end he serves as chairman of the Council for a Livable World.

Jonathan A. Leonard is a graduate of Harvard, a science writer and the former editor of an international public-health journal.

Henry T. Nash is Professor of Political Science at Hollins College, Virginia, and a former analyst with the U.S. Department of Defense. He is the author of *Nuclear Weapons and*

International Behavior (1975) and *American Foreign Policy: Changing Perspectives on National Security* (1978).

Emma Rothschild is Associate Professor in the Science, Technology, and Society program at the Massachusetts Institute of Technology and author of *Paradise Lost: The Decline of the Auto-Industrial Age* (1973).

Dan Smith is Research Officer in the Department of Economics, Birkbeck College, and author of *The Defence of the Realm in the 1980s* (1980).

E. P. Thompson, historian and writer, is the author of *The Making of the English Working Class* (1963), *The Poverty of Theory* (1978), and *Writing by Candlelight* (1980).